THE ART OF
MILITARY DECEPTION

by

MARK LLOYD

LEO COOPER

LONDON

First published in Great Britain in 1997 by
LEO COOPER
190 Shaftesbury Avenue, London WC2H 8JL
an imprint of
Pen & Sword Books Ltd,
47 Church Street,
Barnsley, South Yorkshire S70 2AS

A CIP record for this book is available from the British Library

ISBN 0 85052 510 1

A CIP record for this book is available
from the British Library

Typeset by Phoenix Typesetting,
Ilkley, West Yorkshire.

Printed in Great Britain by Redwood Books Ltd,
Trowbridge, Wiltshire

CONTENTS

INTRODUCTION

The art of military deception is as old as warfare itself. It has long been regarded as a force multiplier and has been employed by virtually every successful campaigner in military history. Inevitably early attempts at deception were constrained by the severe limitations in command, control and communications available to their authors. Nonetheless tacticians such as Sun Tzu, a Chinese general who lived more than 2,400 years ago, were able to practise the art to devastating effect.

Deception at Jericho

The Old Testament provides a fascinating insight into early military history, with many examples of the use of deception. During the thirteenth century BC, when Joshua and the Israelites were laying siege to Jericho he sought the aid of divine inspiration. The instructions which he received were indeed strange (Joshua 6: 2-5):

> 'And the Lord said unto Joshua, See, I have given into thine hand Jericho. . . . and ye shall compass the city, all ye men of war, and go round about the city once. Thus shalt thou do six days. And seven priests shall bear before the ark seven trumpets of rams' horns: and the seventh day ye shall compass the city seven times, and the priests shall blow with the trumpets . . . And it shall come to pass, that when they make a long blast with the ram's horn, and when ye hear the sound of the trumpet, all the people shall shout with a great shout; and the wall of the city shall fall down flat. . . .'

Joshua obeyed his unlikely orders; on the seventh day the priests duly blew their trumpets, the people dutifully shouted and the walls were indeed breached. Nobody has ever established precisely why Joshua's tactics were so successful. It has been suggested that the rhythmic step of the besiegers' feet sent shock waves through the ground, but this is unlikely in the extreme. It is possible that an earthquake shattered the city walls at the precise moment that the Israelites readied their assault, but again this is most improbable.

It is more likely that the actions of the Israelites lulled the citizens of Jericho into a state of complacency. The attackers' daily march around the walls, while initially alarming, would after a few days have become a matter of tedious and noisy routine. Indeed, it is highly possible that by the seventh day it had become so much a matter of routine that the change in length and intensity of the by now regular ceremony would have passed largely unnoticed by the defenders. They would probably not have stood-to, and would therefore have left the ramparts largely unmanned. This would have enabled the Israelites, on a given order, to storm the walls, which they were then closely surrounding, with little immediate opposition.

As warfare became more static the initiative passed firmly to the defenders. Lacking weapons heavy enough to destroy the ramparts of the great fortifications then in existence, the attackers could only hurl themselves against the weaker points of the ramparts in the hope of wearing the defenders down in a campaign of bloody and often pyrrhic attrition.

Where possible the more versatile attackers resorted to deception. The story of the Trojan Horse is well known and will be recounted in greater detail in Chapter Three. It was not unique. Thot, a general of Thutmose III, captured the strongpoint of Jaffa by seemingly surrendering and then, when the inhabitants opened the gates, rising and storming the city. In 1288BC, during the Battle of Kadesh, the Hittites sent two 'deserters' to Ramses II to feed him false information about the state of morale of their army. Ramses was lured northwards into a trap from which he was lucky to escape.

When generals fail to learn the lessons of the past, history surely repeats itself. Two millenia later, in 1879, the British forces in

Zululand allowed themselves to be lured into a false sence of security by three 'prisoners' who had been planted by the enemy king, Catewayo. The Battle of Isandhlwana which followed represented one of the greatest humiliations in the history of the British Army.

Sun Tzu and the Art of War

Sun Tzu produced the first great treatise on the art of war. It is now considered too simplistic for the prosecution of modern combat. However, it was studied to great effect by Mao Tse Tung during his campaign against the Nationalists, and remains an important influence on today's Peoples' Liberation Army.

Little is known about the early life of Sun Tzu save that he was a probable contemporary of Confucius. He was born about 500BC and followed his father, Sun Ping, into the military. Sun Tzu regarded war as more than a mere competition between military forces. He saw it as a comprehensive struggle embracing politics, economics, military force and diplomacy, which would allow the victor to survive while condemning the vanquished to ruin.

Sun Tzu saw war as a matter of deception in which the enemy had to be thrown into a state of confusion by the sudden introduction of unexpected factors, such as specially trained troops employing irregular tactics. They had to be disguised as conventional troops and could only be committed once the enemy's weaknesses had been established.

The principles of surprise were used to excellent effect by Tian Dan, a local warlord, in 279BC. When besieged in the city of Jumo he collected more than 1,000 oxen and covered each with a colourful cloth. He then tied daggers to their horns and dried reeds dipped in oil to their tails. He assembled 5,000 of his best soldiers all disguised as monsters, and when night fell lit the reeds on the oxens' tails. The oxen stampeded towards the enemy camp followed by the 5,000 specialist soldiers. The enemy, taken by complete surprise, were thrown into utter chaos and annihilated.

In 205BC Han Xin adopted the principles of Sun Tzu when forcing a crossing of the Yellow River. Having established an obvious crossing point, he made very patent preparations to force a bridgehead there. Once the enemy were committed to defending the area he moved the majority of his forces in complete secrecy to an alternative, virtually unguarded fording point. Having forced a crossing without resistance he quickly moved to attack the enemy from the rear. In 1944 the Allies employed a similar deception when they convinced German Intelligence that the principal invasion of France would be directed against the Pas de Calais and not Normandy.

Sun Tzu advocated the employment of a permanent espionage service, spying on enemies and neighbours alike. He introduced a rigid hierarchy of spies to include local spies, internal spies, converted spies and 'condemned spies'. He equated espionage with deception in the usage of war and argued that both should be regarded as honourable, with agents granted access to their political and military leaders at all times.

He claimed that captured agents should be treated with compassion, 'tempted with bribes, led away and comfortably housed'. He realized that if such men could be turned they would not spread disinformation. Instead they would be in a position to report on their previous master's strengths and weaknesses. So called 'condemned spies' were less fortunate. Unknown to them they were fed completely false information by Sun Tzu's agents, sent into enemy territory and if necessary compromised. When they were captured and tortured, the information which they were able to divulge was wholly incorrect, leading the enemy to miscalculate his response. When the enemy learned of the deception the spy was put to death, but by then it was invariably too late.

The Battle of Shijiazhuan

Old deception plans are often relevant to new wars and the thoughts of Sun Tzu were regularly put into practice by the communist armies of Mao Tse Tung. In October, 1948, the Nationalist 94th Army attempted to stage a large scale raid into Shijiazhuan Province, which was then guarded by no more than two Peoples' Liberation Army (PLA) garrisons and a few training regiments. The defenders knew that they could not hope to defeat the raid and therefore decided to counter it by deception. Local radio broadcasts made it clear that the raid was anticipated and at the same time grossly exaggerated the PLA strength in the area.

Mindful of a trap, and apparently dismissive of the possibility of deception, the Nationalists slowed their advance giving the defenders sufficient time to construct dummy fortifications along the 94th Army's proposed line of advance. At the same time such PLA forces as there were in the area were deployed to attack the Nationalist 49th Division moving to reinforce the 94th Army.

General Hu Yi, in command of the Nationalist forces, learned of the destruction of his reinforcements at the same time as he received aerial reconnaissance reports of the new fortifications. By nature a nervous individual, the General did not bother to check the authenticity of the defensive works, nor the actual strength of the enemy dispositions. Instead he called off what, had it been executed with vigour, would almost certainly have proved to have been a successful campaign.

The Tactical Withdrawal

Armies have long practised the deception of feigning a retreat to win ultimate victory. It is possible that, in 1066, the Normans staged their withdrawal at the Battle of Hastings to lure the English from the security of their positions on the high ground. What is certain is that over a century later, during the Third Crusade, the Saracens under the command of the brilliant tactician Saladin frequently used local deceptions to lure the heavily laden crusaders into killing areas of their own choosing.

Unlike the European knights, who were heavily armoured and whose strength lay in the heavy cavalry charge, the Saracens were more lightly equipped with lighter and faster horses. Their main strength lay in their horse-archers who, in addition to their bows, carried a small round shield, a sword and a lance. Their tactics favoured loose formations, kept just out of reach of the enemy until an exploitable situation arose. They would occasionally feign retreats for days on end in order to wear the crusaders down and lure them into unfavourable terrain.

During August and September, 1191, Richard the Lionheart attempted to advance with a force of 50,000 Crusaders along the coast towards Ascalon. The English King's planning and logistics were superb and his tactical and strategic abilities were without peer, yet Saladin succeeded in harrying the Christian force throughout, attacking the flanks and encouraging his cavalry to cut

5

off the stragglers, or those who could be drawn from the security of their main force.

In 1192 Saladin executed a masterful withdrawal towards Jerusalem, destroying all crops, grazing land and wells in a devastating scorched earth policy as he retired. Richard was forced to the conclusion that he was simply too weak to take Jerusalem and he was thus compelled to withdraw to the coast. Saladin continued his campaign of deception and minor engagements until Richard at last concluded a treaty, leaving Jerusalem firmly in Muslim hands.

Marlborough's March to the Danube

In 1704 John Churchill, Duke of Marlborough, one of the greatest ever masters of the art of deception, both at tactical and strategic level, changed the course of European history. Charles II of Spain had died childless in March 1700. In November of that year Philip of Anjou, the second grandson of Louis XIV of France, had been proclaimed Philip V and had assumed the throne of Spain. Fearful of the consequences of too powerful a Franco-Spanish alliance, Britain and the Netherlands had intervened on behalf of Leopold I of Austria, who had claimed the throne of Spain on behalf of his second son, the Archduke Charles.

In 1703 Marlborough, in command of the British forces on the Continent, was placed in a most difficult position when France and Spain were joined by Bavaria. The Allies were now split, the Dutch and British in the north, and the Austrians, isolated and threatened, in the east. Marlborough decided to reopen communications with Austria via the Rhine, but to do so he had not only to placate the nervous Dutch, whose permission he required to absent his armies from the Low Countries, but had to fly in the face of British policy which favoured a direct assault on Spain.

In order to confine the enemy to a land strategy, and as part of a large scale deception, Admiral Sir George Brooke was dispatched to the Mediterranean. He successfully attacked Toulon, captured Gibraltar and landed a small force in support of Huguenot rebels operating in southern France. However, these operations were largely diversionary. The main Allied effort was destined to concentrate on the Danube Valley.

6

In May, 1704, leaving about 60,000 men to protect the Netherlands, Marlborough, without informing the Dutch of his intentions, marched toward the Rhine Valley. He took with him a force of 35,000 men, of whom less than one-third were British and the remainder German forces in British pay. Marlborough moved fast, before Villeroi in command of the local French forces could react and attack his dangerously exposed flanks.

Having firmly seized the initiative, he added to the French confusion by introducing a large-scale and brilliantly executed plan of deception. He amassed a large supply depot at Coblenz, from where the enemy tacticians confidently expected him to march up the Moselle towards France. Instead he crossed the Rhine and marched up the right bank of the river. In order to convince the French that this was nothing but a flanking movement, and that his aim was ultimately to recross the Rhine, he had a bridge of boats thrown across the river at Phillipsburg, some 195kms upstream of Coblenz. Tallard, in command of the French forces in Alsace, drew up his army in anticipation of the impending attack. Instead Marlborough continued on south to the Danube, leaving the armies of Tallard and Villeroi, who had marched south from the Netherlands to cover the Moselle, wrong-footed and impotent.

By the time that Marlborough's intentions became clear it was too late for the French to react. On 10 June the Englishman was joined by his allies, Prince Eugene and Louis of Baden, for a planning conference at Mondelsheim, half way between the Rhine and the Danube. Three days later Eugene turned west to prevent the advance of the French armies, allowing Marlborough, now reinforced by Baden, free to advance eastward.

Marlborough's advance to the Danube is a textbook example of great administrative foresight and planning. Nothing was left to chance. Permission was sought of the various German princes whose lands he was to cross, provisions were assured and credits arranged with German bankers. Routes were checked and bridges and strategic points reconnoitred. When secrecy could no longer be maintained deception was used on a grand scale. The construction of the bridge at Phillipsburg was nothing less than masterful.

Seven years later Marlborough again employed deception on a strategic scale when forcing the French *Ne Plus Ultra* Line. He realized that if he were to breach the line with minimum casualties he would first have to take a fort which commanded the causeway through marshy terrain at Arleux, some 25km east of Vimy Ridge. He appreciated that a direct assault on Arleux would telegraph his intentions too clearly to the French. He therefore attacked and captured the fort, lightly garrisoning it with his own troops. He thereupon allowed the French to recapture the fort, sacrificing the garrison in the process, whereupon the French immediately destroyed the fort, assuming that it played some significant part in Marlborough's future intentions.

Reports were 'leaked' to the French intimating that the destruction of Arleux had completely frustrated Marlborough's plans. At the same time the Anglo-German army was pulled back slightly to an area to the west of Vimy Ridge, where it was drawn up as if in anticipation of a frontal assault on the French. That night, as Villeroi confidently awaited the attack, Marlborough silently struck camp, marched over 30km to the east, took Arleux and the causeway with little resistance and penetrated the *Ne Plus Ultra* Line. In the morning the French woke to find their defensive policy in tatters and Marlborough, with his entire army behind them, free to advance virtually at will.

Later that year the alliance began to crumble and on 31 December, 1711, Marlborough was relieved of his command, ending his military career. Given the comparatively limited resources available to him, Marlborough had proved himself not only a great tactician, but one of the most effective exploiters of the art of deception in the history of warfare.

The Age of Napoleon

Until the advent of the telegraph warfare was constrained by the inability of large armies to communicate. Orders were given by runner, flag, hand signal or trumpet, and, unless simple and wholly unambiguous, were open to misinterpretation. In 1854 the written order which led to the destruction of the Light Brigade at Balaclava may have appeared clear to Lord Lucan commanding the cavalry division, but were equally clearly misunderstood by Lord Cardigan commanding the brigade.

Commanders who released detachments from their main armies

could not guarantee to effect their return in an emergency. In 1863 General Robert E. Lee, in command of the Confederate forces at Gettysburg, sent no less than eight messengers to locate and order the return of Jeb Stuart's cavalry. They were located days later, having undertaken an unauthorized raid, hundreds of kilometres from where their presence had been anticipated.

One of the few generals to overcome this difficulty of communications was Napoleon Bonaparte. By dividing his armies into five or six corps, each a semi-autonomous and self-contained organization with its own staff, infantry, cavalry and artillery under the command of a trusted general, he extended his control over a far greater area. This enabled him to avoid stereotypes and develop individual tactics for every campaign in such a way that his enemies could rarely anticipate his intentions.

Nonetheless, by his own admission, his theories were based on a series of simple principles and strategic concepts. Napoleon endeavoured to win a campaign before the first shot was fired. Where possible he would combine rapid marching with skilful deception to outmanoeuvre his enemies, forcing them to fight at a disadvantage. Outstanding among his successes using these simple tactics were the Battles of Marengo, Ulm and Jena.

To deceive and confuse his enemies, who invariably outnumbered him, Napoleon kept his forces spread out until the last possible moment. Then, concentrating rapidly, he would bring superior forces to bear at a critical point. Where relevant he would endeavour to place his concentrated army between two hostile armies, defeating them in turn. He attempted this tactic at Waterloo, and might well have succeeded had it not been for the below par performance of a number of his subordinates and the sheer determination of Blucher not to leave Wellington isolated.

Great War Advances

The Great War of 1914–1918 was the first to employ radio communication on a large scale. Message scrambling was non-existent and it had to be assumed that each side was intercepting the transmissions of the other. Complex codes were introduced, and occasionally broken. When it became apparent that this had happened the codes were immediately changed, and it therefore became important to lull the enemy into a false sense of complacency.

Cipher Wars

The Royal Navy quickly became expert at the art of cipher deception. Under the direction of the future Director of Naval Intelligence, Captain (later Admiral) Reginald 'Blinker' Hall, an elite band of top-secret code breakers began to intercept and decrypt radio messages between the German fleet and its home bases.

Germany started the war with three principal codes, and within four months the Admiralty was in physical possession of copies of all of them. One fell into British hands on 11 August, 1914, when the German- Australian steamship *Hobart*, unaware that war had been declared, was seized off the coast of Melbourne. A second was captured by the Russians when the cruiser *Magdeburg* ran aground off the coast of Estonia. The third was retrieved when a lead box jettisoned by the commander of the destroyer *S.119*, sunk in an engagement with the cruiser *Undaunted*, was dredged up by a British trawler.

At first Room 40 relied upon the Post Office, a number of Marconi wireless stations, the Admiralty listening station at Stockton and three enthusiastic amateurs for its intercepts. After a few months, however, matters improved when the coastguard station at Hunstanton, on the Norfolk coast, linked with Stockton to form the core of 'Y' (Interception) service. From these humble beginnings the service grew until, by 1918, it could intercept virtually every naval and diplomatic message transmitted by the German authorities.

Having captured the genuine German codes, British Intelligence arranged for bogus British codes to be left unattended in a courier's luggage in neutral Rotterdam. The luggage was searched by German agents and the codes copied and returned. During the following months accurate but low-grade information was transmitted using these codes, leading the Germans to believe in their authenticity.

They were subsequently used in 1915 to convince the enemy

that the British intended to make a landing on the island of Sylt, on the north coast of Germany, and later, during the Battle of the Somme in 1916, that they planned a seaborne invasion of the Belgian coast. The latter ruse caused the German High Command to move thousands of troops north to coastal defensive positions where they could take no further part in the battle. Ironically, this caused an invasion scare in England, where the British military authorities had not been advised of the activities of Room 40 and thus put a wholly inaccurate, if understandable, interpretation on the German troop movements.

The Western Front

For the first three years of the land war in Europe there was little attempt by either side to deceive the other as to its intentions. Offensives were telegraphed by the large scale movement of troops and supplies to a given area, and were invariably heralded by several days of relatively ineffective artillery barrage against the sector chosen for the assault.

On 1 July, 1916, on the Somme, the British infantry of Rawlinson's Fourth and Allenby's Third Armies dashed themselves against the highly organized defensive positions of the German Second Army. Small gains were made, but by nightfall the British had sustained 60,000 casualties, 19,000 of them dead – the greatest one-day loss in the history of the British Army. Several factors led to these appalling losses, not the least the fact that the Germans had been fully expecting the attack. The French, attacking in smaller numbers to the south, suffered less and made greater advances, quite simply because the enemy had not expected them to take part in the initial support and had been taken by surprise.

It was only in 1917 that the Allies began to appreciate the need for deception. Haig, under considerable pressure from the French to take over more of the line and from the Government to neutralize the German U-boat bases in the channel, determined to break through on the Ypres salient. He appreciated that success could only be gained if the dominating Messines Ridge were first taken and delegated responsibility for its capture to Sir Herbert Plumer, commander of the Second Army and one of the most competent generals of the war.

Plumer abhorred unnecessary casualties and did all in his power to disguise his proposed attack from the enemy. In almost total secrecy a series of 21 mines were dug, or in the case of a few old workings extended, under the German positions. The spoil, much of it comprising blue clay very different to the topsoil, was bagged and removed at night so as not to leave telltale deposits at the shaft entrances. The enemy, who were also mining the area extensively, knew of the British subterranean activity, but had no idea of its intensity, nor of its implications. Even the British infantry holding the ground above were not told of the existence of the mines until a few hours before they were due to attack.

To maintain the element of surprise Second Army reinforcements were wherever possible brought forward at night and their new positions camouflaged. The tanks, which were destined to play a key part in the attack, were brought forward at the last minute, the noise of their tracks drowned by low-flying aircraft.

The Battle of Messines began conventionally with a 17-day artillery barrage. Thereafter, at 3.10 am on 7 June, 1917, at the precise moment when Plumer anticipated that his troops would have sufficient light to see the enemy at 100 metres, 19 of the mines, containing collectively 430,920kgs of high explosive, were blown and nine divisions of infantry ordered over the top. Surprise was absolute. The British and Commonwealth troops gained their objective for a cost of 17,000 casualties. German losses were 25,000, including 7,500 prisoners.

The initiative, so brilliantly gained with the help of surprise and deception at Messines, was shortly afterwards squandered in the quagmire of the Ypres Salient. During the Third Battle of Ypres, better known as Passchendaele, tactics were abandoned in favour of attrition as Haig once again tried to bleed the German Army dry with minimal regard for his own.

By now the United States had entered the war and many on the home front were beginning to question the necessity for further blood-letting before the arrival of fresh U.S. forces. In a series of heated and often ambiguous meetings with Prime Minister Lloyd George, Haig was left in no doubt that the government would no longer tolerate massive losses without obvious material gains.

There is considerable evidence to suggest that Haig did his best to deceive Lloyd George as to the state of the enemy and the ground taken in order to preserve his position and continue the offensive.

After two months of fighting (by which time Allied losses had reached 88,700 killed, missing and wounded) Lloyd George decided to make one of his rare visits to the front and was taken to see some German prisoners. However, he was not told that, in order to underline the point that the Germans were beaten and almost at the end of their tether, someone had that morning given the order that the most unprepossessing and unfit of the prisoners should be segregated into a separate cage and that to this cage, and no other, he was to be conducted.

Operation Michael

During the winter of 1917–1918 Germany realized that her only hope of winning the war lay in an early victory on the Western Front, before United States manpower could have a significant effect.

The first American troops had arrived in theatre soon after the United States' declaration of war. They had been fine, fit young men, who had paraded proudly and to great applause through the towns and villages of France. They had been projected as an advertisement for trans-Atlantic might, yet their presence had been a sham to bolster wavering French morale. The United States was a naval power with an army scarcely large enough for her own protection. She had to build an expeditionary force from scratch and inevitably this took a number of months. Indeed, it was nearly a year after their arrival before United States troops were able to play a significant part in the ground war.

On 22 December, 1917, peace talks between Russia and Germany opened. Thereupon Ludendorff felt it safe to reduce his garrisons in the east and at once began the movement west of as many divisions as possible in preparation for an all-out spring offensive. He knew that France and Britain would be anticipating his actions and therefore did nothing to disguise the movement of the troops west. He did, however, do everything in his power to keep the Allies guessing as to the precise form, size and timing of the attack.

Recognizing the diversity of interests within the Allied camp (the

French wished to defend Paris at all costs, the British to preserve their communications with the Channel ports) he decided to drive a wedge between their two armies and thereafter to destroy the British in a series of subsequent assaults.

Tactical surprise became of the essence. Assault divisions moved towards the front at night and during the day hid from the prying eyes of Allied reconnaissance aircraft in woods or villages. When railways were used troops were not allowed to dally at the rail-heads, but were dispersed within minutes of their arrival.

The stores and ammunition dumps required to sustain the 800,000 troops and over 6,500 guns destined to take part in the assault were hidden and dummy sites created in the south to intimate that the main assault, when it came, would fall on the French. The first offensive, on 21 March, 1918, took the British completely by surprise. Haig had been expecting to be attacked, but on a narrower front and by far weaker forces. The French, convinced that the attack in the north was a diversion and that they would ultimately prove to be the main target (they were eventually attacked along the Chemin des Dames, but not until 27 May), refused to release their strategic reserve in support of the British for a week.

The assault began well for the Germans. At 4.40am the offensive was launched along a 70km front. After five hours the barrage began to creep forward. The elite storm troopers followed close behind, using the prevailling thick fog as cover. No limits were set to the advance, each division being free to press as far and as fast as possible. The British Fifth Army collapsed, and by the end of the first day the Germans had seized as much ground as the British and French had recovered in the entire Somme offensive of 1916. They took 21,000 British prisoners and 500 British guns at the expense of 11,000 of their own killed and 28,000 wounded.

Tactically Operation Michael, the code-name for the final German assault, was a great success. Like Messines a year earlier it had emphasized the need to incorporate surprise and deception in any major plan. Strategically, however, it failed. It bled the German Army dry of reserves both in men and equipment. When the Allies began their inevitable counter-offensive in July Germany was left too weak to resist it.

The Turkish Campaigns

With the exception of the Crimean War, the Gallipoli expedition of 1915-1916 was the most poorly mounted and ineptly controlled operation in modern British military history. Surprise was surrendered well before the landings when a British naval bombardment of the outer Dardanelles alerted the Turks and Germans to the interest that the Allies were showing in the region. The defences in the area were strengthened until, by the time of the first landings, the peninsula was virtually impregnable.

Two landings were made on the Dardanelles, on 25 April and 6–8 August, 1915. Both were marked by their sheer incompetence. On 15 October General Hamilton was replaced by General Sir Charles Munro who immediately recommended an evacuation. Fighting withdrawals from a beachhead are invariably costly. In this instance, however, good planning and management prevailed. By 10 December all supplies and many of the troops had been moved out. The remaining nucleus of 35,000 men slipped away under the eyes of the unsuspecting Turks, the last of them on the night of 8-9 January, 1916, completing a masterpiece of deception without the loss of a single man.

Routine at the front was maintained to the last possible minute. Fires were left burning and rifles rigged with improvised delay mechanisms to fire the occasional shot throughout the night. The Turks had no reason to suspect an evacuation. Taking this fully into account, Munro milked the enemy's misconceptions to the full. In a campaign of marked ineptitude the final withdrawal stands out as an example of what can be attained with resolve, daring and initiative.

The so-called Third Battle of Gaza, which effectively secured the British advance into Jerusalem, was one of the most completely successful deception plans of the war. Having cleared the Sinai Peninsula of Turkish resistance in January, 1917, the British made two unsuccessful attacks on Gaza, which, with Beersheba, represented the two natural gateways to the region.

When General Sir Edmund Allenby assumed command of the Allied troops in the area he allowed his intelligence officer, the brilliant South African Lieutenant Colonel Richard Meinertzhagen, to introduce a plan of deception. The Turks would be persuaded that a third attack was to be launched against Gaza, but in fact the main attack was to be against Beersheba.

The plan, which took two months to implement, relied upon collateral to afford it added authenticity. Initially Meinertzhagen arranged for a known double- agent to deliver a letter to the head of Turkish espionage in the area. The letter, which contained money and a note of thanks for services rendered, was taken instead to Turkish Intelligence. The spymaster was tried summarily and shot without being given the chance to prove his own innocence.

Thereafter a series of minor security breaches were introduced to the routine radio traffic to enable the German analysts to break one of the British codes. A series of messages were then sent using the compromised code, in which it was intimated that the attack would be launched on 4 November against Gaza and would be supported by a small seaborne landing at Beersheba. Details of the true attack, planned for 31 October against Beersheba, were transmitted using still secure codes.

As a final assurance that the Turks would fall for his deception, Meinertzhagen embarked upon a very personal and potentially risky subterfuge. Accompanied by a guide he rode out into the desert, ostensibly on a reconnaissance patrol near Beersheba, until he encountered a mounted Turkish patrol. When the patrol fired at him he pretended to be hit and dropped a number of personal possessions including a pair of binoculars, a water bottle, a rifle and a blood-smeared haversack, as he made his escape. The haversack contained the personal documents of a fictitious officer, including a letter from his wife announcing the birth of a child. It also contained operational orders, a marked map and a notebook relating to Allenby's would- be attack on Gaza on 4 November.

To alleviate German and Turkish scepticism urgent instructions were sent by radio in the code known to be broken by the Germans. Thay were addressed to all brigades and battalions and instructed all ranks to be on the lookout for the haversack with instructions for its speedy return if found. Patrols were even sent into the desert to search the area where the haversack had been lost.

Further credibility was gained when two British soldiers, taken prisoner and interrogated by the Turks, admitted that they knew of the existence of the haversack and that British Headquarters regarded its loss as a disaster. They were wholly unaware of the deception and were thus being perfectly truthful.

On 27 October preparations were made for a naval bombardment of the Gaza area. At the same time Allenby ordered three divisions into the area, moving the rest of his army secretly to Beersheba. Surprise was complete, but a further tactical deception was required to ensure total victory. While the infantry assaulted the Turkish defences from the front, the Desert Mounted Corps swung wide to the east, before turning on the city. At dusk an Australian cavalry brigade rode over the Turkish wire and trenches into the rear of Beersheba itself, capturing the water supply essential for the successful continuation of the offensive.

Allenby then turned west towards the coast and the Turks were forced to evacuate Gaza to avoid being cut off. He successfully entered Jerusalem on 9 December, 1917. Nine months later Allenby entered into the last great deception of the war. In September 1918, as a prelude to a coastal breakthrough he moved three divisions from the Jordan Valley and the Judaean Hills to the coast in complete secrecy. Once in position the new units were well camouflaged, and where possible were bivouaced with existing units to disguise their recent arrival.

Meanwhile steps were taken on the right flank to make it appear that an attack was imminent. Recently vacated camps were left standing while new ones were pitched. The horse lines were filled by 15,000 dummy horses made of canvas, while sleighs drawn by mules kept the area constantly dusty to frustrate observation. At night bonfires were lit and lights shown in the deserted lines to give every appearance of normality. Battalions marched openly towards would-be assault positions by day, returned to their bases by lorry at night and repeated the procedure on the next and subsequent days.

When Allenby's attack was launched the Turks were taken by complete surprise and victory was absolute. The British build-up along the coast had taken place entirely undetected, while many Turkish units had been moved inland to meet the non-existent threat from the British right flank.

CHAPTER ONE:
The Unworthy Foe

Generals rarely, if ever, set out to lose battles. The fact that they do nonetheless can be attributed to a number of factors. Most of these fall into the catagories of bad luck, bad judgement or ineptitude. However, occasionally a campaign is doomed from the start. As often as not this is due to the fact that one adversary has completely underestimated the worth of the other.

For centuries Europeans have assumed that it is their right to wage war successfully, particularly against non-European adversaries. Traditionally, even within Europe, certain countries have regarded their armies as inherently superior to others. In 1415 the French allowed themselves to be lured into bloody defeat at Agincourt by giving battle to the 'inferior' English in a muddy field of the latter's chosing. Prevented by the terrain from deploying, and forced by the atrocious conditions to advance at no more than a trot, the French cavalry elite were massacred by the English and Welsh bowmen before they could even join battle.

Over 450 years later the French again paid a terrible price for underestimating the worth of their enemy. In 1870 they allowed themselves to be duped by Bismarck into declaring war on Prussia, and in a few months of bloody fighting were soundly defeated on all fronts. In an ignominious peace they were forced to cede the province of Alsace and most of Lorraine, agreed to pay reparations of five billion francs, and suffered the indignity of an army of occupation until they had done so. Prussia had proved the worth of her Army in highly successful campaigns against Denmark in 1864 and Austria in 1866, but France had refused to learn the lessons of history and had instead chosen to rely on the unproven, and in this instance patently untrue, preparedness of her armed forces.

In 1940 French complacency, and an unerring belief in the infallibility of her tired and largely outdated army, led to its wholesale destruction at the hands of the Nazi panzers. German tactics should not have come as a shock to the Franco-British allies. They had been well documented by Heinz Guderian in 1937, yet they had been ignored by the traditionalists who had refused to allow for the possibility of military evolution.

Latterly the Americans have found themselves guilty of the same self-deceipt. In Vietnam they failed to differentiate between technology and ability, and assumed that they had a right to defeat the peasant armies of the Communist North. When they found themselves in an environment in which their technology was of little use, and in which victory or otherwise depended on the skills and resolution of the individual soldier, they were heavily defeated.

In many cases self-inflicted defeat has occurred when an imperial power has failed to appreciate the worth of a colony or former colony. Thus it was with Britain in the later 18th century when her American colonies began to flex their muscles and demand greater fiscal autonomy.

Disaster in the Americas

With the Treaty of Paris in 1763 and the end of the French wars, both Britain and the colonies looked forward to a period of stability. However, this was not to be, and peace brought with it new-found tensions. Nearly bankrupted by the war, Britain found herself having to station 10,000 extra troops in the American colonies which were now expanding fast to fill the void left by the French. Britain felt that the cost of these troops should be met by the colonists. They, on the other hand, resented the presence of the Redcoats whom they saw more as a restraint on territorial growth than a protection against the frontier Indians whom they had earlier proved inept in fighting. More fundamentally they were adamant that, by providing excellent militia throughout the war, the costs of which had been borne locally, they had contributed more than adequately to the campaign and should not now have to suffer higher taxation.

In 1773, in response to the recently passed Tea Act, a group of colonists stole aboard a number of tea clippers in Boston harbour and threw their precious cargoes into the sea. When Britain retaliated by closing the harbour and placing Massachusetts under military rule confrontation became inevitable. Determined to resist military rule, the Massachusetts Provincial Congress began to stockpile ammunition and supplies in Concord, a small settlement some 32km from Boston. General Gage, commanding the British garrison, reacted forcefully, sending a force of 700 men to seize the illegal stores.

However, the minutemen, an elite among the militia, were forewarned and formed on the village green at Lexington to block the advance. A brief firefight ensued after which the militia retired having sustained eight dead. The British proceeded to Concord but during their return to Boston were harried throughout by militia snipers. The British regulars had to call upon the assistance of a relief force to secure their safety and suffered 276 casualties. The militiamen suffered 95 dead and injured, a demonstration of the latter's excellent use of guerrilla tactics. Within days the key forts of Ticonderoga and Crown Point were seized by the rebels.

The militiamen had proved themselves excellent adversaries who were clearly determined to fight the war on their own terms. Notwithstanding, the British continued to fight the insurrection by the tried and tested tactics of large-scale set-piece battlefield engagements. Foreseeing the need for a regular, disciplined force to protect the colonies against the inevitable onslaught, the settlers' Continental Congress adopted the irregular New England Army assembled around Boston and appointed George Washington its Commander- in-Chief.

At the outset the Continental Army consisted almost entirely of infantry supplemented by irregular cavalry and artillery. However, in striking contrast to the British who failed to adapt, the Americans set up a training programme which was highly professional, comprehensive and adapted specifically for American conditions. Cadres returned to their units to inaugurate local training programmes, thus ensuring that the new tactics were disseminated throughout the Army.

After five years of sporadic fighting, and the intervention of the French, the British were forced to surrender. Had they attempted to adapt their tactics to the environment their logistical advantages might well have proved decisive in forcing a different outcome.

Their failure to accept the worth of the local insurgents proved fatal. It would do so again.

African Adventures

During the course of the late 19th century Britain involved herself in a series of disastrous brush wars in southern Africa. In each case Imperial might should have prevailed. However, the failure of the establishment of the day to realize the potential of the enemy led the British to neglect a series of fundamental military tenets with fatal consequences.

When the Zulus began to menace the Boer settlements in the Transvaal the Boers, however unwillingly, sought the protection of the British military. The British High Commissioner, Sir Bartle Frere, determined to destroy the Zulu forces and, acting on his own initiative and against the wishes of the Government in London, ordered Lord Chelmsford to march into Zululand in January, 1879. The Zulu people had, by then, acquired a formidable military organization under successive warrior kings, yet Chelmsford deceived himself that their destruction would be a mere formality. His arrogance was to cost the lives of 1,600 men, half of them British.

Chelmsford advanced deep into enemy territory in search of the main camp of the Zulu king, Cetewayo. Common sense dictated that the British should have reconnoitred well ahead but they did not. Instead they allowed a Zulu army of 20,000 to remain undetected. When Chelmsford did receive a confused and wholly inaccurate report that the Zulus were massing some distance away he split his command, moving out to meet them with approximately half his strength. The rest, six companies of the 24th Regiment, two guns, some Colonial Volunteers, and some native contingents, about 1,800 men in all, he left at his base camp at Isandhlwana.

On 22 January, 1879, with Chelmsford too far away to come to its assistance, the Zulus burst upon the unprepared camp. The British commander formed a hasty perimeter, but the Zulus broke through; the native contingents broke ranks and fled, but were chased and killed. True to their orders the 21 officers and 534 soldiers of the 24th Regiment stood their ground and died where they fought. No more than 50 Europeans and 300 Africans escaped.

The British position was made worse by the refusal of the quartermasters to release ammunition reserves before the battle. When attempts were made to break into the heavy wooden boxes holding the ammunition it was found that some of the screws had rusted making release difficult. Also, prevailing regulations would not allow the two quartermasters to open more than one box at a time, as every cartridge had to be accounted for. When the Natal Native Horse sent for ammunition at the height of the battle they were refused it and sent elsewhere by the quartermasters of the 24th Regiment.

Staggeringly ,when Lieutenant Smith-Dorrien, later a First World War corps commander, began to break into an ammunition box and shovel cartridges into his men's helmets he was requested to stop by a regimental quartermaster until he was able to provide the right requisition papers.

Two days later a company of the 24th Regiment based at the missionary station at Rorke's Drift successfully withstood an attack by some 4,000 Zulus. They were no better equipped than their colleagues had been at Isandhlwana. They were, however, fully alerted to the proposed attack and allowed adequate ammunition resupply throughout the battle. The massacre at Isandhlwana temporarily halted the invasion of Zululand until Sir Garnet Wolseley and 10,000 reinforcements arrived from Britain. The Zulus were eventually overwhelmed, but not until the British had committed a further series of blunders, through one of which the Prince Imperial (the only son of Napoleon III), who had volunteered for the British Army, was killed.

Just over a year later the Transvaal, now free from the Zulu threat, rose in rebellion, and between December, 1880, and February, 1881, inflicted a series of humiliating defeats upon the British garrison. General George Colley, the British Governor of Natal at the time, was a brilliant soldier. He was, however, new to the area and had to rely upon his subordinates to advise him of the worth of his enemy. In this he was tragically ill- served.

Colonel Lanyon, Administrator of the Transvaal since 1879, gave Colley a wholly inaccurate assessment of the Boer military strength. He advised the Governor that the Boers were incapable of any united military action, that they were mortal cowards and that the mere sight of British regulars would be enough to make them sue for peace. In this Lanyon made the cardinal error of underestimating his enemy. The Boers had no standing army. However, they had a strong tradition of frontiermanship and had fought at times fanatically against a series of native enemies, including the much- vaunted Zulus. More fundamentally, with only 1,760 troops in the area, the British were badly outnumbered.

The first British encounter with the Boers proved catastrophic. On 20 December, 1880, a detachment of 264 soldiers from the 94th Regiment was stopped by a 1,000-strong commando dug in on the surrounding hills. The British were given the opportunity to retire, but declined and instead decided to fight it out. Their column was decimated with 77 soldiers killed and over 100 wounded. The Boer sharpshooting was astonishing and should have sent a warning to Colley. It did not. Instead, against all the rules of war, the British general decided to 'invade' the Transvaal, even though his enemy outnumbered him two-to-one, was well entrenched and knew the terrain well.

Soon thereafter the British suffered a further reverse at Laing's Nek, close to the Boer main encampment, suffering 160 casualties out of a force of 480 officers and men. Colley must have known by now that he had underestimated the Boers, but refused to change his tactics and decided upon revenge. Majuba Hill, 2000 metres high, overlooked the Boer position and commanded their defences on Laing's Nek. He reasoned that if the British were to take the Hill the Boers would be forced to evacuate Laing's Nek and ultimately their entire position.

In the course of a night march he occupied the hilltop with 490 soldiers and 64 sailors. From the peak the enemy camp was less than 2km away and the effect of overlooking the Boers made the commander and his men over-confident. Rather than maintain the element of surprise groups of Highlanders heralded the daybreak by waving and jeering at the enemy below. Incensed by the behaviour of the soldiers and by the fact that the British had taken the hilltop on a Sunday, a day kept holy by the ultra-religious farmers, the Boers opened effective fire at once, causing casualties among the British who had not bothered to dig in.

Colley, who had fallen asleep as soon as he had reached the peak of the hill, could not believe that the Boers would not evacuate their camp. Instead they sent a picked force of 180 marksmen, most of them teenage farm workers, to climb the hill while covering fire from another 1,000 troops kept the British pinned down. Majuba was a convex hill, and without the protection of slit trenches the British could only engage the climbing enemy by exposing themselves to the fire from below.

Even when Lieutenant Hamilton, later to command the disastrous 1915 campaign in Gallipoli, woke Colley to advise him that at least 100 Boers had reached the summit of Majuba the General refused to accept the gravity of the situation. Instead he continued to doze, presumably to refresh himself for his ultimate occupation of the Boer position! When eventually Colley did appreciate his predicament and ordered the formation of a skirmishing line his men were shot to pieces by the Boer marksmen.

Within an hour of reaching the summit of Majuba Hill the Boers had completely routed the British, killing 93 soldiers, wounding 133 and taking 58 prisoners for the loss of one dead and five wounded. Colley himself was killed, reputedly by a twelve-year-old farm lad. The British had suffered a humiliating and unnecessary defeat, caused totally by their failure to appreciate the true military qualities of the boys and irregulars whom earlier Lanyon had referred to as 'mortal cowards'. Less than twenty years later the British were destined to suffer a further series of humiliating defeats at the hands of the same enemy.

The Second Boer War of 1899-1902 symbolized Britain's towering imperial status, but at the same time exposed potentially crippling weaknesses in her military machine. The British public were told by their government that the war was being fought to protect the Uitlanders, a pro-British minority in the Transvaal, from Afrikaner tyranny. The Afrikaners of the Transvaal and Orange Free State believed that Whitehall, in support of the expansionist policies of Cecil Rhodes, had hatched a plot to strip them of their independence and subordinate them to the British Empire.

The opposing sides were, on the face of it, ludicrously unequal. Britain, arguably the greatest power in the world, her navy invincible and ubiquitous, her overseas trade colossal and her global influence all-pervasive, completely surrounded the Boer colonies. The war should have been over by Christmas, and might well have been had the British military not deceived itself as to its own strength and its enemy's inabilities.

Britain put 448,000 troops into the field; the Boers could at no time call upon more than 70,000 men, and probably never had more than 40,000 on active service. Moreover, the Afrikaner forces were almost exclusively composed of civilians under arms. Only a small standing infantry force and their artillery was uniformed and the latter, according to the British, was unskilled in close-battery warfare. (Another self- deceipt, it was in fact Prussian trained and highly effective.)

The British forces, despite their numerical advantage in South Africa, had scarcely profited from their humiliation during the earlier Boer War. They possessed no general staff to plan and co-ordinate tactics and strategy, and a paltry £11,000 a year was spent on the maintenance of the Intelligence Division. The generals, most of whom still regarded brains as a dangerous commodity, saw the 'ideal British battle' as one invoving the frontal engagement of lightly armed natives, such as the Dervishes who had smashed themselves against the British lines at Omdurman in 1898. Kitchener, the victor of Omdurman, was later to complain in South Africa that the Boers would not 'stand up to a fair fight'.

The British Army closed its eyes to the potential of mounted infantry. Ten per cent of the imperial troops in South Africa were admittedly mounted, but these were mainly cavalry who, although they carried carbines as well as sabres and lances, had little idea how to use them. Only later did the War Office listen to its self-governing colonies and accept their invitation to send units of experienced horsemen.

Deficiencies in British training and tactics were made apparent to all in the space of one week when three independent columns suffered bloody maulings at the hands of the Boers. Better leader-ship coupled with a greater respect for the enemy would have saved precious lives, but at that time the British still harboured the deceipt that the Boers, as soldiers, offered no greater potential threat than the Dervishes.

Attempts to relieve the sieges of Ladysmith, Mafeking and Kimberley met with disaster. The advancing columns were stopped at Magersfontein, Stormberg and Colenso and slaugh-tered. During the course of what became known as 'Black Week' the British Army sustained 7,000 casualties for the gain of no appreciable ground. Their maps were innacurate, their compasses faulty, and in most instances their reconnaissance was non-existent.

So low was their regard for their Boer opponents that the officers in command ignored every basic rule of combat. During the Battle of Colenso Colonel Charles Long, an artillery officer with a great deal of military experience in India, supported by Brigadier Barton's infantry, decided to charge the enemy with his twelve 15-pdr field guns and six naval guns. While nearly 5km from the enemy position he ordered his guns to gallop forward, leaving Barton's covering infantry fire behind. When only 1,000m from the Boer position, and having left the naval guns 600m behind and the infantry a further 750m behind them, he ordered his guns to take post. They did so with all the precision and discipline of a regiment deploying on the parade ground at Woolwich and were slaughtered by the combined might of 1,000 Boer rifles.

At the same time Major General Hart, as brave a man and as great a fool as Long, ordered his Irish Brigade to advance in broad daylight shoulder-to-shoulder towards the Boer positions. Even when the Boer marksmen opened fire and the Irish began to take heavy casualties Hart refused to allow them to deploy into skir-mishing order. By the time that Hart withdrew his brigade had suffered 532 dead and wounded, one of the most futile operations of the entire war in South Africa.

Only later did the British concede the worth of their enemy. They then introduced a series of new and wholly uncompromising tactics which, although they were to lead to victory, were to cause immense suffering among the civilian population which might have been averted had the British, at the beginning, not deceived them-selves as to the military competence of the 'armed farmers' whom they were facing.

Between 1904 and 1905 Imperial Russia fought the Japanese for control of Manchuria and Korea. In a series of battles the Japanese proved themselves not only superior but utterly ruthless. During the siege of Port Arthur (May, 1904, to January, 1905) the Japanese General Nogi ordered a series of frontal assaults on the Russian defensive positions. The Japanese suffered 16,000 casual-ties in a single unsuccessful assault, and in so doing laid the principle of the Kamikaze – willing to die without question for the Emperor.

The Japanese finally succeeded in taking Port Arthur, and subsequently sunk the Russian fleet at Tsushima. The Russians were forced into negotiating an ignominious peace which led to considerable unrest in their armed forces and ultimately to the Revolution. The military analysts of the day deceived themselves that the Russians had been the wholesale authors of their own downfall. They refused to accept the worth of the Japanese or the beginnings of a new military power in the East. For more than 30 years Western strategists argued that the Japanese could not wage war; they were too small and too weak, they could not close one eye to aim their rifles, which in any case were of too small a calibre to seriously injure a healthy European.

A series of Japanese victories against the Chinese in the mid-1930s should have alerted the West to the dangerous subjectivity of its attitudes, but did not. By late 1941 a war of expansion between Japan and the United States and Britain had become inevitable. Even so the Western militarists did not take the threat seriously. The British deceived themselves that their naval base at Singapore was impregnable. The base had been slowly constructed during the 1930s but had never been completed. It was well protected against sea attack by coastal artillery, although the coastal guns could, and did, fire inland.

British tacticians had argued that the immensity of the jungle to the north, in which European troops had never felt at ease, made the area impregnable to a modern army. They simply did not accept that the Japanese could operate a coherent force within it. When the Japanese landed on the Malay coast and began to advance rapidly through the jungle the British were thrown into confusion. By the time that the Japanese had reached the Johore Straits the morale of the British and Imperial forces was shattered.

Singapore island surrendered on 15 February, 1942, at which time some 16,000 British, 14,000 Australian and 32,000 Indian troops were taken prisoner. Ironically they outnumbered the Japanese forces to whom they surrendered. Indeed the latter had not intended to fight a pitched battle for the island and had contemplated a withdrawal had the Imperial forces put up a serious resistance. Had the siege been better fought and assessed, and the worth of the Japanese not been initially discounted and later exaggerated, what Churchill was forced to describe as 'the worst disaster and largest capitulation in British history' might never have happened.

The Korean Experience

The Korean war began in June, 1950, when the Democratic People's Republic of (North) Korea invaded the Republic of (South) Korea. Ultimately it was to involve a further seventeen combative nations and resulted in the deaths of an estimated 5 million. Korea was seen as a springboard for communist expansion by the Soviet Union and China, and as a bastion of democracy by the West.

At the end of the Second World War the Allies had agreed that the Soviet forces would accept the Japanese surrender north of the 38th degree of latitude in Korea, while the United States would accept the Japanese surrender south of that line. In 1949 both the Soviet Union and the United States withdrew all but a few hundred advisory troops from the Korean Peninsula, leaving the ideologically opposed fledgling régimes to face each other across an increasingly hostile border.

On 25 June, 1950, the North Koreans, on the prompting of the Soviet Union and without Chinese knowledge, unleashed a carefully planned attack across the 38th parallel. South Korea and the West were taken completely by surprise. They should not have been. For the previous three years the North had been training and arming for an obvious conflict. Yet the United Nations, its member states still exhausted from six years of global bloodshed, had chosen to ignore the signs, arguing instead that the North would not risk the consequences of an invasion. On 17 March, 1949, less than three months after withdrawing its occupation forces, the Soviet Union had concluded a reciprocal-aid agreement with North Korea under the terms of which it had agreed to furnish heavy military equipment including a tank brigade. As early as 1946 the Soviets had begun to send thousands of Koreans to the U.S.S.R. for specialist training and between 1949 and 1950 the Chinese had transferred about 12,000 trained soldiers from their army to the North Korean forces.

Too late to act as a deterrent, the United States rushed troops from its garrison in Japan to the peninsula. Too few in number, too lightly armed and far too inexperienced, they were pushed back by the tactically and numerically superior Northern forces. By 4 July, 1950, the communists had taken Seoul, Inchon and the lower reaches of the Han river. By 14 July they had advanced to Kunsan, and by early September had forced the South Koreans and their American allies into the Pusan peninsula in the extreme south-east.

It was now North Korea's turn to suffer from its own complacency. Intoxicated by the totality of its success it discounted the United States' willingness to expend American lives to regain lost territory. On 15 September General MacArthur counter-attacked, catching the Communists on the flank by a daring amphibious landing at Inchon, on the coast west of Seoul. Described by Liddell Hart as one who enjoyed, 'strong personality, strategic grasp, tactical skill, operative mobility and vision', MacArthur was a class above his peers and proved himself ideally suited to the task of regaining the initiative.

The Communists were taken completely by surprise. Thousands were trapped and over 125,000 taken prisoner. By 1 October the US forces, now reinforced by troops from over a dozen countries, were back on the 38th parallel. Despite warnings from the Chinese that they would intervene if U.N. troops crossed the border, on 7 October the UN General Assembly approved a resolution to permit entry into North Korea with the intention of enforcing a reunification. Despite the massive presence of over 1,500,000 Chinese troops on the border the United Nations forces continued advancing north. On 20 October they took P'yongyang, the North Korean capital, and on 26 October reached the Manchurian border at the Yalu River.

On 24 November MacArthur announced a 'home by Christmas' offensive. The next day over 180,000 Chinese 'volunteers' entered the war, driving the UN force back to the 38th parallel. There followed two years of bitter fighting until, after months of negotiation, an armistice was concluded on 27 July, 1953.

Each side had badly underestimated the other and had suffered accordingly. First North Korea and later the United States had deceived itself that its enemy was beaten, and that in winning a battle it had won a war. The United States lost 33,629 dead in action, South Korea 47,000 and the UN forces 3,194; Chinese losses were estimated at 900,000, and North Korean at 520,000. The ground gained by either side was insignificant.

The Korean War established a precedent for United States intervention to contain Communist expansion which ended in disaster in Vietnam. However, it was in Europe that the greatest threat to the West lay, and it was for a war in this continent that the West trained for three decades.

The Threat to Europe

In the spring of 1948 the United Kingdom, France and the Benelux countries signed a treaty of mutual assistance to counter the threat from the Soviet Union, which had kept much of its armed forces on a war footing. This was followed by a wider Brussels Treaty which included the original signatories as well as the United States, Canada, Denmark, Italy, Iceland, Spain and Portugal.

In Washington, on 4 April, 1949, the signatories ratified what became known as the North Atlantic Treaty Organization. In so doing they reaffirmed the principles of collective defence and drove a deeper wedge between themselves and the communist East. In 1951 the original signatories invited Greece and Turkey to join them, and in 1955 admitted West Germany. Furious, the Eastern bloc retaliated, on 14 May, 1955, with the formation of the Warsaw Pact. The scene was now set for a thirty-five-year-long Cold War in which each side greatly deceived itself as to the potency and intentions of its adversary.

Convinced that it was surrounded by enemies, and determined never again to suffer the horrors of invasion, the Soviet Union surrounded itself with satellites. Trusting none of them fully, it established proxy governments throughout and stationed large garrisons in each of its allies to ensure their wholesale compliance. When Hungary and later Czechoslovakia demurred it restored Marxist order savagely.

In the eyes of the Soviet Union it was merely protecting its territory, but in the eyes of the West it was constantly planning for a surprise attack. NATO responded by positioning heavily armoured divisions along the so-called Inner German Border

(IGB), and by introducing a series of tactics designed to frustrate a far larger force attacking from the east. 'Kill zones' were introduced into which Soviet armour would be channelled and destroyed by NATO tanks and artillery, and nuclear release points, beyond which the Warsaw Pact would not be allowed to advance without strategic intervention, were openly discussed. Major national and NATO exercises were undertaken on a regular basis, during which the enemy advanced according to a set pattern, ground was surrendered, the forward line of own troops (FLOT) established and the enemy driven back, with or without nuclear release.

It would now appear that many of these exercises were deeply flawed. They assumed a level of competency within the Warsaw Pact that has since been shown to have been vastly overstated. Soviet airborne potential was justifiably respected by the NATO planners, but all too often the fact that the Soviets only had the transport aircraft potential to carry a quarter of their airborne force at any one time was discounted. When faced with the realities of combat, Soviet conscripts in Afghanistan proved less than efficient, and it was only when elite Spetsnaz and airborne units intervened on a large scale that the Soviets succeeded in gaining the initiative away from the major cities. Equally, the modern Russian Army has proved often ill-trained and less than effective in its dealings with the Chechen irregulars.

More dangerously the presumed effectiveness of NATO tactics which, when tried elsewhere in battle, proved less than satisfactory. Exercises were controlled by money and timing. They were extremely expensive to plan and administer, and when ground troops were involved were highly disruptive to soldier and civilian alike.

Exercises were planned for set periods, usually seven or eight days. Once planned they were rarely curtailed and could not be lengthened without causing administrative chaos. Troops were often brought over from Britain and the United States to participate, flights to and from Germany were planned months in advance and could not easily be changed. When reserves or reservists participated, as they did in virtually all major exercises, it was imperative that they be returned home by an agreed date to enable them to return to their civilian employment.

To ensure that exercises ran to a more-or-less pre- ordained timetable both 'blue' (friendly) and 'orange' (enemy) losses had to be monitored carefully, and in some cases doctored heavily to ensure that the 'battle' ran to plan. Orange air defences were often ignored or discounted if it became necessary to slow down the enemy by destroying a heavily defended bridge or supply route, while communications, one of the most fickle aspects of the modern battlefield, rarely, if ever, failed. Equipment, never tested in battle, gained a fearsome reputation for potency and reliability, while tactics, only ever practised in peacetime, came to be regarded as sound.

Gulf War Consequences

The Gulf War quickly shattered NATO's self- deceptions and complacency. The Iraqi Air Force was a hybrid, largely purchased on credit and with little in the way of reserves. It operated from twenty-one main bases and thirty dispersed bases, some of them up to 9,000 acres in size (over twice the size of Heathrow Airport). The Coalition Air Forces aimed to gain overall air supremacy within seven to ten days, and to suppress the Iraqi ground forces within three weeks. But first they would have to destroy the Iraqi airfields.

The RAF, with forty-five Tornado GR1 jet bombers in the Gulf, was given the task of attacking the heaviest defended of the airfields with JP233 airfield-denial bombs. The RAF had developed the tactics of low-level bombing – down to 50 feet during daylight to avoid radar when attacking heavily defended targets – and used the same tactics during the first few days of the Iraqi air war. However, true to the maxim 'no plan survives contact with the enemy', the RAF quickly began to suffer casualties, losing four aircraft in as many nights before switching to higher-level tactics. By then they had flown only 4 per cent of the Coalition air missions, but had sustained 25 per cent of the aircraft lost.

The RAF asserted its willingness to return to low level bombing should the Iraqi air defences prove too strong, but these were quickly rendered impotent by the US Air Force flying F15 fighter bombers equipped with ALARM (Air Launched Anti-Radar Missiles). To compound British discomfort early intelligence reports quickly established that the Iraqi airfields, which had been excellently camouflaged, were simply too big to be closed down by bombing.

It has been suggested that elements within the Ministry of Defence resisted requests by the RAF to move to higher-level bombing, as to do so would have impacted too drastically on the RAF's future strategy for Europe. Whether or not a high-ranking official did in fact do his best to ensure that reality did not interfere with theory will probably never be publicly known. What is certain is that, if war is to be properly simulated in peacetime exercises, it is imperative that those in control accept reality for what it is, however unpalatable.

CHAPTER TWO:
Politics, Self-Deception and Carnage

When an enemy does not exist it is occasionally necessary to invent one. The causes of war are rarely simple; they may be truly 'honourable,' but as often as not they are economic or political. Professional soldiers will not fight well without motivation and citizen armies will often not fight at all. It is necessary therefore to inject a broad ideal, albeit one of self-preservation, into warfare. If it is to be prosecuted to its full potential by the working masses who, at the end of the day, may well gain nothing from it, they must first be deceived into a frenzy. They must come to believe that their government's enemy is their enemy and that his defeat is worth dying for.

If the enemy is pictured as somehow less than human he becomes easier to kill; indeed if he can be successfully depicted as an enemy of God his murder may be turned into devotion. His death becomes a blow for truth, goodness and freedom. Like the inquisitor who tortures heretics to make them confess their error, the warrior doing righteous battle against the enemies of God may come to see himself as their saviour rather than tormentor.

Crimean Blunders

In 1854 Britain and France went to war against Russia. The immediate cause of the Crimean War was the refusal of the Turks to accept a Russian demand to protect Christians within the Turkish Empire. The longer-term causes were more complex, having their roots in the Russian intervention in the Hungarian Revolution of 1848-49 and in the Tsar's proposal for the eventual partition of the ailing Turkish Empire. France had no intention of letting Russia gain the ascendancy in the Middle East while Britain opposed any change in the balance of power. Equally the shadow of Russia, already a formidable force in Asia, was beginning to creep ominously over India.

The need to resist Russia was plain to the British Government, which regarded Czar Nicholas I as the cornerstone of despotism in Europe. Superficial attempts were made at mediation, but at the same time it was made clear to the Turks that in the case of war Britain would intervene to protect Constantinople and stop the Russians from seizing the Bosphorus. In June, 1853 the Cabinet ordered the British fleet to Besika Bay, outside the Dardanelles, in an obvious show of support. War was not yet certain. The Czar, alarmed by the threat of Franco-British intervention, sought a compromise but this was rejected out of hand.

On 4 October the Sultan declared war on Russia. The Russians reacted with an onslaught against the Turkish fleet off Sinope, in the Black Sea. Indignation flared in England, where the action was denounced as a massacre. The hawks in the British Cabinet used this as an excuse to foment anti-Russian feeling in the populace as a whole until war became inevitable. Stories of Russian aggression and massacre of innocent Turks filled the news-sheets. Jingoistic songs were heard nightly in the music halls and began to reflect the common sentiment of a population which could hope to gain nothing from war, yet which was being duped into one by the self-interest of a few politicians.

Prime Minister Aberdeen, a dove among hawks, did all he could to stem the cry for war, but in the end was overcome by it. 'I will say that war is not inevitable,' he wrote in February, 1854, 'unless, indeed, we are determined to have it; which, for all I know, may be the case.' The British people had been swept away by jingoistic self-deception, fuelled by the desires and exaggerations of a few ministers. The war which followed was to have far reaching consequences for the British Army.

It is unlikely that the population of Britain would have been quite so keen to commit its armed forces to war had it realized quite how far its army had deteriorated in the previous four decades. The Army which had vanquished Napoleon on the field of Waterloo had quite simply stagnated. Its great chief, Wellington, had died in 1852. During his long reign as

Commander-in-Chief at the War Office nothing had changed. Nor had his successors in office seen any need for reforming the Army which the Duke had led. The conditions of service were intolerable, the administration bad, the equipment scanty and the commanders of no outstanding ability.

Britain had introduced a military academy half a century earlier, yet its senior officers still deceived themselves that war was a sport to be played by gentleman with the common soldier as his pawns. Professionalism was despised, the intellectual officer shunned. Raglan, in command of the Army in the Crimea, made it clear that he would not accept professionalism in his ranks, complaining that it 'smacked of murder'.

War is as physically demanding as it is violent. The physical condition of the men required to carry out its many aspects is crucial, yet in the Crimea the senior officers so neglected the health of the soldiers under their command that the army's efficiency suffered disastrously. The French and British between them had only 45,000 troops in the Crimea in the terrible winter of 1854-55, yet they suffered 14,000 hospital cases, of whom many died for want of medical supplies. The British commanders in particular deceived themselves that the plight of their men, whom they largely despised, was adequate, or at the very least that nothing could be done to improve it. Throughout the siege of Sebastopol the Army survived without tentage or in many cases cover of any kind, half-starved and disease-ridden. The troops had neither transport nor ambulances, and thousands were lost through cold and starvation, yet seemingly no one considered the possibility of laying down five miles of light railway from the port of Balaclava to the front line.

The War Office was shaken from its complacency and self-deceptions of normality, albeit unwillingly, by William Russell, a war correspondent sent to the Crimea by J.T.Delane, the editor of *The Times*. His reports so shocked the nation that the government was forced into action. In March, 1855, Sir John McNeill and Colonel Alexander Tulloch were dispatched to the Crimea to assess the position. Their report shocked the British people out of its complacency. In particular the causes and effects of scurvy had been well known, yet throughout the previous winter the troops had subsisted on a diet of salt meat and biscuit. Even the supplies of these had been minimal, and on some days non-existent. The fault was laid firmly at the feet of Commissary- General Filder whose men had made no attempt to provide fresh meat or newly baked bread to the troops. For reasons of greed and apathy they had deceived themselves that a soldier's daily food supply, although *less* than that provided for a convict in a British prison, had been adequate.

The French had established bakeries and were supplying their men with fresh bread. The British could easily have done this had anybody taken the trouble to organize it, but the Commissariat had preferred to do nothing, blaming the climate for the record number of patently diet-related casualties sustained by the rank and file.

When fresh fruit had arrived on board the *Harbinger* in November, 1854, it had been accompanied by the wrong documentation, and had been allowed to rot before being thrown into Balaclava harbour, while the Commissariat had argued among itself as to who should take responsibility for its unloading and distribution. A month later the *Esk* had arrived at Balaclava, her holds full of lime juice. Yet it had remained on board ship for three months because, as Filder later claimed, it had not been his job to tell the Army that it had arrived. Although improvements followed, and by April, 1855, the troops at least had fresh bread, the Army later closed ranks in an attempt to protect its image.

It deceived itself that the Crimea had been a victory (true, Russia had been forced to offer concessions, but for reasons little to do with the battlefield), that all had been well and that any faults had lain with others. The Army failed fully to reform itself for another fifteen years, by which time the American War between the States had fundamentally transformed the theories and practices of warfare.

Deceptions of Grandeur

Until comparatively recently commanding officers felt the necessity to send their men into action in uniforms more suited to the parade ground than the battlefield. Sartorial elegance was considered more important than strategic expediency. The British dressed their Rifle Brigade in green in the 1790s, but for a further century refused to allow the line infantry to abandon their red coats, even when it became clear that the white bands across the red tunics gave enemy marksman an ideal aiming point for the heart. The British introduced khaki after the First Boer War, but it was not until the final stages of the First World War that officers serving in the trenches were allowed to wear other ranks' jackets with their badges of rank removed from the cuff to the shoulder.

Last to suffer from the self-deception of grandeur were the French, who regarded their uniforms of red kepis (caps), red trousers, blue jackets and blue greatcoats as quintessentially Gallic, and refused to abandon them in the face of obvious military reality. During the Balkan Wars of 1912-13 the Minister of War, Adolphe Messimy, accepted the advantage of dull colours in the field and set about introducing them into the French Army. His action, which Messimy regarded as both professional and humane, nearly cost him his position within the Government.

French domestic reaction was as immediate as it was hostile. National newspapers pilloried the suggestion that their troops should be dressed in 'muddy, inglorious' colours. Instead they claimed that the '*élan vitale*' of the French *poilus* (infantryman), his self- assessed (but never tried in battle) ability to charge down and defeat the enemy with the bayonet, would prevail in any future war. The words of a former Minister, Alphonse Etienne, '*Le pantalon rouge c'est la France*' were adopted as the catch phrase of every conservative in the country until change became impossible and was finally abandoned.

Public opinion even denied the troops the protection of a hard hat. The French insisted on keeping their soft kepis, ridiculing the German *pickelhaube* (spiked helmet) which later saved thousands of German casualties. In despair Messimy wrote prophetically, 'That blind and imbecile attachment to the most visible of all colours will have cruel consequences.'

During the Battle of the Marne in 1914 he was proved tragically right. The 246th Regiment, in an attempt to cross an exposed plain on a bright sunny day, highlighted themselves against the yellow background of the fields. Even at 1500 metres the red and blue of their uniforms stood out so clearly that the opposing Germans were almost dazzled by the scene. To compound their folly the French then unfurled their regimental standard and brought their band forward to play them into close-quarter battle, rendering them virtually impossible to miss in the process. Inevitably, and wholly avoidably, the regiment was annihilated during the first few hours of its committment to battle. During the month of August, 1914, alone the French sustained 206,515 casualties, many of them unnecessary. Even then they failed to learn. Men were sacrificed by the thousand in fruitless charges against positions strengthened by barbed wire and machine guns, weapons which the French tacticians had earlier discounted as irrelevant.

It was over a year before the French infantry was able to convert to a more realistic uniform. Until then tradition was allowed to overrule common sense throughout. The Foreign Legion continued to wear its distinctive kepi blanc (white headdress), while the Zouaves and Spahis, elite infantry and cavalry regiments formed from the North African colonies, wore extraordinarily colourful uniforms, as ill-equipped to protect the wearers against the northern French winter as they were to camouflage them from the enemy.

The French Cuirassiers wore shiny breastplates and long horse-hair plumes on Grecian helmets, but in this madness they were not alone. Other armies were equally fanciful: the Belgian cavalry of 1914 wore green tunics and purple breeches, the Austrian horsemen yellow breeches, Austro-Hungarian officers yellow sashes and bright sword scabbards.

It has been claimed that 1915 heralded the death of military innocence. It certainly witnessed the demise of the military deceit of sartorial elegance in battle. But by then countless thousands of men had died needlessly, all because a few powerful traditionalists such as Etienne had earlier deceived themselves that war was somehow a romantic entity to be fought by gentlemen. In so doing they had ignored the realities of modern firepower and the introduction of new weapon systems and had chosen to ignore the obvious lessons of wars in Africa, the Far East and even the Balkans; no doubt arguing that, because these had not been exclusively Western European in their prosecution, they were of no consequence.

The Schlieffen Plan

It should not be thought that the German commanders of the day were themselves somehow free of the sin of complacency. The Schlieffen Plan, which formed the basis of the German attack in 1914, was as brilliant as it was audacious. Introduced in complete secrecy in 1905 by Chief of the General Staff Count von Schlieffen, amended annually by him until his death in 1913 and then modified and reduced by his successor, General Helmuth von Moltke, it was also far too optimistic.

The object of the plan was to knock France out of the conflict in precisely 42 days, before the Russian steamroller could mobilize and come to her aid. It accepted the risks of an early Russian move westward and a French attack on Alsace and Lorraine, in order to unleash five armies – three quarters of the entire German Army – in a gigantic westward sweep across Belgium and Luxembourg, followed by a wheel south into France.

After a series of striking successes the German advance, by now exhausted, was brought to a halt on the Marne. Quite simply von Schlieffen had underestimated the strength of the Russians and the near-panic that their advance would cause in Berlin, the power of Belgian resistance, the effectiveness of the British Expeditionary Force and the importance of the French railway system in bringing up reserves.

Equally, the plan failed to take into account the realities of human endurance. The men of Kluck's First Army on the German left had to cover 30 to 40km per day, as a result of which their supplies quickly became over- extended and their communications unreliable. It became impossible for Kluck properly to reconnoitre the areas through which he was advancing. When the German IV, III and IX Corps under his command encountered the British II Corps at Mons on 23 August, 1914, the lack of reconnaissance proved critical.

The Germans had discounted the worth of the British on account of the relatively small size of their Army, its lack of European warfare experience and its poor showing in the Boer War. Yet, by 1914 War Secretary Richard Haldane had transformed the British Army. Composed of volunteers enlisted for a seven year period, stiffened by reserves recalled to the colours, and led by well-qualified officers, its morale, discipline and steadiness were second to none. With a few exceptions the 150,000 men of the British Expeditionary Force (BEF) were armed with the legendary .303-inch Short Magazine Lee Enfield rifle, and all were trained to fire fifteen aimed rounds per minute at a target up to 300 yards away. Unaware that the British had established themselves in skirmishing order among the slag heaps and houses to the south of the Mons Canal the Germans advanced in close order and were slaughtered by the concentrated fire of the British infantry. Many who survived would not believe that the British had no more than two machine guns per battalion and had little idea of how to deploy these.

The British, although undefeated, were forced to continue their retreat from Mons when General Lanrezac's French Fifth Army withdrew, leaving their left flank exposed. Kluck was therefore able to recover much of his lost momentum, convince himself that the British had been neutralized as a fighting entity, and continue the German First Army's advance across the border into France. Three days later Kluck was again rebuffed when the BEF attempted a second stand to relieve the exhausted II Corps troops at Le Cateau. General Horace Smith-Dorrien's Corps was heavily outnumbered in men and more particularly artillery, yet in the largest battle that the British Army had fought since Waterloo it successfully fought off a double envelopment by the full strength of Kluck's army. The survivors successfully disengaged at nightfall. The cost was high; 7,800 casualties out of 40,000 engaged, but the Germans were slowed yet again and the Schlieffen Plan was struck a near-mortal blow.

When Bulow's German Second Army to the south was mauled by the French and sought assistance Kluck, thinking the British to be out of the equation, and unable to communicate with high command 240km away in Luxembourg, abandoned the remnants of the Schlieffen Plan. Ignorant of the French reserves massing in Paris, and of the speed with which they would ultimately be able to move, he shifted his direction of march to the south-east across the Marne, his own right flank wide open to counter-attack from the massing French reserves.

The French took the offensive on 5 September, 1914. In five days of bitter fighting they stopped the larger, though now utterly exhausted, German armies, forcing them to regroup north of the Marne. The short but bitter war of mobility ended as both sides consolidated and dug-in.

Obtuse Consequences

Smith-Dorrien's decision to stand and fight at Le Cateau had saved the BEF, but it had been made in defiance of orders given by Field Marshal Sir John French, in overall command of the BEF, to go on withdrawing. General Douglas Haig, in command of I Corps, had retreated at such a pace that he had completely lost touch with the enemy, exposing Smith- Dorrien's flank in the process. The resultant wholly irrational grudge which Haig and French bore against Smith-Dorrien as a result of his showing up their spinelessness in this way, and their lack of regard for his social standing, had much to do with his subsequently being sacked.

In December, 1915, French, too, was sacked, and replaced by Douglas Haig. Haig's rise owed more to influential connections than to natural ability. A personal friend and ADC to the King, in 1905 he married the Hon. Dorothy Vivian, one of Queen Alexandra's maids of honour. Although a graduate of the Staff College he had failed to pass the entrance examination and had been forced to rely upon the patronage of the Duke of Cambridge, an acquaintance of his elder sister, Henrietta, to have the formalities of an examination waived. Perhaps not surprisingly he had failed to shine in the final examination, attracting unfavourable comment from General Plumer (later his subordinate), who was conducting it.

Yet Haig quickly became accepted by the social and political elite to whom breeding was more important than brains. His often-expressed opinions that the cavalry would have a larger share of action in any future war, that the artillery was of little worth save against raw troops and that the machine gun was overrated, all dangerous self-deceptions, became accepted without question by the old guard and did much to cause the chronic imbalances and weaknesses in materiel experienced by the BEF in the early stages of the war.

The Cavalryman's Lament

When the Armistice came into effect on 11 November, 1918, the regular armies of the world sighed with relief and looked forward to demobilizing all the conscripts and 'getting back to the gentlemanly art of soldiering'. High on their agenda was the restoration of the proper peacetime pecking order, with the cavalry at the top of the pile.

It did not matter that the First World War had been a humbling experience for the horse soldiers, who had seen their premier position usurped by the other arms while they had spent much of the conflict waiting for the breakthrough which never came until the war was virtually over. As soon as peace prevailed they were quick to point out that the conditions in France had been an aberration, never likely to occur again.

Palestine, they argued, had been more typical. In defeating the Turks Allenby had shown that in open country the horse still had many advantages. Many of the horses used in the desert had not been bred for the cavalry. Indeed many of the Yeomanry mounts had been ex-Hackneys, some over twenty years old. Purchased in an emergency in England, they had been shipped abroad and had performed as well as their better-bred neighbours.

In the wave of good will towards the cavalry, it is hardly surprising that when the inevitable post-war retrenchment came the cavalry generals were able to ensure that the regular establishment for cavalry regiments remained virtually intact. In the eyes of its commanders the greatest enemy of the cavalry was the tank, to be belittled and denigrated at every opportunity. The fact that Field Marshal Haig, in spite of the appalling slaughter caused by metal against flesh on the Western Front, still deceived himself that there was an important rôle for horse cavalry on future battlefields, did much to slow down the process of mechanization. Tanks and armoured cars were slow and unreliable, he argued, and could not hope to usurp the cavalry, particularly in its traditional rôle of reconnaissance. Furthermore they lacked panache, were noisy and unromantic and they were simply not a mode of transport suited to gentlemen.

Among the Allies bias against the tank led to its being degraded as a weapon of war. In the United States the Tank Corps was disbanded in 1920 as part of the Defense Act. The majority of the 1,200 tanks in service were scrapped or moth-balled, and the balance designated 'Infantry' and parcelled out to act purely as support troops. From a potent and independent force they were limited to one armoured company per infantry division, plus five battalions and a headquarters group in Army reserve.

In France the *Artillerie d'Assault* succumbed to the conservatives even before the war had ended and by 1918 had been relegated to infantry support. In 1920 the surviving tanks, most of them small Renault two-man vehicles, were dispersed throughout the army as independent battalions attached to infantry regiments. Only in Britain, where ironically the cavalry tradition was strongest, was a true Tank Corps allowed to remain in existence and by 1924 even it had dwindled to about 150 tanks.

Throughout the 1920s and early 1930s the dispute continued over the method of deploying the tank. The cavalry saw it as threatening its traditional roles of reconnaissance and flank protection and thus continued to deceive itself that the tank was too slow and unreliable to replace the horse in such work. Even when Fuller, Guderian and others proved the fallacy of this argument the self-deception was allowed to continue. The infantry wanted the tank solely as a mobile pillbox and gun-carrier to accompany them at a slow walk across no-man's-land and punch a hole in the enemy's trenches. The cavalry accepted this return to a patently redundant style of warfare, as it would have been they who would have exploited the breakthrough created by the infantry. As a result the Allies were destined to squander their numerical superiority in tanks in the early stages of the Second World War (3,310 against 2,439). While the Germans planned for Blitzkrieg the Allies committed their armour piecemeal, losing it any advantages that its numbers might otherwise have provided. Only in Arras, and then by accident, did Allied and German armour meet on equal terms.

The tanks of Major-General Harold Franklyn's First Army Tank Brigade were caught in the open by German Stukas and badly mauled. The survivors were pursued into Arras by the German Panzers, who ran into a trap, albeit entirely unplanned. The French 3rd Light Mechanized Division was waiting for the BEF's arrival, and they, with their heavier guns and stronger armour, achieved the only Allied tank victory of the campaign.

Had the cavalry not deceived itself into believing that nothing had changed, and had the infantry not followed the tradition of trying to fight the new war using the previous war's tactics the Allies would have been far better placed to meet the German onslaught. In defence of the cavalry, it should not be thought that the rôle of the horse was over by 1918. There are none so devout as the newly-converted, and in their enthusiasm for their new concepts of war the tank enthusiasts often over-reached themselves, and in so doing made more enemies than friends. Despite their high degree of mechanization the German Army never lost sight of the potential of the horse, but used it in its proper place. Throughout the Second World War more guns were towed and ammunition moved by horse transport in the German Army than in any other.

CHAPTER THREE:
Deception and Human Vanity

Little is known of the fall of Troy, save that it was sacked by the Greeks during the eleventh century BC. The intercession of the gods during the siege and the part played by the wooden horse are pure fable. Nonetheless the story of the Wooden Horse of Troy serves as a salutory warning to those warring nations who would drop their guard and, in their longing for peace, allow themselves to be deceived by a more ruthless enemy.

After ten years of fighting the siege of Troy was at a stalemate. Turning to subterfuge, Odysseus, the king of Ithica and a renowned warrior, ordered a great number of trees to be felled and the timber to be carried back to the Greek camp. There a high wall was built to hide from the Trojans the activities of the Greek Army. The timber was cut and shaped into a vast wooden horse. Its belly concealed a hollowed area large enough to accommodate thirty fully armed men. The horse was constructed on wheels and was deliberately made too high and wide to pass through any of the city gates.

As soon as the horse was finished Agamemnon, commander of the Greek Army, ordered the siege camp to be raised and his forces to put to sea. They left behind Odysseus and thirty of their finest troops hidden in the belly of the horse. The Trojans rejoiced at the ending of the war and at their good fortune. Believing that the horse would make their city impregnable they tore down a section of the wall and towed it to the courtyard before the temple of Athena.

That night, as the entire city rejoiced, the Greek fleet stole back to the beaches. On a given signal Odysseus and his men climbed down from the horse, crept through the by now silent streets, killed the few sentries on duty and opened the gates of Troy to Agamemnon and his army. There followed a night of terrible slaughter, during which death fell on the Trojans before they were awake and able to arm.

Over three millenia later another wooden horse proved equally successful in the deception of a too complacent enemy. In 1943 two RAF officers and an army officer dug a shallow tunnel, and by means of it contrived an audacious escape from the German prisoner of war camp, Stalag Luft III. Uniquely their tunnel did not begin in the solid floor beneath the stove in their living accommodation nor in the foundations of a washroom or other permanent building. Instead it began in the open, less than 40 metres from the wire.

To cover the digging the trio built a wooden vaulting horse. It stood 1.38 metres high, the base covering an area 1.5 metres by 90cm. The sides were covered with 60cm square plywood sheets from Red Cross package cases, the top was of wooden bed-boards padded with bedding and covered with white canvas used originally to pack cigarettes from England. There were four slots, 10cm long by 7.5cm wide, cut into the plywood sides through which rafters were pushed to enable the horse to be carried by four men in the manner of a sedan chair.

Once constructed, the horse was kept in the canteen where the Germans could, and occasionally did, inspect it. For the first week of its use the horse was employed conventionally. Teams of volunteers spent up to two hours a day in vaulting practice, occasionally deliberately knocking the horse over in sight of the guards to prove that there was nothing hidden inside. After a few days two jump pits were built in the exercise area, ostensibly to make the vaulters' landings easier but in reality to ensure that the horse was positioned in precisely the same place each day.

After a week, once the guards had become used to the sight of the horse, it took on its real purpose. First one and later two tunnellers were hidden inside and carried out on each vaulting session. Once the horse was in position and vaulting had commenced they began to dig, first vertically to a depth of about a metre, and then horizontally towards and eventually under the wire. Before the exercise session ceased and the horse was removed the tunnel entrance was disguised with loose boards and covered with grey sand similar to that in the exercise area. The spoil was carried away in improvised sacks made from the sewn-up legs of old trousers.

Shortly before the escape was due to take place the vaulters increased their training sessions to twice a day, no mean feat for men who were weak with hunger. In late October, after four months of digging, the three escapers were carried to the tunnel entrance, one in the morning session and two in the afternoon. Once in position the three moled the last few metres to freedom, breaking surface after dark but before evening roll- call. By the time that they were missed they had already caught a train and were safely en route to Hanover. All three made it safely back to England.

It is impossible to tell the full story of the escape from Stalag Luft III in a few paragraphs. Certainly the trio were lucky, the tunnel suffered a partial collapse on at least two occasions and one of the tunnellers was hospitalized for a week with exhaustion. Nonetheless theirs is a classic example of what can be done with resourcefulness and daring, particularly when the enemy is complacent and all too willing to accept a deception at face value.

Although wartime escapes from Occupied Europe were not unusual, those from Germany itself were comparatively rare. This was due in no small part to the German psyche. Prisoners were inevitably travelling with forged or stolen papers, and in clothes which would not stand up to rigorous inspection. Most Germans have an eye for detail and will quickly pick out the unusual. They will then invariably question it in a manner which other Europeans will find obtrusive, and will carry on doing so until satisfied. Many prisoners were apprehended when forced into conversation by a fellow traveller on a bus or train, or by a local in a village or small town. Not satisfied with the escapers' attempted deception the local would quickly inform the authorities. Investigation and arrest would quickly follow.

The Sykes-Picot Agreement

Not every government deception has been so honourable. In the summer of 1916 Hussein, the Sherif of Mecca, flung hia armies in open rebellion against the Turks. The Allies, sensing an advantage, offered help. They provided assistance in the form of advisers, including the mercurial T. E. Lawrence, but gave little in the way of material assistance. Unaided, the Sherifian forces overran the Turkish garrison in Mecca and took Jeddah, but then dissipated their energies against the fortifications at Medina.

Fearful that Hussein might withdraw his forces, and that elements of them might even sue for peace, the British and French entered into a shameful deception. In 1915 the diplomat Ronald Storrs was ordered to offer Hussein a vague assurance of British support in the cause of a Hashemite 'Arab nation'. When Hussein subsequently demanded as a reward for his venture against the Turks an enormous slice of territory, almost all the Arab-speaking lands between the borders of Iran, the shores of the Mediterranean and the Persian Gulf, Britain and France intimated their agreement.

Sir Henry McMahon, the British High Commissioner in Egypt, accepted virtually the entire demand, save that large parts of Syria were to be exempted and French interests were to be considered in any final settlement. At approximately the same time Britain and France entered into the secret Sykes-Picot agreement, by which the entire area was carved into zones of influence agreeable to the major European Allied powers.

There was to be a 'Blue' zone, north of Acre and west of Damascus, which would be run by France, and a 'Red' zone stretching from the Persian Gulf along the river valleys to beyond Baghdad, which would be British. Zone 'A', a triangular area incorporating Homs, Damascus and Tiberias, and Zone 'B', east of the Dead Sea and Jordan Valley, although nominally independent, were to fall under French and British influence respectively. Palestine would come under a British, French and Russian condominium, while Russia would herself take the Dardanelles, including Constantinople. Even Italy, a relative latecomer to the war, was offered Smyrna and southern Anatolia.

As far as Paris and London were concerned, promises made to Arab leaders, whom few diplomats understood and most despised, were of little import. It was never intended that Hussein should gain a kingdom from the Allied victory, nor indeed would many of his potential subjects have wanted it. Nonetheless the fiction was perpetuated in order to keep the Arab armies in the field. Pro-Arabists such as Lawrence were denied the truth, while less scrupulous diplomats actively perpetuated the fable of local independence long after they knew it to be a sham.

The Allies gained considerably from this deception, which effectively led to the opening of a new front behind the Turkish lines. The Arabs in their turn gained little. The Turks were expelled from their lands but were quickly replaced by Europeans who neither understood their lifestyles nor sympathized with their aspirations.

One More Push

All too often in recent history military commanders have fallen victim to the sin of self-deception. They have allowed their sheer desire for victory to overcome their better judgment and in several instances have even massaged the truth to suit their theories. The losses during the major battles of the First World War were horrific, yet there is ample evidence to suggest that they might have been less had the commanders listened to their subordinates, studied their casualty figures more sympathetically, and believed less blindly in the success of 'one more push'.

By 1914 all the major powers had adopted a general-staff system more or less along the lines used so successfully by the Prussians during the Franco-Prussian War of 1870-71. Yet even the German High Command failed to exploit the system fully when its findings contradicted their social or political bias.

The British Army had suffered a number of ignominious defeats during the Second Boer War, yet it had been rebuilt by Haldane in the years that had followed and by 1914 was a potent, if small, fighting machine. Germany ignored these improvements and continued to regard the British army as 'contemptible', ill-disciplined, poorly equipped and liable to be swept into the sea on the first contact. The realities were very different. The British Expeditionary Force (BEF) of over 100,000 men was all-professional, a fairly equal combination of regular soldiers or reserves recently returned to civilian life and called back to the colours. It quietly but efficiently crossed the Channel within days of the outbreak of war, moved into Belgium and was mentally and physically prepared for combat when it met the advancing German First Army at Mons on 23 August, 1914.

Von Kluck, on hearing that his route was being opposed by the British, deceived himself into believing that they would offer little resistance. Ignoring the basic lessons of manoeuvre, he moved his men forward at speed, in tight formations and without reconnaissance. The British forces, all capable of firing fifteen aimed rifle shots per minute at a range of 300 yards, poured volley after lethal volley into the massed ranks of the advancing Germans. Heavily outnumbered, the British were eventually forced to concede ground, but not until they had taught the German General Staff a salutory lesson in the evils of complacency.

For the next few days the BEF, hard-pressed, vastly outnumbered and almost entirely lacking in heavy artillery, fought a series of daily rearguard actions. On 27 August it became engaged in the biggest battle that the British had fought since Waterloo when, at Le Cateau, General Smith-Dorrien's exhausted II Corps fought off a double envelopment by the full strength of von Kluck's army. Its losses were high, yet its sheer professionalism caused the by now disillusioned enemy facing it to slow their advance and reconsider their tactics.

It must be conceded that the bloody stalemate on the Western Front which followed soon after was caused much more by territorial limitations and weapon power than by poor leadership. Yet all too often the failure of the senior commanders to appreciate that a battle had not had its desired effect, and their tendency to sacrifice reserves when common sense dictated that the enemy was too strong to effect a breakthrough, compounded the carnage.

Typical was the carnage suffered by the British during the months following the Battle of Neuve Chapelle. The initial attack at Neuve Chapelle, delivered on 10 March, 1915, had been well planned, but thereafter the battle had been mishandled. Poor management had prevented an adequate follow-up and within three days the Germans had re-established the line.

The planners conceded that they had made a mistake and deceived themselves that they had rectified it. Realistically they had done no such thing. Fundamentally they ignored the potency of concealed machine-gun nests sited 800 to 1,000 metres behind the front line. In so doing they failed totally to address the problems faced by massed manpower when it enters a position defended by intelligently applied firepower. They ignored the fact that the

Germans, recognizing the need for a change in tactics, had adopted an elastic defence, in two or three widely separated lines, each independent of the others and highly organized with machine guns and artillery support in depth. In the Battle of Aubers Ridge, and in late September, 1915, at Loos, the British took the German front lines with comparative ease only to be decimated by the fire from the supporting lines and pounded by heavy artillery beyond the range of their own guns.

Field Marshal French was relieved of command and replaced by General Haig on 17 December, 1915. Matters might have improved, but did not. Like his predecessor Haig regarded the machine gun as a much over-rated weapon and could not be convinced that a battalion should be issued with more than two. A cavalryman to the last, he firmly believed that victory lay in the massed assault.

Haig accepted that surprise should always be of the essence, yet all too frequently ignored advice when warned that the element of surprise had been lost. After the first day of the Battle of Loos, which had gone relatively well for the British, Haig, then commanding 1st Army, ordered that the 21st and 24th Divisions, both fresh from training and untried in battle, should attack the German second position, some 8km behind the front line.

Not only was the venture ludicrously over-optimistic, but it was attempted against all prevailing advice. Intelligence, which had earlier accurately predicted the German dispositions, warned that the enemy were capable of bringing at least five reserve divisions into the second line before the attack could be launched. Common sense dictated that the second attack should be abandoned. Yet such would have been its effect on the war had it succeeded in forcing a break-through that Haig convinced himself that it was feasible.

The British divisions left the protection of their trenches in broad daylight with no gas or smoke cloud to cover them and with no dedicated artillery support, and proceeded to assault a position more strongly defended than had been the German front line at the commencement of the battle. Both were slaughtered.

Lessons Learned

On 11 November, 1918, the last shot of the First World War was fired. It had been the most destructive war in history. Nearly ten million human beings had been bombed, gassed, blown apart, buried alive or machine- gunned; another twenty-two million had been wounded or maimed; five million civilians had died from starvation, exposure and disease, another ten million from the war-spawned plague of Spanish Influenza. Less than twenty-one years later the first shot of the Second World War was fired and set off a firestorm destined to consume more lives than any other war in history.

Technology and tactics improved tremendously during the two decades of the interbellum. The principles of blitzkreig practised so successfully by the Germans during *Operation Michael* in the spring of 1918 were expanded and, under Heinz Guderian, were honed to perfection. The effects of blitzkrieg, and the willingness of Germany to practise total war, should have been no secret. On 25 April, 1937, Luftwaffe pilots flying in support of Franco bombed the northern Spanish town of Guernica with the loss of many non-combatant lives. During the same year Guderian published his widely acclaimed textbook, *Achtung! Panzer!* in which he openly advocated the creation of independent armoured formations with strong air and mechanized infantry support. Each corps would be comprised wholly of elite troops, highly trained and capable of penetrating the enemy lines with minimal loss.

Britain, and to a lesser degree France, regularly monitored German military radio traffic during the late 1930s and must have known of the creation of the panzer formations, yet both chose to ignore this new and terrible form of absolute warfare. Instead their leaders deceived themselves that nothing had changed and that the might of the French Army, so nearly brought to its knees in 1917, would protect them against the growing threat of German aggression.

The way in which the British and French governments were deceived by Hitler at the time of the Munich crisis was shameful. Equally alarming was the way in which the military leaders of the day allowed themselves to be deceived into a policy of near-inactivity before and immediately after the commencement of hostilities.

Between 1929 and 1934 France constructed a series of fortresses along her eastern frontier from Longwy, on the Luxembourg border, to Switzerland. Named after the Minister of War, Andre Maginot, the fortifications were not continued along the Franco-Belgium border, because of Belgian objections and because a group of French strategists held that the Germans could not penetrate the densely wooded Ardennes.

When war came in September, 1939, Belgium and Holland both maintained strict neutrality, a fatal concession to political expediency which prevented any co-operation with French and British military planners. A British Expeditionary Force of nearly 400,000 men was moved across the Channel where it was forced to construct a series of wholly inadequate anti-tank ditches along the Franco-Belgian border.

There followed nearly nine months of 'Sitzkrieg' or 'phoney war' during which the Allies, instead of taking the initiative and attempting a breakthrough which might well have succeeded, did nothing. Instead they relied upon a policy of blockade, economic strangulation and defensive fortification to exhaust the German Army which, in reality, grew stronger by the day.

The Allied planners continued to argue that a big push would win the war eventually, yet failed totally to plan for one. More fundamentally, they continued to deceive themselves that the Ardennes remained impassable for large modern armies and declined to place more than nine divisions, only two of which were up to strength, in the sector. Hitler and the German High Command fully realized the recklessness of this complacency. Top secret plans were implemented for a lightning strike through Belgium and around Sedan. The attack, when it came, proved highly successful.

What had appeared to the Allies to be solid lines of defence were breached with little opposition by the sheer violence and speed of the blitzkrieg tactics. Von Rundstedt's Army Group A in particular, moving through the Ardennes, swept aside a weakened and unprepared enemy, pouring men and munitions into the Allied rear. The BEF and French left flank, instead of looking across the front line to face the enemy, were shocked to discover German tanks behind them.

Left with no option but to retreat Lord Gort, Commander of the BEF, withdrew towards the sea and began to implement previously laid plans for a mass evacuation. Calais, with its harbour, long gently sloping beaches and proximity to England would have proved an ideal base, but German troops were moving in fast and attempts a few days earlier to embark men there had been entirely thwarted by air attack, at the cost of many lives.

Operation Dynamo

It quickly became clear that Dunkirk offered the only possibility of an evacuation. The story of Operation Dynamo, the removal of 338,226 Allied soldiers from the mole and beaches of Dunkirk, is well known. It might never have occurred had it not been for the massive deception played by the British Government against its French Allies and for an incredible decision taken personally by Adolf Hitler.

On 26 May, 1940, Hitler ordered his panzers to halt and pull back. It has been suggested that he was motivated by Goering's plea that the Luftwaffe be permitted to administer the *coup de grâce* and thus share fully in the glories of victory. Others have argued that, even at the eleventh hour, Hitler hoped to make peace with Britain and realized that the wholesale humiliation of his fellow Anglo-Saxons would make this more difficult.

Whatever Hitler's motives the reality was very different. Not for the last time Goering allowed himself to be deceived into over-estimating the potency of the Luftwaffe. The Germans in the air met an unrelenting attack from RAF fighters based in southern England, and in a series of spectacular air battles were temporarily neutralized. At the same time the British resolve to fight on, spurred on by the new Prime Minister, Winston Churchill, grew daily stronger. It took Guderian two days to convince Hitler to change his mind and resume the assault, but by then it was too late; the British defences around Dunkirk had hardened.

Deception on the Eastern Front

At 3.00am on 22 June, 1941, Hitler invaded the Soviet Union. Stalin was taken completely by surprise but should not have been. For months British Intelligence had been monitoring German troop movements east and had been using every means possible short of a direct approach to warn the Russian dictator. Details of the impending attack had been fed to the NKVD via the Lucy spy-ring in Switzerland. Richard Sorge, a reliable Russian spy in Tokyo, had warned the Kremlin of the coming invasion weeks ahead of the event. German officials in Moscow had begun to pack their possessions and had sent their families home. Yet Stalin had chosen to ignore the warnings, believing that they were a crude British attempt to undermine the Molotov-Ribbentrop Non-Aggression Pact of August, 1939. In an environment in which disagreement was regarded as criticism, and had all too often resulted in liquidation, none of his closest advisers had dared to argue with him.

By the summer of 1941 Stalin was sure that war with Germany was inevitable, but equally knew that his armies were in no state to withstand an assault. Over 35,000 of his senior officers had been purged in 1937-38 to ensure the unquestioning loyalty of the remainder. Only 27 per cent of the Red Army fleet of 24,000 tanks were fully operational and all but 1,500 were obsolete.

Stalin planned a steady build up of his forces during the winter of 1941/42, but until then determined to do nothing to provoke his hugely more powerful neighbour. He ordered that the terms of the Non- Aggression Pact be adhered to rigidly and, until the very morning of the invasion, continued to send train- loads of grain and oil to the Reich.

Crucially, he ordered that Soviet reconnaissance planes were not to provoke the Germans by being too intrusive. The final preparations for the assault therefore went entirely unheeded, even by the forward units which were overrun within hours of the invasion. Those units that were strong or disciplined enough to put up even a token resistance were ordered not to. When General Pavlov in Minsk reported to Moscow the bombing of every major city in the area he was ordered by Marshal Timoshenko, Commissar of Defence and one of Stalin's oldest aides, to take no retaliatory action. Specifically he was not allowed to deploy his artillery, nor was he allowed to fly reconnaissance missions more than 60km behind German territory.

It was a ludicrous response. Most Soviet planes had already been destroyed on the ground and Pavlov's forces were in full retreat. Yet it exemplified the sheer depths to which Stalin had allowed himself to become deceived.

By the spring of 1942 Stalin had recovered from the shock of *Barbarossa* and was in buoyant mood. Against all the evidence he convinced himself that Moscow remained the Nazis' principle target, even when the plans for *Operation Blau*, the proposed German assault deep into the Ukraine and the Caucasus, fell into his hands. Eleven days before the German attack General Georg Stumme, the commander of XL Panzer Corps which was destined to play a major part in the attack, briefed his three divisional commanders. Strictly against orders he issued detailed written plans, a copy of which fell into Soviet hands when a light plane carrying Major Reichel, the chief of operations of 23rd Panzer Division, crash-landed.

The plans gave Stalin the German order of battle and details of where they would strike first. Yet when they were shown to him he regarded them as so contrary to his own belief that Moscow would be the sole target for the forthcoming event that he dismissed them out of hand as 'planted evidence'. Stumme was court-martialled and imprisoned, though he later returned to action. Stalin, a man incapable of finding fault in himself, no doubt found a scapegoat on his general staff.

Hitler was as capable of self-deception as Stalin. By the time of *Operation Blau* his front line forces were under-strength. Only eight divisions out of the 160 in the field were fully fit for an offensive; 48 could sustain limited action, 73 were suitable only for defence, 29 were so badly depleted that they could not even defend themselves and two were non-operational. The German army in the east was short of 500,000 men and was rapidly haemorrhaging while the Soviets grew stronger. The Red Army was much better armed and motivated than had been anticipated, with far greater reserves both in men and materiel.

To any leader lacking Hitler's self-confidence these factors would have weighed heavily against a spring offensive. But Hitler was determined to capture the oilfields of the Caucasus and the grain harvest of the Ukraine, and, for no other reason than economic needs, discounted the very real caveats of his generals.

Having himself assumed supreme command of the German army in December, 1941, Hitler was determined to assert his authority by imposing his own battle plans. He decreed that *Operation Blau* would comprise a two-pronged offensive, with one army thrusting eastward towards Stalingrad (though not the city itself) to destroy the Soviet forces on the Don and Volga rivers, and the second assaulting south into the Caucasus. He blatantly ignored the advice of his strategists who argued that the two prongs would be too far apart to support each other, and instead asserted that they would split the Soviet forces, which would thus be unable to stop either thrust.

To realize his grand scheme Hitler ordered a huge mobilization programme which resulted in the commitment of over half of Germany's Eastern Front forces to one battle. The initial success of *Operation Blau* was due in no small part to Stalin's refusal to accept that it was more than a feint. Contrary to all advice he continued to regard Moscow as the prime Nazi target. Only in the second week of July, when no offensive against Moscow had materialized, did he take defensive action. He ordered his forces in the south to withdraw to defensive positions on the Don to avoid encirclement, and to stand firm on the Volga. The advancing German armies captured ground easily but took few prisoners, a factor which Hitler wholly discounted to his later cost.

Hitler's belief, against all military experience, that *Blau* had succeeded in full led him to make some disastrous changes of plan. He transferred five divisions from the Crimea to Leningrad and moved two crack divisions to France, arguing, again without military support, that an Allied invasion there was imminent. At the same time he extended the scope of the advance south to the Caucasus, ordering Hoth's IV Panzer Army, originally part of the dash towards Stalingrad with VI Army, south to the Don.

Had IV Army remained on its original course it is likely that Stalingrad could have been taken with minimal resistance. By the time that Hitler had changed his orders yet again, and had sent Hoth back to Stalingrad, Stalin had formed a massive front around the city and had ordered that it be held at all costs. The folly of

Hitler's policies now became apparent. By disposing his armies too thinly, and by alloting them objectives hundreds of kilometres apart, he had lost the initiative and allowed the Red Army to reform. In so doing Hitler virtually single-handedly laid the foundations for Germany's eventual defeat.

On 23 August, 1942, the German VI Army, supported by the IV Panzer Army to the south, began the battle for Stalingrad. Their target was not as easy as Hitler had deceived himself into believing it would be. The city, with its population of 500,000, was well positioned for defence. Its massive factory complexes in the north were quickly turned into fortresses while in the centre the 100m high Mamayev Kurgan (a burial mound) offered natural cover. Further to the south ran the 60m deep gorge through which flowed the Tsaritsa river en route to the Volga. The entire population had been either evacuated or mobilized with orders to fight to the death. Stalingrad could be supplied, albeit with difficulty, from across the Volga, while German supply was meagrely maintained by a single rail line, completely inadequate for the situation.

Under the overall command of General Georgi Zhukov, who had masterminded the defence of Moscow a year earlier, the Soviets began a long-term strategy in which Stalingrad became the bait in a huge military trap. General Vasili Chuikov's Sixty-Second Army was charged with holding the city at all costs, and was given just enough men and supplies to survive. In the meantime, and quite unknown to Hitler, massive reserves were built up to the north and south-east.

Within two months Zhukov had a million men, 13,500 heavy guns, 900 tanks and 1,100 aircraft at his disposal and was ready to spring his trap. On the night of 19/20 November four fresh and fully equipped Army Groups began a massive pincer movement to the north and south of the city, cutting through the meagre Romanian, Hungarian and Italian forces protecting the German lines of communication. Within forty-eight hours von Paulus was completely encircled. A spirited attempt by the IV Panzer Army to come to his rescue from the south was fought to a bloody standstill, leaving von Paulus and the VI Army with no option but to force a breakout or face annihilation.

Von Paulus requested permission to withdraw. Hitler refused and instead accepted Goering's offer to supply the VI Army from the air. On 24 November, to the horror of his senior military advisers, Hitler signalled von Paulus: 'I will do everything in my power to supply it (VI Army) adequately, and disengage it when the time is convenient.'

The airlift was put into effect, but it was immediately obvious that Goering's promise was mere fantasy. The VI Army would require 165 aircraft loads of fuel and ammunition and 75 aircraft loads of food per day to survive, yet the Luftwaffe had already committed the bulk of its transport planes to North Africa. The only airfields available were at Gumrak and at Pitomnik, 24km from central Stalingrad and vulnerable to Soviet attack. The Luftwaffe suffered heavily in its valiant attempts to supply its comrades on the ground but was never able to provide von Paulus with more than half of his daily needs, and on several occasions was unable to fly at all due to heavy fog.

In Stalingrad itself conditions became steadily more horrific. Back in Germany the plight of VI Army was either ignored or denied. When Hitler's liaison officer reported the imminent collapse by radio, Goering dismissed the report out of hand as Soviet propaganda, arguing that the transmitter must have been captured. In a final orgy of self-deception, on Christmas Day Minister of Propaganda Joseph Goebbels transmitted phoney messages from the Stalingrad garrison to their relatives at home in an attempt to prove that all was still well.

The Soviets offered von Paulus terms of surrender on 8 January, but, faithful to his Führer the General fought on. Even when the airfields fell Hitler refused to concede the true plight of his VI Army and absolutely forbade surrender. On 30 January, 1943, he made von Paulus a Field Marshal. His motives were transparent: never in the history of Germany had a Field Marshal surrendered. In Hitler's estimation von Paulus was now left with only two possible causes, to fight to the death or to commit suicide. He did neither. On 2 February, its food and ammunition exhausted and with most of its positions overrun, he ordered the VI Army to surrender.

Hitler's obstinacy in refusing von Paulus the right to withdraw had cost him in all 300,000 men. Von Paulus and 93,000 survivors were taken into captivity, of whom no more than 5,000 ever saw Germany again. Hitler accused von Paulus of being 'a characterless weakling' for preferring captivity to suicide. As a prisoner, the Field-Marshal turned against the Nazis, organizing military opposition and broadcasting pleas to his former colleagues to defect. He remained in Russia after the war, returning to East Germany in 1953 where he became an adviser to the East German Army.

Monty's Double

In September, 1939, Clifton James volunteered to return to the colours. He had seen service as a private infantryman during the First World War, had been wounded in action in 1916 and had lost a finger. Between the wars he had become an actor, appearing in a number of successful repertory productions, although never becoming a well-known figure on the West End stage. He had not unreasonably assumed that the Army would wish to exploit his theatrical talents. Instead they commissioned him into the Royal Army Pay Corps.

James did not complain, but instead settled down into a job which, by his own admission, he regarded as routine and boring. In early 1944, to alleviate the monotony, he volunteered to join an RAPC drama group then giving Sunday performances to the troops in London. While performing at the Comedy Theatre he was approached by a reporter from the *News Chronicle* who remarked upon his likeness to General Montgomery. James agreed to have his photograph taken saluting and wearing the distinctive Royal Tank Corps beret readily identifiable with the general.

James thought little more of the incident until 14 March when the photograph appeared in the newspaper under the caption 'The man who brought the house down'. James waited in nervous anticipation for a severe dressing down for the unauthorized impersonation, but when none came he forgot the matter. Unknown to him, however, the photograph had been seen and filed by MI5.

A few weeks later James was summoned to London to meet Lieutenant-Colonel David Niven of Army Kinematography and Colonel Lester of MI5. His likeness to Montgomery was discussed, as was the possibility of his passing for the General at close quarters. Thereafter he was transferred to 'Special Pay Duties', a non-existent unit within the RAPC, and ordered to join

Montgomery's staff in Portsmouth. To reduce the possibility of prying questions, while attached to the staff he was given the identity and uniform of a Sergeant in the Intelligence Corps, although he was allowed to revert to his own rank and insignia in London, a potential for confusion which he manfully overcame.

James spent approximately two weeks in the close proximity of Montgomery, both at his headquarters and while the General was holidaying in the north of Scotland. During that time he learned to ape his subject's voice and mannerism to near perfection. Finally his missing finger, which had been shot off on the Somme in 1916, was replaced with a replica.

When all was ready James was dressed in the uniform of a general and flown, via Gibraltar, to North Africa. Wherever he went he was dogged by deliberately lax security. His flight from RAF Northwood was leaked and widely photographed by the press. His stop-over in Gibraltar, where he stayed as the guest of the Governor, one of the few men aware of the deception, was witnessed by large numbers of Spaniards, many with Nazi sympathies. He was even introduced to two high ranking Spanish officials with known Abwehr connections, in whose hearing he was injudicious enough to discuss 'Plan 303'.

The plan was wholly fictitious, yet the agents were so convinced by it that German Intelligence subsequently wasted massive resources in attempting to discover its secrets (both agents later changed their identities and fled, rather than be summoned to Germany to face Nazi wrath).

James travelled from Gibraltar to Algiers where his identity was scrutinized by at least two Italian agents and a former major in the French Foreign Legion known to be in German pay. Only once did he feel threatened. When in Gibraltar he was forced to snub a valet who had previously spent many loyal years in the service of the General. At all other times the deception worked perfectly. The German High Command became obsessed with the idea of an invasion through the Mediterranean and retained a number of key divisions in the Balkans long after it should have been obvious that the Allies' interest was with northern Europe.

James remained in North Africa until after D Day. His eventual return home, as a subaltern in the Royal Army Pay Corps, was considerably more laborious, and certainly less glorious, than his journey to Africa had been as a General. At his own request James returned to his original RAPC posting in Leicester and to his devoted wife with whom he had been forbidden to communicate for several months.

Operation Market Garden

There were occasions during the Second World War when the British were as guilty as any of the sin of self-deception. By the summer of 1944 the outcome of the war was beyond reasonable dispute. Victory was only a matter of time and the Allies were becoming impatient. When Montgomery proposed that his British 21st Army Group and Bradley's 12th United States Army Group should combine into a single 40-division mass to thrust northwards through the enemy defensive positions into the heart of Germany his plan was vetoed by Eisenhower.

Disappointed but not defeated, he formulated an alternative, more audacious scheme. By seizing a succession of bridges between the Dutch frontier and the Lower Rhine he argued that the British 2nd Army would be able to smash its way through Holland on to the North German plain. Five major bridges over three rivers, the Maas, the Waal and the Lower Rhine, and two canals, the Wilhelmina Canal some 30km beyond the Dutch border and the Zuid Willems Vaart Canal 15km to the north, would have to be captured intact.

One airborne division would be landed in the 30km stretch between Eindhoven and Uden to secure the two canal bridges and the road between them. A second division would be assigned to the Maas bridge at Grave and the Waal bridge at Nijmegen. A third division, the British 1st Airborne, would have the hardest task of all, to drop at Arnhem to secure the crossing of the Rhine.

Planning for Operation *Market Garden – Market* referring to the airborne corps' activities and *Garden* to the follow up by the British 2nd Army – was completed in only six days. It is during this time that British Intelligence began to commit a series of critical blunders. Ignoring the necessity for objectivity at all times it began to see what it wanted to, and submitted a series of reports stating that enemy activity along the intended corridor was light.

Enemy forces along the route to be followed by 30th Corps,

spearheading the 2nd Army advance, were reported to consist of a small force of six infantry battalions supported by a limited quantity of light artillery and armour. Initial reports from the Dutch Resistance indicated that a further six battalions, comprised of medically downgraded troops, were stationed in the area of Nijmegen and that a number of under-strength armoured units, which were refitting and reorganizing, were based around Arnhem.

Collateral intelligence reports from 21st Army Group intimated that all units in the area were understrength, short of equipment and suffering from low morale. Throughout the early stages of the operation 21st Army Group continued to maintain that both the northern and southern areas of Holland were only lightly held by the enemy.

Their optimism was such that, when the Dutch Resistance submitted more up-to-date reports indicating the presence of SS troops, including armour, near Arnhem, Intelligence staffs at both formations refused to regard the report as reliable. Two days before the landings were due to begin the Chief of Intelligence at SHAEF, Major General Sir Kenneth Strong, reported to the Chief of Staff to the Supreme Allied Commander, General Eisenhower, that the 9th *Hohenstaufen* and 10th *Frundsberg* SS Panzer Divisions were in the area of Arnhem. Both had been withdrawn from Normandy and were in the process of refitting. They were considerably understrength, but even so would be more than a match for lightly armed paratroopers.

Smith brought the information to the attention of Eisenhower and advised him that a second airborne division should be landed in the Arnhem area. Eisenhower gave the matter his urgent consideration, before delegating the decision to General Montgomery in command of 21st Army Group. Smith's fears fell on deaf ears when he sought an interview with Montgomery at his headquarters in Brussels, so much so that the British general flatly refused to countenance any alteration to his plans.

As the planning for *Market Garden* reached its final stages the intelligence staffs at 21st Army Group, 2nd Army and 1st Allied Airborne Army became increasingly convinced that the enemy forces in the region of Arnhem were approximately one brigade in strength. To have thought otherwise might have led to the postponement, and almost certain cancellation, of the entire operation.

The 1st Airborne Division had not taken part in the Normandy landings. It had been trained to a fine edge and due to enforced inactivity was now in danger of losing it. It was ready and willing to accept anything and was not about to let the 'ifs' and 'buts' of a few pessimists stand between it and combat.

One individual at Headquarters 1st Airborne Corps refused to allow the prevailing optimism to overcome his professional objectivity. Major Brian Urquhart, the GSO 2 (Intelligence), was convinced that there was a large concentration of armour in the Arnhem area. He was in possession of current Dutch Resistance reports and aerial reconnaissance photographs which confirmed his belief, and was sufficiently concerned to request a low- level photo-reconnaissance sortie to be flown over an area of reported Panzer activity.

The results, in the form of five low-oblique photographs clearly showing camouflaged tanks, were brought to the immediate attention of Lieutenant-General 'Boy' Browning. The corps commander, however, made light of the photographs and dismissed Urquhart's fears. When the Major persisted he was removed from his post, diagnosed as suffering from nervous exhaustion and returned to Britain.

Arnhem was one of the most glorious failures in British military history. Almost from the outset *Market Garden* proved to be over-ambitious. The US 82nd Airborne Division assaulting the Nijmegen Bridge encountered unexpectedly stiff resistance and was held up for far longer than anticipated. Thereafter the tanks of the Guards Armoured Division spearheading Lieutenant-General Brian Horrocks' XXX Corps were forced to proceed almost suicid-ally along a single raised road ideally suited to defensive warfare.

Many bitter lessons were learned from the battle for Arnhem Bridge. Over-reliance on initial air-photo reconnaissance, coupled with a failure to fully master the art of stereoscopy, led to an in-correct appreciation of the ground and selection of dropping and landing zones. Taking into account the lessons learned by the 6th Airborne Division during the Normandy landings, dropping para-chute troops some 13km from their objective was little short of lunacy. Communications within the division were wholly in-adequate, with commanders at all levels out of contact with their formations and units. Close air support was almost entirely lacking until the final stages of the operation, while the provision of the wrong crystals for the ground-to-air radios meant that air resupply could not be diverted to alternative dropping zones when those originally designated were overrun. Above all, the planners' failure to appreciate the true strength and dispositions of the enemy in the area proved critical.

The failure of the Arnhem phase of *Market Garden* did not detract from the magnificent performance of the airborne forces. Ordered to hold the bridge at Arnhem for forty-eight hours against less than a brigade of understrength infantry, the British 1st Airborne Division and Polish 1st Airborne Brigade held on for nine days against two battle-hardened panzer divisions. In all 7,578 paratroopers were killed, wounded or captured out of a total of 10,005 men dropped or landed at Arnhem before the survivors were forced to retire across the Rhine leaving the bridge destroyed and the town in enemy hands.

Even the enemy were guilty of self-deception. The British landings took the German High Command completely by surprise. Field Marshal Model had envisaged a thrust by the 2nd Army across the Maas and into the Ruhr, but had discounted completely the use of airborne troops west of the Rhine. When paratroopers began to fall in the area of his headquarters in Oosterbeek he became fixated with the idea that the whole operation had been planned to capture him. Had he and his Chief of Staff, General Krebs, not reacted quickly and evacuated in haste to the safety of Arnhem, they might well have become General Browning's first prisoners.

During the height of the battle for Arnhem a full set of plans showing the British intentions and order of battle was discovered in the fuselage of a wrecked glider. They were taken at once to German headquarters where they were dismissed as a ruse. The British, it was argued, would not have been so stupid as to take a set of top secret plans into battle!

The Ardennes Offensive

Despite the Allied setback at Arnhem, by the end of 1944 the tide of war was running firmly against Germany. The Red Army was advancing everywhere along the Eastern Front and was exacting terrible revenge against the civilian population. In Italy the Allies were ready to advance across the Rome-Rimini line, and in the west were closing up to the Rhine.

Hitler saw a window of opportunity. The Allied armies, massed in the north-west of Europe, were being supplied through the port of Antwerp. If an attack could be launched through the Ardennes, as it had been in 1940, the panzers could cross the Maas, reach Antwerp and split the Anglo-American forces. The winter offensive came to be known as the Battle of the Bulge and involved four armies and three special units, including a group of commandos recruited in great secrecy by Otto Skorzeny.

The commandos were employed as shock troops to confuse the enemy on and soon after D Day, which was set for 5.30am on 16 December. Speed was of the essence throughout. It was estimated that the infiltration of commando troops dressed as Americans, some in the uniforms of military police, would not only spread panic among the enemy but would ensure that the roads were kept open for the advancing panzers.

Skorzeny recruited two battalions for this deception. Volunteers had to be fit, mentally alert and with strong personalities. They had to be trained in hand-to-hand combat, speak English and have a working knowledge of an American dialect. Ultimately Skorzeny selected ten volunteers with a perfect mastery of American-English, including idioms, over thirty with a good knowledge of English, 150 who could understand the language and some 200 with command of a few phrases.

The commandos, who were eventually reduced to a force of 160 men, were subdivided into sets of agents carrying out three types of mission: sabotage, reconnaissance and infiltration. Their task was to cause confusion to the enemy by changing road signs, removing minefield indicators, relaying rumour and false information and issuing conflicting orders. Where possible they were to intercept enemy radio signals and issue their own conflicting counter-orders on the net.

To add to the deception the armoured battle group with which they were to operate, 'Panzer Brigade 150', was to be equipped as far as possible with captured and disguised enemy equipment and was to act like a US armoured group fleeing in disorder from the advancing Germans.

Ultimately the commandos played little part in the Battle of the Bulge, although their presence undoubtedly unnerved some of the less experienced American troops. An American tank battalion was sent in the wrong direction and an infantry unit was bluffed into withdrawing from a village which it held. Telephone lines were cut and an ammunition dump blown. Of the nine teams deployed, seven were able to infiltrate successfully and one reached the River Meuse. Commandos from one of the captured units, the Einhert Steilau, were court-martialled and shot.

The War at Sea

British naval codes and ciphers were easily penetrated during the early stages of the Second World War. Well before the outbreak of hostilities the German Kriegsmarine developed its 'B-Dienst', or '*Beobachtung-Dienst*' ('Observation Service'). The service was minute and had little contact with the other German codebreaking agencies, yet its subsequent success was out of all proportion to its size.

When war eventually came 'B-Dienst' enabled German surface raiders to elude the British Home Fleet, spared German heavy ships from chance encounters with superior British forces, permitted surprise attacks on British warships and helped sink six British submarines in the Skagerrak area between June and August, 1940. Astonishingly the Royal Navy failed totally to appreciate the extent of German interception. Instead they deceived themselves into believing that they were suffering from nothing worse than bad luck. Even when, in July, 1940, the German merchant raider *Atlantis* captured a copy of the 'BAMS code' used universally by British merchant shipping, together with a series of super-encipherment tables, Royal Naval Intelligence failed to make a connection between this and the subsequent increase in U-boat successes and did nothing to change the codes.

The Germans also became adept at the use of 'Q' ships or armed merchant cruisers. Unlike British armed merchant cruisers, which were cruise liners hurriedly pressed into service in the early stages of the war to provide convoy protection, these were raiders which masqueraded as merchant ships to decoy and sink genuine merchant ships. Arguably the most fascinating of these was the ex-British steamship *Speybank*, captured by the Germans in 1941, renamed the *Doggerbank* and put under the command of Captain Paul Schneidewind. Equipped as a minelayer but in outward appearance still a British merchantmen, she was selected for Operation *KO*, the covert laying of mines in Cape Town Harbour.

In every outward respect an innocent merchant ship, she was allowed to sail unmolested into the harbour, where she successfully laid her mines before sailing out, still unchallenged. Allied complacency caused them to suffer two ships sunk, three ships badly damaged, 200 casualties and serious disruption to their supply lines which took months to repair.

Subsequently, while minelaying in the nearby Agulhas Bank, Schneidewind deceived the Royal Navy twice, once when *Doggerbank* was challenged by the light cruiser HMS *Durban*, the second time when challenged by the armed merchant cruiser HMS *Cheshire*.

When approached by HMS *Durban* at night he initially failed to recognize and respond to the coded order to identify himself. Fortunately for Schneidewind British merchantman were notoriously bad at responding to coded messages and the warship therefore repeated the order in plain language. When Schneidewind flashed back '*Levernbank* from New York to Durban,' the cruiser, which had been badly damaged in action against the Japanese and was thus in no condition for action, and which had no reason to doubt the merchantman's story, bade the raider good night and sailed on.

The next day, when challenged by HMS *Cheshire*, Schneidewind claimed to be the *Inverbank* sailing from Montevideo to Melbourne. *Cheshire*, which was carrying a large consignment of troops bound for the Middle East at the time, had no reason to doubt this deceit and let the German sail on.

The ease with which the British warships allowed themselves to be deceived should not be construed as negligence on the part of their captains. The larger German raiders were extremely potent and had to be approached with considerable care. Several would have been a match for the damaged *Durban*, which could bring only one gun to bear, or the under-armed and over-laden *Cheshire*.

Some four months earlier, on 19 November, 1941, the

Australian cruiser HMAS *Sydney* had sighted and challenged a lone merchant ship, from which she had received a garbled response, and had closed to within 2km for greater clarification. She had paid a tragic price for her carelessness. The pseudo-merchant ship had been the *Kormoran*, the largest of all the disguised German ocean raiders. As HMAS *Sydney* approached, *Kormoran* torpedoed her. Although the cruiser was mortally stricken her guns remained operational, and had sunk the *Kormoran* at close range before being blown apart by a great explosion. None of the Australian ship's crew survived. Indeed the Royal Navy would have known nothing of the action had not some of *Kormoran's* crew , escaping in lifeboats, reached the West Australian coast where they were taken prisoner.

On 3 March, 1942, in an ironic twist of fate, Schneidewind's daring caught up with him. *Doggerbank* was torpedoed by the German submarine *U-43*. In strict adherence to orders the U-boat made no attempt to pick up survivors. Several died of their wounds or of exposure. Of nearly 200 men on board only one lived to tell the terrible tale.

During the Second World War a considerable number of British 'irregular' naval formations came into being to perform certain special tasks beyond the normal naval ambit. They were commanded by the DDOD(I) or Deputy Director Operations Division (Irregular), Captain Frank Slocum RN, who had been seconded to MI6 in 1937 but had 'returned' to the Naval Intelligence Division in 1940. The formations included a small unit designed specifically to deceive the enemy as to where a landing was to take place, and a larger outfit tasked with the infiltration and exfiltration of agents and other personnel to and from enemy held territory.

Although the latter had fast patrol boats at its disposal, where possible it used converted French or Belgian fishing vessels, a number of which had come over with refugees after Dunkirk. The first boat to be requisitioned was a former Brittany trawler, then acting as a patrol boat in Newhaven where she had been registered with the Newhaven number *N51*. She was taken to Falmouth for a refit after which she was moved in complete secrecy to an isolated anchorage in the Scilly Isles. There *N51*, as she continued to be known, was painted in the appropriate French colours and given the false registration of a tunny fishing vessel typical of those operating under German licence off the Concarneau region of Brittany. Her volunteer crew consisted of two officers and six ratings who were dressed in the manner of local French fishermen, but who nonetheless optimistically carried British identity cards in case of capture. *N51* was fitted with a radio capable of receiving SOE agent traffic and was lightly armed with a number of hand guns, together with an anti-tank weapon to disable the engine of a challenging patrol boat if necessary.

N51's first mission was to liaise with a small fishing smack and take on board a French agent, Colonel Gilbert Renault, who had returned to France by air in order to evacuate his wife and family. Not only was the mission successful – Renault his wife and four children were safely evacuated – but it proved that a regular line of communications could be maintained with occupied Europe. During her time in French waters *N51* had been spotted by numerous genuine fishing boats, not all with crews sympathetic to the Allied cause, and by a number of German patrol boats. Yet none had questioned her; on the face of it she had been fishing in permitted waters and they had had no reason to challenge her *bona fides*. Once again well-planned deception, supported by enemy lethargy, had proved a potent weapon.

N51 was later joined by two other trawlers and by a small motor torpedo boat converted to resemble a Brittany fishing boat. As the flotilla grew it was designated with the cover name Inshore Patrol Flotilla, although its craft continued to appear in the Navy List as Motor Fishing Vessels. Using one boat or another, the flotilla continued to operate until the end of the war in Europe, usually carrying out one trip a month in the moonless period.

The Fallacies of Aerial Warfare

In May, 1917, a formation of German Gotha bombers attacked the Kent coastal town of Folkestone and the neighbouring army camp at Shorncliffe. Their bombs killed ninety-five people and injured 175. The seventy-four British aircraft which were scrambled to intercept them managed to shoot down only one. Three weeks later, on 17 June, twenty-one Gothas mounted a second daylight attack. Seven bombers attacked small towns in Kent and Essex, while the remaining fourteen flew on in diamond formation to attack London itself. 162 people were killed and 432 injured. A third attack on 7 July killed sixty-five people and injured 245.

It was the inauguration of strategic aerial bombardment and led to a panic among the British politicians and press, if not the population at large. Prime Minister Lloyd George appointed himself and General Smuts as a committee of two to study the way ahead for Britain's air forces. In the event Smuts conducted the inquiry single-handed, with the assistance of Army and Royal Flying Corps officers. His report, completed on 17 August, 1917, became the foundation upon which the Royal Air Force was born, and enabled a succession of 'experts' to argue that future victory lay in the air and not on the ground.

Fifteen years later the British politician Stanley Baldwin argued that 'the bomber will always get through!' Supporters pointed to the panic caused by the Gotha bombers in 1917 and by the Allied bombers which attacked Germany extensively in 1918. As the size and range of bombers increased, the argument ran, a bombed and fear-crazed population would compel its government to sue for peace before its ground forces had even seen action. In the words of Chief of Air Staff, Sir Hugh (later Lord) Trenchard, 'it (will not be) necessary for an air force, in order to defeat an enemy nation, to defeat its armed forces first.'

If the RAF could create such devastation abroad, then equally, it was argued, her enemies could wreak havoc at home. In 1937 a secret Whitehall forecast claimed that Britain would suffer a massive 150,000 civilian casualties in the first week of hostilities alone, a figure which happily proved wildly pessimistic. Between 1936, and December 1937, when Britain transferred her priority to fighters, the British and German air forces changed beyond all recognition as they vied with each other to produce larger fleets of bombers in the unsubstantiated belief that these alone would win wars.

In September, 1939, Britain entered the war with 608 first-line fighters against the 1,215 of the Luftwaffe, and with 536 bombers against 2,130. The inability of the aircraft of the day to breach the enemy's front line and create havoc with his economy quickly became apparent. On 18 December, 1939, twenty-four Wellington bombers attacked the German naval base at

Wilhelmshaven. The enemy defences were slow to respond. The German *Freya* radar picked up the sortie 50km from its target but the sighting was dismissed as a flock of seagulls. Luftwaffe fighters were scrambled only after the raid had taken place, but even so fourteen of the bombers were destroyed.

By the spring of 1940 Bomber Command had come to realize the suicidal nature of unescorted daylight raids and had switched to night operations. On the night of 11/12 May an attack was mounted on the Mönchengladbach railway junction on the west bank of the Rhine. Four nights later ninety-three bombers struck at oil plants and blast furnaces at Duisburg. On the night of 25/26 August 1940 British bombers raided Berlin for the first time in a tit-for-tat retaliation for the bombing of London which, ironically, had taken place strictly against Luftwaffe standing orders.

News of the Berlin raid heartened the British whose newspapers carried widespread reports of the resultant devastation. The truth, however, was very different. Air reconnaissance photographs repeatedly revealed very little damage to the designated targets. In July 1941 the Butt Report admitted that only one aircraft in three was dropping its bombs within 8km of its aiming point, and that for heavily defended targets the figure was closer to one in ten. Disillusioned, in early 1942 Bomber Command switched to a policy of 'destroying the morale of the civilian population and, in particular, of the industrial workers'. Area bombing had arrived with a vengeance.

Crucially for Bomber Command new aircraft types were by then coming off the production line. In 1936 the Air Ministry had issued specifications for four-engined heavy bombers and twin-engined 'heavy medium' bombers which, by 1941, had manifested themselves into the Stirling, quickly followed by the Halifax, the Manchester and its ultimate modification, the Lancaster.

Germany and France, on the other hand, had throughout the 1930s devoted their resources to the production of light and medium bombers primarily for army support. Both the German Army and the Luftwaffe were so deeply imbued with the doctrines of mobile warfare that they discounted the need for the heavy bomber. Hitler in particular remained obsessed with the fighter bomber. From the Stuka in 1939 to the Me262 jet in 1944 he frustrated every serious attempt to produce an adequate four-engined long-range bomber. He failed totally to appreciate that the format for land-air support which so suited the tactics of blitzkrieg would not lend itself to strategic bombing. When the Luftwaffe attempted to unleash squadrons of Stuka fighter bombers over Britain in 1940 they were shot down with consummate ease by the RAF.

Air Marshal Arthur Harris was appointed Commander in Chief Bomber Command on 22 February, 1942, eight days after the Air Ministry introduced its policy of saturation bombing. The blanket bombing of cities by the Luftwaffe in 1940 had failed to bring Britain to her knees, indeed it had been welcomed by Churchill for bringing respite to his hard-pressed airfields. Yet for the remaining three years of the war the policy was to be adopted by the British and Americans with increasing ferocity.

Harris began with a series of night attacks on the industrial city of Essen before launching his true curtain raiser – the destruction of the medieval city of Lübeck on 28/29 March. Rostock was destroyed a month later, as was Cologne in a 1,000 bomber raid at the end of May. Hungry for revenge, the British public became intoxicated with stories of the devastation, most of them grossly exaggerated. By the end of 1942 Harris had won for the RAF the top priority in factory production and had become firmly convinced that his Command alone could bomb Germany into submission.

In 1943, Harris's great year of area attack, 200,000 tons of bombs fell on Germany, five times the weight which had been dropped in 1942. In a minute to the Prime Minister dated 3 November, 1943, Harris listed nineteen German cities which he claimed had been 'virtually destroyed', by which he implied that they had become 'a liability to the total German war effort vastly in excess of any assets remaining'. He also listed a further nineteen cities which had been 'seriously damaged', and claimed that 36 percent of production had been lost in twenty-nine towns attacked.

This vastly over-optimistic piece of self-deception could not have been further from the truth. In reality the German armaments production index rose from 100 in January 1942 to 153 in July, to 229 in July 1943 and to a staggering 322 in July 1944. No more than 9 percent of German production was lost as a result of bombing in 1943, a figure which rose to only 17 percent in 1944.

In the words of Nazi Production Minister, Albert Speer 'the total damage suffered by the armament programme as a result of aerial attack during 1943 was not considerable.' Despite the fearful damage which it sustained, Hamburg lost no more than 1.8 months production. During the huge attacks on its works in Essen, Krupps lost no more than three months production from all air attacks up to and including the spring of 1944.

After the war, Speer professed himself astonished by the inconsistency of the Allied air attack. 'The vast but pointless area bombing,' he said, 'had achieved no important effect on the German war effort by early 1944.' In too many instances the Allies had convinced themselves that their targets were important simply because they had been destructible. Prior to the Dambusters raid in May, 1943, the Ministry of Economic Warfare in London had correctly judged that the Möhne and the Sorbe Dams were the key to the Ruhr water supplies. But after destroying the Möhne 617 Squadron used its remaining bombs to wreck the Eder Dam which was quite irrelevant. Bomber Command had merely judged it more breachable than the Sorbe and for no other reason had designated it a prior target.

When the Allies found a target of significance, they tended to attack it only once in the case of the RAF, or on a few occasions in the case of the American Eighth Air Force, and then leave it alone to recover. Had the Allies adopted a more cohesive plan of attack they might well have crippled the German war machine. No serious effort was made to bomb the Nazi electricity generating plants, nor were the synthetic oil plants attacked until the spring of 1944, and even then only by the Americans. Bomber Command might have been better served had Harris been less single-minded in his desire to wreak vengeance on Germany as a whole, and had chosen his targets with more circumspection.

The Lessons of Indo-China

In 1945 Britain, France and to a lesser degree the Netherlands began an unequal struggle to retain the vestiges of empire in Africa and the Far East. In South-East Asia they found themselves facing growing armies of communist nationalists, convinced that western armies were far from invincible and hardened by over four years of unrelenting guerrilla warfare against the Japanese. Nowhere was the threat to empire stronger than in the French colony of Indo-China. French mastery of Tonkin, the northern province of modern Vietnam, had never been absolute. Yet in 1946 the authorities in Paris convinced themselves that the area, which had been under communist Viet Minh control since the Japanese surrender in the previous August, could be returned to imperial control.

In March, 1946, French troops re-entered Hanoi and at once set about engineering a series of provocative incidents aimed at destroying the power and influence of the Viet Minh. For three years they were largely successful, until in April, 1949, the Viet Minh, now under the control of the brilliant Vo Nguyen Giap, went on to the offensive, successfully attacking a series of outposts which the French had constructed north of Hanoi. Within months the French was forced to evacuate the border area losing over 6,000 troops in the process.

However, subsequent attempts by Giap to organize his irregulars into conventional units for an attack on Hanoi met with less success. Quick to recover and now reinforced by a number of elite units, the French constructed a series of defended positions around Hanoi. In a series of attacks the Viet Minh lost heavily on one occasion sustaining over 3,000 casualties in a single five-day action.

In April, 1953, Giap invaded Northern Laos forcing the French to commit their limited reserves to the Plain of Jars to protect the Laotian capital. Thereafter, fearful of over-extending their fully stretched resources, the Viet Minh, having secured the annual opium crop, withdrew to the comparative safety of its northern strongholds.

The French now countered by entering upon a series of self-deceptions destined ultimately to condemn them to total defeat in the area. Inexplicably they came to interpret Giap's patent act of regrouping as a victory and came to reason that he was no longer strong enough to attack a fully protected defensive position. Accordingly, they decided to entice him into battle by creating an artificial target against which his forces might pound themselves into oblivion. They chose the village of Dien Bien Phu, close to the Laotian border, as an ideal killing ground, and in so doing condemned the bulk of the French colonial army to certain annihilation.

Dien Bien Phu had a number of advantages and would have proved an ideal defensive position against a conventional enemy. It straddled a Viet Minh supply route and could not therefore be ignored. It had its own primitive airstrip and was surrounded by a series of fortifiable hills. It was, however, overlooked by high mountains and, but for the airstrip, was completely cut off from Hanoi, some 280km away.

Giap pondered on what action to take and eventually decided to accept the French challenge to battle, but upon his own terms. Instead of rushing his nearest available conventional troops into early combat against the elite French paratroopers and Legionnaires, he instead put into effect one of the finest logistical moves of modern history. Completely unknown to the French, he ordered the mobilization of two distinct armies. While he force-marched three regular infantry divisions and an artillery division – about 50,000 men in all – towards Dien Bien Phu, a second army of 20,000 men, women and children began to hack new routes through the jungle for weapons and supplies.

During the months of preparation, and completely unseen by French aerial reconnaissance, the Viet Minh support army manhandled over 200 artillery pieces – mostly 105mm howitzers and anti-aircraft guns – through the jungle. By super-human effort involving nothing more sophisticated than muscle and sweat, relay teams roped to the guns pulled them centimetre by centimetre – 800 metres a day – through 80km of jungle. In the space of a few weeks they turned Dien Bien Phu from a fortress into a prison.

The French had expected an attack, but when it came they were overwhelmed by its ferocity. Unknown to them, Giap had amassed a fighting force over three times superior to theirs. The communist artillery, perfectly secreted in caves and trenches in the hills, over-looked the French, making daylight movement above ground suicidal.

The French position was quickly made hopeless. Attempts at resupply from the air, wholly inadequate at the best of times, ceased when the airstrip fell to the Viet Minh. One by one the outlying strongpoints of the Dien Bien Phu defences fell to a combination of mining, well-directed artillery fire and direct assault. The final assault overran the starving defenders as their last ammunition was expended on 7 May, 1953, the 55th day of the siege.

Of the 15,094 troops who defended Dien Bien Phu 9,500 began a forced march into captivity which few were to survive. Not for the first time in their history the French had allowed themselves to be deceived by their apparent strength. In moving a fully equipped army into the T'ai mountains, Giap had done what the French had discounted as impossible. In so doing he had recognized the French challenge for what it was, had discovered in it weaknesses which the French had not appreciated and had exploited them to the full.

Never again would it be safe for a Western power to deceive itself that it would automatically be a match for irregular soldiers operating in their own environment. A few years later, again in the jungles and paddyfields of Vietnam, the United States was destined to learn this lesson the hard way.

The Harsh Lessons of Vietnam

Vietnam was a dirty, uncompromising war fought without scruples. The terrain, the enemy and his tactics, indeed almost everything he was faced with was alien to the young American conscripts.

By 1965 Washington had privately conceded that the South Vietnamese Army could not beat the growing Communist threat without a massive input of United States manpower and materiel. The draft was extended and young conscripts, with an average age of only nineteen, were shipped to Vietnam in increasing numbers. It soon became clear to those on the ground that many Stateside lessons learned by these green recruits would have to be unlearned quickly if they were to survive. However, the only classroom available for many was the battlefield itself. As a result the vast majority of casualties among the young GIs was sustained during their first two months in the field, before they had been given a chance to learn the basics of self-preservation.

Ironically, at the time both good will and experience abounded among the United States' allies. France had fought a protracted and bloody war in the same theatre while Britain had recently defeated the Marxist insurgents in Malaya. The British in particular had become experts in the field of psychological operations, particularly in the art of winning over the 'hearts and minds' of the non-combatant majority. Both France and Britain offered covert, and indeed overt, assistance. Their overtures were rejected by an all too self-assured Pentagon. Later, however, the United States came to realize the true worth of 'hearts and minds', and attempted to introduce the concept to the battlefield. Tragically, by then, it was too late.

Many United States instructors preferred to make their own mistakes, or to draw on their wholly redundant experiences gained in Korea, and even in some cases as far back as the Second World War. There were even those who made the fundamental mistake of drawing a non-existent parallel between the Vietnamese and Japanese on the naive assumption that as Orientals they both shared the same psyche.

The United States Army's lack of experience in Vietnam was compounded throughout the war by the Establishment's blinkered adherence to the twelve month roulement policy. Young men were called up soon after their eighteenth birthday and spent the next year in basic training. Thereafter they spent the remaining twelve months of their service in Vietnam before returning home to almost immediate discharge. Men who had come to trust each other during the rigours of basic training were not kept together and posted en masse in the manner of a European army. Instead they were broken up and sent out piecemeal to their designated active units in order to fill the gaps left by casualties or returnees. This inevitably led to friction. 'Veterans' of twelve months' warfare – who in terms of professional soldiering were only then beginning to master their trade – were suddenly replaced by green recruits to the inevitable detriment of squad morale. The position of officers was potentially even worse. Although they too served a twelve month tour in Vietnam, half of this was likely to be spent in a staff appointment, leaving them with only six months in the field. The resultant scarcity of combat-experienced officers led to gross over-promotion which often resulted in companies in action being led by second-tour captains with less experience than half the men under their command.

The Pentagon simply would not accept that the draftees of 1965 who found themselves fighting in the paddyfields of Vietnam were far from prepared. The lack of training of the soldiers, the inexperience of the officers and the almost wholesale lack of a strong senior NCO cadre led to uncertainty, brutality and even to the occasional atrocity. The cruellest of all recorded examples of brutality occurred in the village of My Lai on 16 March, 1968, when American soldiers from Company C, 1st/20th Infantry massacred over 300 old men, women and children on suspicion of pro-communist involvement. Lieutenant Calley, in command of the patrol, was tried for murder and spent four years in prison. In all other respects the Establishment closed ranks around the other participants, none of whom was punished.

As time went on, particularly after the 1968 Tet Offensive and the 1969 announcement of US troops withdrawals, the Army in Vietnam declined drematically. President Johnson's refusal to involve more than a handful of National Guardsmen or Army Reservists in the fighting had the effect of alienating the conscripted soldiers. More and more people began to question the direction and morality of the war. Conscientious objectors and draft dodgers were lauded on school and college campuses. For the first time in American history returning troops were openly abused in the streets. Drug abuse, racial fights, even the occasional 'fragging' of unpopular officers, became the regular diet of those left to patrol the paddyfields and villages of Vietnam. The Vietnamese became 'gooks' and all 'gooks' became the enemy.

The United States Army was soundly beaten in Vietnam. Yet for years the cause of the defeat was largely ignored by the American population as a whole. The Army went into decline both socially and professionally as it sought a solution to its malaise. The Pentagon did eventually learn from its mistakes and in the twenty years following the war completely restructured its army. However, these mistakes need never have been made. Had the United States Government and its senior military advisers shown more respect for the enemy, accepted the advice willingly offered by the French and British, and realized that there are circumstances in which technology cannot defeat a dedicated enemy the United States' losses in the most fruitless war of her history might have been halved.

CHAPTER FOUR:
Second World War Deceptions

After Dunkirk Britain found herself facing the imminent threat of invasion. Although she had managed to extract the majority of her Expeditionary Force from France it had been compelled to abandon its heavy equipment. The ten squadrons of mainly Hurricane fighter aircraft sent to bolster the French had been all but destroyed, leaving Britain's defences vulnerable in the extreme.

Churchill, refusing to countenance defeat, was determined to convince Hitler that Britain would be able to meet and defeat an invasion of her beaches. To this end deception, then the responsibility of the Director of Camouflage, part of the Ministry of Home Security, was called to the fore. Research was undertaken at the Camouflage and Training Centre, Royal Engineers, at Farnham in Surrey, and at a number of independent centres throughout the country.

Camouflage Field Companies, Royal Engineers (later known as Special Field Companies, RE) constructed a web of dummy pill boxes, tanks, guns and defensive emplacements round the coast and home counties. German reconnaissance aircraft were allowed to photograph these emplacements, the presence of which was supported by a number of turned agents described in detail below.

Meanwhile the RAF constructed a number of fake airfields on which it was hoped the Germans would waste a large proportion of their bombs. Dummy flare paths and fake lighting effects had been constructed in the proximity of actual airfields prior to the war and were now expanded. In June, 1940, electrically-lit dummy flares were introduced to confuse enemy reconnaissance. Fictitious obstructions were added and car headlights introduced to simulate aircraft lights. Later, lights were rigged up on carriages and propelled on wires along the 'runway' to simulate landing aircraft.

Great care was taken to ensure that the dummy airfields, or 'Q' sites as they were formally known, were not too obvious. They were lit when enemy aircraft were known to be in the vicinity but were turned off once it was felt that they had been spotted. Occasionally single lights, acting as notional breaches in the blackout, were left on to offer added authenticity.

Inevitably, as the Luftwaffe became aware of the RAF's various ruses, they became less effective. Nonetheless, during the crucial months of the Battle of Britain the approximately 100 'Q' sites absorbed twice as many bombs as the working airfields. Steps were also taken to simulate airfields in daylight hours. Approximately sixty of these 'K' sites were produced and also played their part in the Battle of Britain, but with markedly less success.

When the 'K' sites were discontinued in early 1942 the 400 dummy aircraft which had been manufactured to add realism were put into storage and later used to simulate aircraft concentrating in support of a major assault.

Four dummy aircraft factories were constructed, two of which were subjected to heavy bombing in August, 1940, leaving the real factories unscathed. While airfields and factories were necessarily the first priority for deception-protection, the maintenance of civilian morale demanded that towns and cities were not neglected. Bonfires were prepared in the countryside close to likely industrial targets and were ignited to give the Luftwaffe false targets. Once lit, they were fuelled with wood or coal and sprayed with paraffin to keep them burning.

The fake fires, which were lit after the first wave of aircraft had dropped their bombs and turned for home, were codenamed 'Starfish' and were only moderately successful. There were, however, a few successes: in Bristol on the night of 15/16 March 1941, local decoys were hit by 100 explosive bombs and a large number of incendiaries during a six hour raid which completely missed its intended target. Later that month sixty-seven bombs intended for Cardiff obliterated the local decoys while only five actually landed on the city.

The Desert War

The British Army in the Western Desert transformed the science of deception into an art. On 9 December, 1940, General Wilson, the Commander-in-Chief of British troops in Egypt, launched a major assault against the over-extended, though numerically superior, Italians. In two days of fighting he destroyed them as a military force, taking 38,000 prisoners, 400 guns and fifty tanks. The assault was launched in complete secrecy. Troops were moved to their assembly positions under the impression that they were about to take part in a major exercise, virtually no written orders were given, and those that were were limited to a few trusted staff officers. Dummy headquarters were constructed to simulate non-existent units, false orders leaked and feints undertaken to substantiate the cover story.

Subsequently General Wavell, Commander-in-Chief in the Middle East, set up a dedicated deception unit in Cairo under the command of the highly experienced Colonel Dudley Clarke.

Clarke's most spectacular exercise in deception occurred in early 1941. During the operation to capture the Siwa Oasis from the Italians the RAF dropped flares, pyrotechnics and dummy exploding parachutists on the oasis at night. Convinced that they had come under attack from a far superior force, the Italians fled, allowing the Long Range Desert Group to motor into Siwa on the following morning without firing a shot.

In December, 1941, General Auchinleck, who had by then replaced Wavell as C-in-C Middle East, launched Operation Crusader to push the Axis forces back from Egypt. Siwa, which was well to the south of the proposed line of advance, was converted into a mock divisional headquarters. Dummy accommodation and adminstration buildings were created, ammunition dumps simulated and signallers installed to indicate the presence of a high- level planning cell. It was subsequently discovered from captured German papers that they had been taken in by the deception. Although they had not actually altered their dispositions they had estimated that Siwa held an infantry brigade, two or three armoured car regiments and an unknown number of Egyptians.

At the same time a dummy railhead was run from Capuzzo to

Mishifa. To add credibility a fake train was even stationed on the track. The 'target' was bombed on several occasions by the Luftwaffe whilst the real railhead was never attacked.

Deception and concealment was practised on a scale previously unheard of during the preparations for the Battle of El Alamein which began on 25 October, 1942. The front was 56km long, flanked by the sea in the north and by the Qattara depression in the south. Despite the Allied superiority at sea and in the air, enemy reconnaissance could not be wholly discounted, nor could the preparations for the impending assault be concealed.

The British line was held by 30 Corps in the north, 13 Corps in the south with 10 Armoured Corps in reserve. They were opposed by one German division and five Italian divisions in the north, with a Panzer division and an Italian armoured division in reserve, and by the 21st Panzer and the 'Ariete' Armoured Divisions in the south. A German parachute brigade was deployed among the Italian formations to give them added resolve.

General Montgomery, in command of the British Eighth Army, resolved to launch his main assault in the north, using four infantry divisions to break in and 10th Armoured Corps to break through. At the same time he planned a holding attack by armour and infantry in the centre and south to draw off the enemy forces. The deception plan, codenamed Bertram, was intended to convince the Germans that the attack would be launched in the south and to indicate that it would take place in mid-November, some fourteen days after its actual date anticipated.

Operation Bertram took many forms. Knowing that the information would be intercepted by the German spy network operating in Cairo the British Embassy and Australian Legation 'leaked' a number of stories intimating that Montgomery would be attacking on about 6 November during the moonless period and not on 23 October during the time of the full moon. Social events involving many of the senior Allied staff were planned for the end of October and rumours were spread that the new Sherman tank was experiencing problems and would not be operational for a number of weeks.

At the same time a series of signals were sent relating to a bogus conference in Tehran, due to be held in October and attended by all the senior officers from the Middle East and Far East theatres.

The bulk of the deception plan was, however, visual. 10th Armoured Corps was ordered to undertake a number of very open training exercises during September and October geared to indicate that the main armoured thrust would be to the south-west. Thereafter the Corps moved to three staging areas, all sited astride a series of tracks leading to the south. No attempt was made to camouflage the staging areas until 20/21 October when the armour began silently to withdraw north. As each real tank was moved it was replaced by a dummy.

It was accepted from the outset that it would be impossible to conceal the dense mass of vehicles concentrating in the northern areas. Instead, as the tanks moved into their harbour areas they were disguised by the 'Sunshield' system, and made to look like ten-ton vehicles. The Grant, Sherman and Crusader tanks were fitted with side and top covers to give them the appearance of lorries from a distance or from the air. A quick-release device worked by the commander enabled the panels to be discarded once the tank started to move.

The 400 25-pounder guns and their tractors and limbers were disguised by poles, wire and garnished nets to resemble three-ton vehicles; tell-tale supply dumps, particularly those holding engineer equipment and ammunition, were hidden as far as possible among the general impedimenta of the area. At the same time dummy supply depots were built in the south and left virtually uncamouflaged. A dummy pipeline was built in the south and filling points and pump houses added. Finally, several decoy gun positions were built in the south. Early in the battle, when these dummy positions were recognized by the Germans for what they were, real guns were brought up to replace the dummies in a final deception.

The manpower required to implement Operation Bertram was formidable. 2,275 Allied soldiers disguised 5,000 tons of stores dumped in the north, displayed 8,000 tons of dummy stores in the south, moved or positioned 4,500 dummy or spare vehicles, and erected 700 'Sunshield' camouflage kits for the tanks and 360 kits for the guns. Success was absolute. Captured enemy documents later confirmed that the Germans had accepted the deception plan at face value and had prepared for an attack in the south. So certain were they that the main thrust would come in the south that they retained two armoured divisions in reserve in the southern sector for four days after the start of the attack in the north.

The Venlo Incident

Nazi Germany practised the art of deception at every level. In October, 1939, shortly after the commencement of hostilities, German Military Intelligence, the Abwehr, pulled off a major coup. Two senior intelligence officers, purporting to be representatives of 'the German General Staff', let it be known that they wished to meet with British Intelligence to discuss the overthrow of Hitler. Two agents, Captain Henry Stevens, SIS head of station in the Hague, and Captain Sigismund Payne Best, were dispatched to neutral Arnhem to meet them.

The British agents met Captain Schaemmel of the Transportation Corps and Captain Hausmann of the Medical Corps, verified their bona fides and escorted them to MI6 headquarters in Amsterdam. While in Amsterdam the Germans were passed a compact wireless set and given instructions to contact London, using the callsign ON- 4, should there be further news of the anticipated coup.

About a week later ON-4 signalled requesting a second meeting, which took place on the Dutch-German border. The British agents were in direct violation of their standing orders which forbade follow-up meetings away from the comparative safety of the Hague or Amsterdam. Nonetheless a third meeting was arranged. The rendezvous was to be for 4.00pm on 9 November at the Café Bacchus in Venlo, only a few paces from the German-Dutch border.

The British agents approached Venlo from the Hague in the company of Lieutenant Dirk Klop, a Dutch Army intelligence officer. As they arrived a German car screeched to a halt in front of theirs. Men standing on its running boards fired at the Dutch guards, fatally wounding Klop. The two Britons were handcuffed and bundled into the car, which roared over the border into Germany.

'Hausmann' was in fact Max de Crinis, a psychologist from the University of Berlin. More crucially 'Schaemmel' was none other than Walter Schellenberg, chief of the Foreign Intelligence section of the SD. Stevens and Payne Best were taken to the cellars at 8 Prinzalbrechtstrasse, Gestapo headquarters in Berlin, and kept in solitary confinement. Although rigorously questioned, they were never tortured. In the weeks that followed they revealed a mass of detailed information, including the identities of fellow agents and the structure of the SIS in Europe. As a direct consequence of the Venlo incident the Hague station had to be closed down. It subsequently became a simple matter for German Intelligence to hunt down and neutralize the SIS stations in occupied Europe.

Operation Gelb

The swiftness of the fall of France in 1940 was in significant measure due to the swift successes of a handful of elite units. Operation Gelb, the offensive into France and the Low Countries, began at 5.35am on the morning of 10 May, 1940, when 135 German divisions struck across the borders of Holland, Belgium and France against a superior Allied force.

Belgium and Holland were neutral at the time. When Britain and France had declared war on Nazi Germany in September, 1939, Belgium had refused to join the old Alliance, preferring to join the Netherlands in a policy of strict neutrality. It had mobilized its forces, placing the majority along the German border, but at the same time had strictly forbidden the Anglo-French to enter Belgian territory to make effective preparations for its defence.

Britain had been forced to construct a series of wholly inadequate anti-tank defences along the Franco-Belgian border during 1939. It was accepted that this created a dangerous gap of some 80km between the southern flank of the British defences and the nearest point of the near-impregnable Maginot Line but this was discounted. The French felt certain that the Ardennes, which occupied the bulk of this area, was impassable to large, modern armies and declined to place more than nine divisions, only two of which were up to strength, to protect it.

Von Manstein and the German High Command recognized the folly of this complacency. They believed that the terrain, despite its lack of roads, presented no insurmountable obstacle. They further appreciated that the key to success lay in fast movement by

Panzer formations driving deep into the Allied rear, supported by Stuka dive-bombers acting as long-range artillery.

Von Manstein realized that his 6th Army would have to pass through Belgium quickly, and to do so would have to secure a series of bridges intact. Four companies of Brandenburgers, a German commando elite containing an unusual number of linguists, were given the task of capturing the most crucial bridges. Their ultimate plan relied upon deception rather than military might.

Prior to the outbreak of hostilities reconnaissance patrols were infiltrated across the bridge to establish the strength and location of the sentries. From February onwards the number of incursions was increased until a complete intelligence picture had been gained.

The 400m Gennep railway bridge across the Meuse was considered the major prize. It stood 3km within the Dutch border and had to be taken before the Dutch could destroy it in order to allow two heavily-laden troop trains, scheduled to cross the border at zero hour, to proceed west towards the main Dutch defences. At 11.30pm on the night of 9 May a small section of Brandenburgers disguised as Dutch military policemen slipped across the border. The group leader, a corporal who spoke fluent Dutch, led his party to a laying up point between the River Niers and the railway.

Just before dawn the Brandenburgers approached the sentries on the eastern approach to the bridge and overpowered them without a struggle. They then telephoned the guards on the far end advising them, in fluent Dutch, that two military policemen would be escorting four German prisoners across. The 'prisoners and escort' then set out, leaving a second party of Brandenburgers holding the eastern approaches. At the bridge's middle the soldiers disguised as military policemen handed over their prisoners to the Dutch and returned to the eastern end. The Dutch, by now thoroughly alarmed, escorted the prisoners to their command post, leaving a single sentry to guard the demolitions. When the first troop train approached a few minutes later the guard hesitated just long enough to allow the Germans on board to jump off and overpower him. The original German 'prisoners' then overpowered their confused captors and the bridge fell into German hands intact allowing the trains to proceed westward. Once again the value of deception as a weapon of war had been proven.

The Russian Campaign

Plans for Operation Barbarossa, the German invasion of the Soviet Union, were laid as early as July, 1940, some eleven months before the attack was actually launched on 22 June, 1941. On 18 December, 1940, Hitler issued Führer Directive No 21 Case Barbarossa setting out definitively his plans for the assault. As ever, deception played a major part.

Hitler was helped in no small part by Stalin's belief in the sanctity of the Molotov-Ribbentrop Non- Aggression Pact of 1939. Despite warnings from the British, supported by sporadic intelligence from his own spies in MI6 and elsewhere, Stalin, as we have seen, refused to believe that Germany would commit herself to the invasion of Britain and an attack on Russia simultaneously.

Operation Sealion, the German seaborne invasion of Britain, was quietly shelved in September but continued as a grand deception to keep the Soviets placated. Germany was heavily involved in the Balkans at the time and was able to some degree to pass off her military build-up in Poland as part of her proposed offensive operations against Greece and the Eastern Mediterranean. Despite the excellence of their own intelligence, even the British were deceived. They moved 60,000 Imperial troops into Greece in February, 1941.

Specific measures were also taken by the Propaganda Branch of the German High Command to deceive both German and Soviet public opinion. Every effort was made to suggest that Germany was using Poland as a convalescent area while retaining her best troops in the west. Get well messages were even transmitted on popular radio programmes wishing fictitious recuperants from non-existent units a speedy recovery.

Fictitious plans were laid to invite Stalin to Baden Baden for a rest cure while a 'secret' (but inevitably leaked) reception was planned for a senior Soviet dignitary.

Immediately before Barbarossa all train movements west were halted and the army put on an alert for an invasion of Britain. Knowledge of the attack was kept from the German troops until the previous evening, although inevitably a few selected commanders were made privy to Hitler's intentions. When three German Army communist sympathizers crossed into Soviet-occupied Poland with a warning that night, the incredulous Red Army was too indifferent to pass the startling news up the chain of command.

The assault units travelled to their forming up areas by night, halting and camouflaging their positions by day. The Soviets were taken completely by surprise. It was not until 1.30am on 22 June, a mere 95 minutes before the attack began, that the Soviet High Command was alerted to its imminence. By nightfall the Luftwaffe had destroyed 2,000 Soviet aircraft, most of them on the ground, and the Army was in places 80km into Soviet territory.

Preparations For D-Day

By early 1944 even the United States had come to accept the necessity for deception. They co-operated fully therefore in Operation Bodyguard, the plan to protect Operation Overlord, the Allied invasion of France in June, 1944. By then Allied Intelligence was intercepting the vast majority of German radio traffic and was fully aware of the fact that Hitler anticipated that the invasion would come across the Straits of Dover. This assumption, although wrong, was inevitable and was fully endorsed by Field Marshals von Runstedt and Rommel and by Admiral Krancke, the commanders in the area. Accordingly Hitler had garrisoned the Pas de Calais with the German 15th Army, the strongest available in the west.

Of necessity the plans for Operation Bodyguard were kept top secret. They were entrusted to the London Controlling Section (LCS) – two naval officers, an RAF officer and five army officers who operated from the privacy of a government underground shelter adjacent to Horse Guards.

It was decided to convince Hitler that land operations would begin in the spring of 1944 with an invasion of Norway. The British, American and Russian participants would then advance into Sweden, turn south into Denmark and enter Germany across the vulnerable plains of Schleswig-Holstein. The main thrust would be in the Balkans and would consist of an Allied invasion of the Peloponnese, followed by an advance into Germany through the Ljubljana Gap. At the same time the Soviets would attack the Ploesti oilfields, denying Hitler a third of his fuel supplies.

If an invasion of France were to come at all it would be subordinate and would be directed against the Pas de Calais. Additionally the Allies would have to convince Hitler that when the landings on the coast of Normandy occurred they were diversionary. It was crucial that, while the British and Americans were establishing their beachhead, the powerful 15th Army should take no part in the initial fighting.

The scale of Bodyguard was such that it defied a single plan. Instead it was divided into geographical sectors each with a subsidiary scheme.

Operation Fortitude was the major subsidiary scheme and was itself divided into two sub-parts. Its aim was to convince Hitler that a massive diversionary attack would take place on the Pas de Calais while the main Allied landing was effected in Norway. Fortitude North was responsible for the creation of the wholly fictitious British 4th Army with its headquarters in Edinburgh Castle and its two corps in Stirling and Dundee.

Under the command of Colonel McLeod a small group of specialist signallers based in the three locations began the steady build up of radio traffic to simulate the movement into position of troop reinforcements. Concurrently the BBC and a number of national and local newspapers began to carry reports of sporting fixtures between non-existent units and reported a series of engagements, and later marriages, between local girls and soldiers serving in these units.

Double agents operating in Scotland reported the arrival of a Soviet officer, Klementi Budyenni, to co-ordinate a Red Army attack, and the setting up of an American liaison staff in Edinburgh representing the 15th (US) Corps in Northern Ireland. As ever, no single piece of information was conclusive. However, when the constituent parts of the intelligence jigsaw were put together, the Abwehr began seriously to believe in the distinct possibility of an invasion of Norway and began to concentrate their assets in that area.

Even neutral Sweden was brought unwittingly into the deception. Air Vice-Marshal Thornton, the pre-war Air Attaché to

Stockholm, was dispatched to see his old friend General Nordenskiold, the Commander-in-Chief of the Swedish Air Force. Thornton flew to Stockholm in civilian clothes and was taken to and from the British Embassy in a car with the blinds drawn. During his visit to Nordenskiold in his headquarters he was careful to enter and leave the building by a rear entrance, knowing that he would be photographed by German agents and identified by the Abwehr.

During his meeting with the Swedish Commander-in-Chief Thornton conceded that the British invasion force would not be able to overcome German resistance quickly enough to prevent the murder of thousands of Norwegian partisans and the destruction of much of that country's infrastructure. He therefore proposed that the Swedish Army should enter Norway, not as an invasion force but as neighbours, in a police rôle to protect the local population.

Nordenskiold was a committed Anglophile and undertook to put the plan to the Swedish Government. The Swedish Chief of Police, however, was pro-German and bugged the General's office. The conversation between the two senior airmen was recorded and passed verbatim to the Germans. Hitler was fully briefed and, soon thereafter, a further 30,000 German troops were dispatched to Norway where they played no further effective part in the war. For this reason alone Operation Fortitude North is justifiably regarded as an unqualified success.

Operation Fortitude South, the ruse to convince the Germans that the Allies would also be invading the Pas de Calais, was equally successful. General George Patton was put in command of the fictitious First United States Army Group (FUSAG), 'stationed' in Kent and East Anglia. Unlike the British 4th Army which was wholly non-existent, FUSAG did contain a number of actual British, Canadian and United States formations coincidentally stationed in the area in preparation for the Normandy landings. In the days following D Day, as these units were fed into the beach-head, their places were taken by further fictional units until, by 26 August, 1944, FUSAG was entirely notional.

A dummy fuel installation was constructed at Dover, large numbers of rubber tanks, guns and vehicles were moved into the woods and fields of Kent and Essex and plywood landing craft were moored in every available bay and inlet along the south-east coast. News of the build up was fed by agents, both real and turned, and supported by the inevitable increase of radio traffic.

Nothing was left to chance. In May, 1944, a month before D Day, the German General Hans Kramer, the former commander of the Afrika Corps and a prisoner of war in England, was invalided home. He was taken by car through Dorset and Hampshire but was told that he was being driven through East Sussex and Kent. He was shown the very real preparations for the invasion and even met General Patton in his rôle as FUSAG commander.

A subsidiary component of Operation Fortitude South, code-named Rosebud, continued after D Day specifically to convince Hitler that the Normandy landings were no more than a complex feint. Radio traffic within Patton's FUSAG intensified as if to suggest that the Group would soon be committed to a further landing. Von Runstedt, in command of the German defences in France, felt certain that Patton would land between the Somme and the Seine with the objective of encircling and capturing Le Havre.

The German 15th Army was retained in the Pas de Calais awaiting an enemy who would never come, while Rommel's hard-pressed 7th Army strove to stem the growing might of the Allies alone. By the time that leading elements of the 15th Army were at last committed it was too late. The Allies had broken out and were across the Seine.

The aim of Operation Zeppelin was to prevent the transfer of enemy troops from the eastern Mediterranean to northern France. The threat of a Soviet attack against Bulgaria and Romania was fabricated, to be supported by a British attack through Greece culminating in a campaign in Austria and a breakout into southern Germany and Central Europe. Fictitious army divisions were moved to North Africa and the eastern Mediterranean and fake invasion dates set, although subsequently postponed.

The plan proved remarkably successful. Although at the time of the Normandy landings there were in fact only thirty-eight Allied divisions in the whole Mediterranean theatre, most of them committed in Italy, the Germans credited the Allies with seventy-one, eleven of which they deemed to be weak. During May, 1944, not a single German division moved from the Mediterranean to northern Europe and none subsequently arrived in time to influence the battle during its first crucial weeks.

The rôle of Operation Vendetta was to maximize the number of German troops committed to southern France. In fabricating a threat to the area it was necessary to strike a reasonable balance. Plans had been set for Operation Anvil, the genuine Allied invasion of southern France, so it was imperative that the Germans did not move additional troops to the area.

The French 1st Army and the 91st US Infantry Division, the latter stationed in Oran, provided the threat. Ironically the redeployment of the 91st Division to Italy, where it was sorely needed, had to be postponed until mid-June to perpetuate the deception.

Enquiries were made at Ambassadorial level to discover whether the Spanish would grant facilities in the port of Barcelona for the treatment and evacuation of casualties in the forthcoming operations. Inevitably details of the request were leaked to the Germans and did much to make Hitler believe that an attack in southern France was imminent. A number of units, including the battle-hardened Das Reich SS Division, were retained in the south until too late. By the time the Allied ruse was discovered and they were moved north the Allies had already consolidated.

The final component of Operation Bodyguard was Ironside, designed to keep the 1st German Army in the Bordeaux area for the first three weeks after D Day. However, the lack of available aircraft and personnel meant that visual deception was virtually impossible and the plan had to rely almost entirely on the German interception of bogus radio traffic. It was the only part of Operation Bodyguard not to meet with complete success, and proved conclusively that strategic deception can only expect to succeed if applied broadly with as much collateral input as possible.

The Use Of Neutrals

The Allies never balked at feeding neutrals disinformation if they felt that it would ultimately find its way to German Intelligence. In one particularly fascinating example, which took place in October, 1940, the Franco Government sought permission for a representative of the Spanish Youth Movement to visit Britain, ostensibly to study the Boy Scout movement but in reality to give a detailed report on the state of British defences and her preparedness for invasion.

MI6 persuaded the Foreign Office to agree to the request and then, in cooperation with MI5, took charge of the plans for his arrival.

The Spaniard's room in the Athenaeum Hotel was bugged and one of the only three operational anti-aircraft batteries in London moved to Hyde Park, close to the hotel, from where it fired continuously throughout every air raid. A visit was arranged to Windsor Castle, where the Royal Family's 'Ceremonial Guard' just happened to be passing as he was being shown the sights (he was not told that it was the only fully equipped tank regiment in the country). Later he was flown to Scotland, where his aircraft was passed en route by 'squadrons' of Spitfires (or, more precisely, by the same Spitfires passing several times in different formations).

Not surprisingly, the spy's report to Berlin counselled strongly against invasion, warning that British unpreparedness was a mere fiction promulgated by the secret services to lure a German expeditionary force into a trap. At a time when the Abwehr regarded the Soviet Union rather than Britain as its natural enemy, such assessments, however spurious, did much to counter the political hierachy's impatience for an invasion.

Agent Turning

The rôle of the secret agent in the Second World War was unglamorous. It involved days, perhaps weeks, of inertia superimposed on moments of extreme danger. Nothing could prepare an agent for his first encounter with an enemy checkpoint, nor for the shock of working constantly in the close proximity of the enemy. The nagging fear that the next knock on the door might be a less than gentle summons to security headquarters played on the minds of most. Not surprisingly a few agents, when captured, agreed to help the enemy to save their own lives.

Both sides used their best endeavours to turn captured agents. Without doubt the single most successful mass agent-turning operation was undertaken by the Germans in Holland.

Like the other nations of Europe overrun by the Germans in

1940, Holland was in a state of bewilderment and disarray. When Queen Wilhelmina fled to London she left Holland in a political vacuum, a country almost wholly without leadership. Dutch Intelligence had made no provision for clandestine organizations, not even secret radio stations, leaving a patriotic people devoid of all but the will to resist. The lack of covert communications in Holland left the Queen and her advisers in exile completely isolated. To compound the problem, during his hasty departure from the capital, the local SIS agent had abandoned an attaché case containing the names and addresses of all his Dutch associates. This was discovered by the Germans, with sanguinary results.

German Intelligence was well aware of the unpreparedness of the Dutch for clandestine warfare. Under the leadership of Herman Giskes, a keenly perceptive man of great energy and subtlety, and with the assistance of a number of V-men, the Abwehr quickly built up a portfolio of potential resistants. V-men were Dutchmen recruited by the German authorities to spy on their fellow countrymen. Many acted as double agents and allowed themselves to be recruited into the embryonic resistance groups only to compromise them to their German masters. Although their presence must have been known to the Dutch, the latter seemed either unwilling or incapable of countering them.

During the summer of 1941 the Germans learned through one of their V-men, Antonius van der Waals, of the existence of an underground radio station near the town of Bilthoven. A *Funkhorchdienst* radio-detection van was quietly moved into the area and the authorities waited. When the clandestine transmitter went on the air the Germans struck. Hans Zomer, a Dutch intelligence operator working both with the SIS and SOE, was captured in possession of a complete radio post, including a pile of back messages, codes and their keys. Zomer steadfastly refused to divulge information to his interrogators, even under Gestapo torture.

However, an SD sergeant, Ernst May, acting on his own initiative, succeeded in breaking the SIS cipher system. May had no training as a cryptanalyst, which made his achievement all the more extraordinary. He not only deciphered the messages but discovered the security check with which every clandestine radio operator was provided. Without the check impersonation would have been practically impossible; with it a transmitter could be 'turned'.

A few months later another resistance cell was penetrated by a V-man and on 13 February, 1942, two more SIS agents, Ter Laak, and a former Royal Dutch Navy radio operator, William van der Reyden, were captured in possession of a second set of codes. Angry and disorientated after his capture, van der Reyden gave a large amount of information to the gentle and sympathetic May, enabling the latter to increase considerably his knowledge of British codes. Disastrously, May also learned of the existence of the security checks and test questions used by SIS and SOE agents to prevent impersonation, thus setting the stage for a deception exercise of massive proportions.

With the help of George Ridderhof, yet another V-man, the Germans next closed in on an SOE group. Thys Taconis, a trained saboteur, and Huburtus Lauwers, his radio operator, were parachuted in on 6/7 November, 1941. Despite some startling irregularities in their forged identity papers the two men successfully settled down to work, Lauwers in The Hague and Taconis in Arnhem. Under the guise of a road haulier Ridderhof befriended Taconis, providing him with transport to remove supplies from his drops. He also supplied the agent with wholly inaccurate intelligence for transmission to London.

Gradually, from snippets of information carelessly divulged, Ridderhof succeeded in unravelling crucial details of the SOE network, including the location of its radio. On 6 March, 1942, while preparing to transmit to London, Lauwers was arrested. Taconis was taken a few days later. Both men were told that their lives would be spared if they cooperated with '*England Spiel*', an operation involving the transmission of disinformation on Lauwers' captured radio set. Taconis refused, even under torture, and was eventually executed at Mauthausen in the early winter of 1944.

Initially Lauwers also refused, but when it was proved to him that the Germans had already broken his codes he concurred, though solely in the belief that London would realize from the lack of certain key security checks that he was working under duress. Tragically they did not, and for two years continued to act on

Lauwers' messages despite their continuous lack of checks and the constant inclusion of netting-in signals (NIS) and other paraphernalia calculated to warn the receivers.

Incredibly, in a post-war investigation SOE excused its extraordinary failure to heed its own procedure by claiming that it had assumed that the agent had been transmitting under other than normal circumstances and had consequently forgotten one of the fundamental tenets of his training. On one occasion Lauwers even succeeded in signalling, in open language, the message 'caught caught caught' within a standard transmission, but to no avail. The listeners at Bletchley simply chose to edit out what they did not want to hear. After a few weeks the fact that Lauwers was omitting his security checks was no longer relayed to SOE headquarters in London.

It was not the messages which Lauwers transmitted – all careful German fabrications – that were important; it was the messages which he received. After only a few days transmission Lauwers was advised by London that an agent named Lieutenant Arnold Baatsen (code-named 'Watercress') would be parachuted on to a drop zone north of Assen on the night of 27 March. Baatsen, a professional photographer, dropped on schedule, along with several containers of explosives and weapons, to be greeted by a number of V-men masquerading as *resistants*. He was arrested and handed over to the Abwehr. Baatsen was furious and talked openly to his captors, adding to their growing knowledge of SOE ciphers and personnel.

Lauwers was ordered to notify SOE that Baatsen had arrived safely, after which other agents followed in increasing numbers. Piet Homberg arrived in the autumn of 1941, followed by Lieutenant Leonard Andringa on 10 March, 1942. On 29 March another team, Hendrich Jordaan and Gerard Ras, were parachuted in, to be followed a week later by Hendrich Sebes and Berend Kloos. Two weeks later, Lieutenant Hendrich van Haas arrived by boat.

On 23 June SOE agents Johannes Buizer and Jan van Reitscoten landed at a field near Assen where they were immediately apprehended by the Abwehr, who by now were not even attempting to mask their activities. At the same time V-men activity accounted for a number of other resistance cells, until, by late 1942, the

Germans controlled six 'turned' radios, complete with operators and security checks.

Despite frantic attempts by Lauwers to warn London, SOE believed that it had no fewer than ten agents safely operating in Holland. Instructions from London arrived almost daily; a captured agent named Gerard Hemert brought with him instructions for the dynamiting of a German naval installation at Kootwijk. Radio instructions to agents to destroy other installations led to reinforcements being sent to those places. Gradually the nature of the instructions enabled German Intelligence to build up a plan of Allied intentions in Holland which they were thereafter able to frustrate.

The Abwehr was painfully aware that a few agents remained free in Holland. However, the strict British policy of 'need to know' prevented agents from associating with each other either during training or in the field and the sudden disappearance of so many did not therefore arouse suspicion.

The Abwehr was faced with a dilemma on one occasion when SOE requested information concerning the progress of an agent not under German control. Rather than prevaricate or ignore the request, Giskes chose to steer a middle course. He cautiously requested additional information from London and, when that arrived, culled through the SOE prisoners for an agent who had been associated with the missing spy. Information from this source made it possible for Giskes to concoct a believeable scenario.

In all *England Spiel* netted fifty-one SOE agents, nine from MI6 and one, Beatrix Terwindt, the only woman in the party, from MI9. She survived Ravensbruck and Mauthausen, but almost all of her male companions were shot. Lauwers himself was spared, and five agents escaped from the concentration camp at Haaren, north-east of Tilberg. Two of these, Sergeant Dourlein and Lieutenant Ubbink (code-named 'Cabbage' and 'Chive'), ultimately escaped to Switzerland, where they made contact with the local MI6 head of station in Berne.

The Germans finally realized that the game was no longer playable when MI6 sent a damning message to its agents in the area, warning of SOE's insecurity and ordering them to break off all contact with the rival unit's agents. The message was intercepted by the Germans, who then began to run down their network.

As a final twist of the knife Dourlein and Ubbink were arrested when they finally reached Britain and held in Brixton Prison. During their laborious journey along the escape line from Switzerland they were denounced as Gestapo agents by the Abwehr using a captured SOE radio set. After a few months both men were released and ultimately decorated by the Dutch authorities.

When the Germans realized that *England Spiel* had run its course they sent a gloating message to the heads of the Netherlands section of SOE:

'TO MESSRS BLUNT BINGHAM AND SUCCESSORS LTD STOP YOU ARE TRYING TO MAKE BUSINESS IN THE NETHERLANDS WITHOUT OUR ASSISTANCE STOP WE THINK THIS RATHER UNFAIR IN VIEW OUR LONG AND SUCCESSFUL COOPERATION AS YOUR SOLE AGENT STOP BUT NEVER MIND WHENEVER YOU COME TO PAY A VISIT TO THE CONTINENT YOU MAY BE ASSURED THAT YOU WILL BE RECEIVED WITH THE SAME CARE AND RESULT AS ALL THOSE YOU SENT BEFORE STOP SO LONG STOP'

The British response to this message remains unknown and would almost certainly have been unprintable. *England Spiel* without doubt constituted the greatest single act of deception in the Second World War, and was one of the most successful in the history of espionage. Had SOE only obeyed its own rules and accepted that an agent as experienced as Lauwers would simply not have made so many continuous errors in his transmissions the tragedy need never have taken place.

Giskes was taken into custody after the war and investigated and interrogated by both Dutch and Allied prosecutors. It was accepted that he had acted honourably and within the Geneva Accords and he was subsequently released without charge.

The Double Cross System

It would be grossly wrong to suggest that the Allies did not also enjoy a great deal of success in the field of agent-turning and deception. The Double Cross System was one of the earliest and most enduring of British Secret Service successes. German agents were arrested, held in secret in a centre in Richmond Park and either 'turned' or their places taken by British radio operators. The system was controlled by the Oxford academic Sir John Masterman at the head of the ad hoc 'Twenty (XX) Committee'.

Masterman was commissioned into the Intelligence Corps in March, 1940, largely because of his ability to speak fluent German, and was posted to the War Office as secretary to the Howard Enquiry investigating the improvised evacuation of the British Expeditionary Force from Dunkirk. He was later transferred to the counter-espionage division of the Security Service, based initially at Blenheim Palace and later less salubriously in HM Prison Wormwood Scrubs.

In December, 1940, Masterman was given the task of debriefing Dusko Popov, a Yugoslav who had been recruited by the Abwehr in 1940, but who had later offered his services to the British in Belgrade. Popov had been sent by the Abwehr to Portugal in November, 1940, but a month later had succeeded in flying secretly to the United Kingdom, where he was interviewed and recruited both by MI6 (code-name 'Tricycle') and by Masterman into MI5 (code-name 'Scout'.). It was this remarkable encounter which led to the development of the Twenty Committee, an inter-departmental body created to supervise double-agent deception operations run by London.

Crucially, on one critical occasion involving Popov, 'Allied' disinformation proved double-edged. The Yugoslav returned to Lisbon where he began to provide valuable intelligence for the British. However, one key piece of information was badly mis-handled. From German sources he obtained detailed information on the proposed Japanese attack on Pearl Harbor. Inexplicably, rather than pass the information to the White House (the United States had no formal foreign intelligence service at the time) the British kept it to themselves. MI5's Guy Liddell (then a Soviet agent) informed the head of the FBI J. Edgar Hoover and arranged for the two to meet in Washington. Primed by Liddell that Popov was a double agent (which he was not), and horrified by his MI6 code-name 'Tricycle' (which Hoover assumed, wholly inaccurately, to have sexual connotations), Hoover took an instant dislike to the Yugoslav, whose wholly accurate information he dismissed out of hand.

Between January, 1941, and his return to the academic world at the end of the war, Masterman chaired a total of 226 weekly meetings of the Double Cross Committee. He later wrote a full report on the activities of the Committee, only to find it heavily censored by the head of post-war MI5, Sir Roger Hollis. The full story has yet to be told, but enough information is now available to establish the full extent to which the British authorities effectively controlled the flow of intelligence, and with it disinformation, to Germany.

Britain's first wartime double agent (code-named 'Snow') was recruited by MI6 in 1936. At the time his connections with German Intelligence had not been appreciated; indeed it was not until a letter from him to a known forwarding address in Hamburg was intercepted some months later, and he was closely questioned on the matter, that his dealings with the Abwehr became apparent. Snow was allowed to continue his association with the Abwehr with little interference from the British, and in return, as war loomed closer, provided the latter with a considerable amount of useful information.

In September, 1939, Snow was served with a detention order and removed to Wandsworth Prison where he agreed at once to transmit to Germany, using a radio set provided him by the Abwehr in the previous January. With Snow's first message from Wandsworth Prison the double-cross system was well and truly launched. Very soon he was receiving a variety of orders and requests for information. German Intelligence was particularly keen to infiltrate the Welsh Nationalist Party which it felt, quite erroneously, was planning a major insurrection. The agent was allowed to travel to Holland to meet his unsuspecting Abwehr 'handler' to discuss a project for shipping arms and explosives to South Wales for use in the insurrection. He was given details of other agents in the United Kingdom and arrangements were made to provide him with a regular income.

During the 18 months in which Snow operated under Masterman's control he aided the discovery of three German agents. More importantly he provided considerable information on Abwehr personalities and their methods of working. He brought to light the embryonic sabotage plans of the Germans and provided the Bletchley code-breakers with a deep insight into German cipher codes and wireless procedures.

Most subsequent attempts by Germany to infiltrate agents into Britain failed, in no small part due to the extremely poor levels of briefing and technical support afforded the agents. In the early stages of the war most agents were generally given about £200, clearly on the assumption that they would only have to maintain themselves for a month or two until the invasion took place, and their clothing, identity documents and the like showed insufficient attention to detail and betrayed every indication of haste and improvisation.

The agents' positions were made no easier by the fact that the identity documents given to them were constructed from information provided by the Snow organization, and were therefore deliberately flawed. This made them relatively easy to detect, but gave British Intelligence clear evidence of the arrival of newcomers.

All captured agents were brought to the attention of the Twenty Committee. Those who had been captured almost immediately and who had not therefore had the opportunity to contact Germany, whose capture had been unobserved by the general public and who agreed to work for Masterman, were 'turned.' Those who failed to meet any part of this criterion were handed over to the relevant authorities, tried and invariably executed.

This policy was opposed by the security services who argued that a live spy, even one useless to the deception plan, still remained a useful source of information to be tapped as necessary. Nonetheless the deaths of at least a few agents was considered necessary, both to satisfy the public at large that the security of the country was being maintained and to convince the Germans that those who had not been apprehended were working properly and were not under 'control'.

In all there were some 120 double cross agents on MI5 records, of whom thirty-nine (with code-names as improbable as 'Mutt', 'Jeff,' 'Lipstick' and 'Peppermint') were caught and controlled successfully from within the United Kingdom. As the war progressed disinformation back to the Germans changed in emphasis from troop dispositions, factory outputs and localized defences to arms build-ups and possible landing sites for the invasion. Signals disinformation constituted a crucial part of 'Operation Fortitude', giving German Intelligence a wholly inaccurate insight into the Allied preparations for D Day.

The Double Cross System proved most successful in the Middle East and North Africa. Working as part of Security Intelligence Middle East (SIME) it succeeded not only in keeping Turkey neutral but in forcing the Germans to keep crucial divisions tied down in the Balkans. SIME convinced German Intelligence that Britain had several new divisions in North Africa poised to strike across the Mediterranean. In reality the divisions comprised nothing more than a few hard-working radio operators sending routine radio messages to each other from relatively inaccessible parts of the Middle East. When tasked by German Intelligence to investigate the source of the increased traffic, 'turned' agents under SIME control reported completely fictitious troop build-ups in the transmission areas. Completely unaware of SIME's activities, the German High Command in the area became obsessed with the idea of invasion through the Balkans.

When captured networks were unable to provide enough disinformation, SIME invented fictitious agents. One, a prostitute named 'Gala', was actually in prison in Palestine, but for the purposes of misleading the Germans was depicted as 'working' in Beirut. She sent reports on a whole string of indiscreet, but wholly imaginary, lovers, including a motley series of Allied officers and a technician secretly working on the preparation of Turkish airfields for Allied occupation.

Not all agents involved in deception were 'turned' or fictitious. Amy Elizabeth Brousse was larger than life and very much her own woman. She was also an excellent deceiver and flatterer of men, and one of the most successful sex spies in modern history. Born in Minneapolis, USA, at the age of 20 she married Arthur Pack, a taciturn and somewhat pompous commercial secretary at the British Embassy in Washington. Due in no small part to the vast difference in their ages and the wholesale difference in their characters theirs was a far from happy marriage. Nonetheless Amy stuck with her husband as his job took him to Chile, Spain and finally Poland.

During the Spanish Civil War Amy Brousse assisted in the escape of a number of Franco supporters and in 1939 offered her services to MI6. While in Poland she gained the confidence of a young aide to the Foreign Secretary, Colonel Beck. From him she gleaned considerable intelligence, some of which led to Britain gaining possession of a top secret German Enigma cipher machine.

When war broke out she was seconded to New York where she was given the code-name 'Cynthia' by Willian Stephenson, the Canadian born head of British secret service in the United States. She was lodged in comfort in Washington where she quickly became an accepted part of the diplomatic social scene. On MI6 orders she renewed the acquaintance of an ex-lover, Admiral Alberto Lais, the Italian naval attaché to the United States, seducing from him detailed sets of codes and ciphers which later proved invaluable in the prosecution of the war in the Mediterranean. Having drained the Italian of his usefulness she dumped him, reporting him as an agent to the FBI and having him expelled as an undesirable.

Cynthia next targetted Captain Charles Brousse, a press officer at the Vichy French Embassy in Washington. Her orders were to obtain as much detail as possible on all correspondence passing between Vichy and Washington, and ideally to obtain copies of the French ciphers. So irresistible did the young man find his new lover that she quickly realized that subterfuge was unnecessary. He willingly gave her details of a secret cache of gold buried on the island of Martinique and helped her to break into the Embassy. He even arranged for her to move into his hotel, where he lived with his third wife.

Later Cynthia was sent to London and attached to an SOE office in Dorset Square. She volunteered unsuccessfully for field service as an assassin. In 1945 her husband committed suicide and Brousse divorced his wife. The couple subsequently married and lived in a castle in southern France until Cynthia's death in 1963. She never showed the slightest degree of remorse for any aspect of her earlier life, regarding her assignations, both genuine and staged, as necessary. Indeed she was immensely proud of the fact that the information gained as a result of her sexual activities had almost certainly saved many hundreds of Allied lives.

It has been claimed that, without the Lucy spy network in Switzerland, the Soviet Union might well have lost the war on the Eastern Front. The network took its title from the code-name of its leader, Rudolf Roessler, an anti-Nazi publisher and expatriate Bavarian who fled to Geneva when Hitler came to power. Roessler was employed by Brigadier Masson, head of Swiss Military Intelligence, who employed him as an analyst with Bureau Ha, overtly a press cuttings agency but in fact a covert department of Swiss Intelligence.

Roessler was required to assess military intelligence relating to a possible German invasion of Switzerland. At the same time he began to send out information to the Soviets, intelligence so valuable that they paid him a large monthly retainer. Aided by an Englishman, Alexander Foote, and a Hungarian, Sandor Rado (then NKVD head in Switzerland), Roessler fed the Soviets highly accurate intelligence on a daily basis relating to Nazi assessments and troop movements down to brigade level for over two years.

No one has ever precisely ascertained how Roessler obtained such high grade-information, but it has been claimed that he received much of the data from a mysterious group of ten Bavarian anti-Nazis high in the German Command. However, Masson had connections with MI6 and it is far more likely that he was fed the information by the British from intercepts of German radio traffic. Churchill was keen to give Stalin every assistance in his prosecution of the war in the East, yet did not wish him to know that Britain possessed the Enigma machine and was able to break German codes routinely. He felt that Stalin would almost certainly discount as untrue any information passed direct by MI6 and was at the time unaware of the existence of the Cambridge spies within British Intelligence. Only later did he discover that Stalin had captured several Enigma machines and was in any case regularly receiving information direct from Burgess, Philby and Maclean.

The Lucy ring continued its activities until late in 1943, with the Swiss Authorities turning a blind eye to the 'Rote Drei' (Red Three). However, as it became clear that Hitler was losing the war and the possibility of invasion ceased, the Swiss reverted to their traditional neutrality. Lucy was wound up and the three agents given short jail sentences prior to deportation.

President Roosevelt supported a secret war against Nazi Germany for two years while the United States was formally at peace. To do so he had to deceive not only Congress but also some of his closest advisers, many of whom were markedly isolationist in their attitude towards Britain.

He was greatly assisted by William Stephenson, the larger-than-life Canadian with overall responsibility for British Intelligence in Washington. Born in 1896, Stephenson joined the Royal Flying Corps in the First World War, serving with distinction until he was shot down. He managed to escape, returning to the Allied lines with a wealth of information on the economic state of Germany.

After the war Stephenson became a pioneer in the world of broadcasting with particular regard to the transmission of photographs. His worldwide commercial interests quickly spread, until by the mid-1930s they had grown to incorporate the manufacture of plastics and steel. He became alarmed to discover that practically the entire German steel output was being turned over to armaments, a fact which few in Britain seemed to regard as significant. One exception was Winston Churchill, who encouraged Stephenson to delve deeper. The two men became confidants, with Churchill inviting the Canadian to join his team of informal advisers.

Shortly after becoming Prime Minister in June, 1940, Churchill appointed Stephenson to the rôle of co-ordinating an informal friendship between the British and United States Intelligence agencies. He was posted to Washington as a Passport Control Officer (by then a rather over-used MI6 disguise), and quietly set about the task of recruiting agents for the twin tasks of propaganda dissemination and intelligence gathering.

Any co-operation with American Intelligence needed to be kept secret, even from the State Department. At one stage anti-British hostility at the State Department was so pronounced that Stephenson suspected that it had been infiltrated by pro-Nazis. It was even feared that Roosevelt was being kept unaware of their existence and of their desire to enter into a peace accord with Germany.

On 20 May, 1940, Special Branch in London took the unprecedented step of entering the apartment of Tyler Gatewood Kent, a cipher clerk attached to the American Embassy. Copies of

1,500 top secret documents cabled between London and Washington, including coded and highly personal messages between Churchill and Roosevelt, were seized. When confronted, Kent conceded that the messages had been passed to Berlin, claiming that he wanted to thwart his President's 'secret and unconstitutional plot with Churchill to sneak the United States into the war'.

Consequently, and wholly without formal instructions, a British agent took it upon himself to burgle the safe of the Under Secretary of State, Mr Sumner Welles. This action, which might so easily have proved catastrophic, met with success when it was revealed that German plans to sabotage British shipping in American waters were being hushed up by the State Department. The agent was forced to flee to Canada, but was allowed to return to the United States after America entered the war.

Stephenson's activities were made somewhat easier by the tacit support afforded him by the Head of the FBI, J. Edgar Hoover. Stephenson knew that Hoover brooked no interference in the management of the FBI, which the latter regarded as his personal fiefdom, and was always careful never to allow his operations to compromise the internal security of the United States.

It is extremely doubtful whether any British agent other than William Stephenson could have handled Hoover so skilfully at that time. Later, others tried but failed lamentably, particularly when faced with Hoover's obsession with communism and his crude methods of combating the perceived menace.

The two men quickly settled down to a working, if at times stormy, relationship. Hoover gave Stephenson the title of Head of British Security Co-ordination (BSC), although the latter seemed happier with his code-name 'Intrepid', which he continued to use as his telegraphic address in Bermuda after he retired. His contacts with the film world enabled him to enrol a surprising number of agents from that sphere. Alexander and Zoltan Korda developed Camp X in Canada, a location in which agents were trained and Hollywood make-up artists employed to create disguises for them.

A number of celebrities worked for 'Intrepid', among them Leslie Howard, tragically shot down over the Bay of Biscay while on a secret mission in 1941.

In mid-1942 an urgent request from British Naval Intelligence presented Stephenson with something of a dilemma. London wanted an immediate disruption of the links between Europe and South America, which were becoming dangerously pro-Nazi. Stephenson was given *carte-blanche*, providing his actions did nothing to jeopardize BSC's somewhat tenuous relationship with Washington. The United States had always regarded South America as within its exclusive economic and political sphere and would have been far from happy at any intimation of British interference in the area.

Stephenson decided upon a plan of deception aimed at frightening the Brazilian government into a state of enforced neutrality. A letter from the Rome offices of General Aurelio Liotta, the president of the Italian State Airlines (LATI), was stolen and sent secretly to the BSC offices in Canada. Stationery identical to that on which the letter was written was manufactured and the letterhead forged. Finally a typewriter exhibiting the precise imperfections of the Italian machine on which the stolen letter had been typed was constructed.

In September a forged letter was produced, notionally written by General Liotta to Commandante Vicenzo Coppola, the airline's regional manager in Brazil. It read:

'Dear Friend:

Thank you for your letter and for the report enclosed. I discussed your report immediately with our friends. They regard it as being of the highest importance. They compared it in my presence with certain information that had already been received from the Prace del Prete. The two reports coincided almost exactly . . . It made me feel proud. . .' There can be no doubt the "little fat man" is falling into the pocket of the Americans, and that only violent action on the part of the "green gentlemen" can save the country. I understand such action has been arranged for by our respected collaborators in Berlin . . .'

Micropix of the letter were smuggled to Rio and blowups carefully leaked to the Government, who with little prompting construed the forgery as part of a fascist-inspired plot to bring about the downfall of President Getulio Vargas, the 'little fat man'. The 'green gentlemen' were a group of well known Integralists openly hostile to his regime.

As a final insult, the letter finished with the sentence: 'The Brazilians may be, as you said, a nation of monkeys, but they are monkeys who will dance for anyone who can pull the string.'

Outraged, the President suspended LATI's landing rights and ordered Coppola's arrest (he was apprehended en route to Argentina with a million dollars of LATI funds). President Vargas, enraged by the Italians and antagonized by the Germans, moved under the United States umbrella. Later he willingly offered his new-found protector bases and ports for launching operations in Africa.

The forgeries had been so well planted that the FBI later claimed, in good faith, that the coup had been theirs. A copy of the letter had reached the US Embassy in Brazil via an FBI agent, where it had been taken as genuine. Stephenson did nothing to disillusion Hoover. Instead he ordered that the original forgeries be destroyed and the rebuilt Italian typewriter taken apart and dropped into a lake.

The Men Who Never Were

Very occasionally it has proved expedient to invent a character to add credibility to a deception. Few intelligence agencies when under pressure are wholly objective in their analysis of a situation and experience has frequently shown that information received from any source will all too often be accepted if it helps to turn supposition into probability.

The story of Alfred Wahring, 'the spy who never was', is particularly interesting. In October, 1939, Captain Gunther Prien, commander of the German submarine *U-47*, entered Scapa Flow, sank the battleship *Royal Oak* with considerable attendant loss of life and damaged the carrier support ship *Pegasus*. At the time it was accepted that Prien, an exceptional seaman and later U-boat ace, had operated alone.

Then, in 1942, Curt Reiss of the Philadelphia *Saturday Evening Post* published a fantastic story in which he suggested that the whole operation had been masterminded by a single agent. He alleged that Captain Alfred Wahring, a First World War veteran who had witnessed the scuttling of the German Grand Fleet in Scapa Flow, had vowed revenge. He had moved to Switzerland where he had applied for a passport under the name of Alfred Oertel. In 1927 he had moved to Britain, had become a naturalized citizen and had set up shop as a watchmaker at Kirkwall in the Orkney Islands, close to Scapa Flow. At the outbreak of war he had contacted Germany, advising them of the lack of adequate anti-submarine defences at the eastern entrance to the Flow. When Prien had been dispatched, Wahring had guided *U-47* into position using the headlights of a motor car.

Walter Schellenberg, head of German Intelligence, exploited and expanded the story, yet there was not a shred of truth in any of it. Neither German nor British records show any trace of a Captain Wahring, nor of a watchmaker named Oertel. Prien died later in the war and could not be cross-examined. However, his log makes no mention of a signal from an agent ashore, but instead intimates that he entered Scapa Flow blind. He did see the flash of a car headlight, but assumed that it belonged to a motorist alerted by the wake of the U-boat's conning tower in the water.

The story of Wahring was a complete fabrication brilliantly planted in the United States by German propagandists. So professional was the plant that for years afterwards Allan Dulles of the CIA incorporated the story of Alfred Wahring into his lecture pack on the worth of the long-term sleeper.

Major Martin RM, perhaps the most famous fictitious man in the history of espionage, was conceived by Lieutenant-Commander Montagu RNVR, of the Naval Intelligence Division.

During the planning of *Operation Torch*, the invasion of French North Africa, the Allies were keen not merely to mask their intentions, but to deceive the enemy as to their target. It was conceded that the gradual build up of shipping at Gibraltar prior to the invasion could not be hidden from the Nazi agents in Spain and was therefore accepted that the Germans would appreciate that an invasion was imminent, but at the same time it was hoped they could be persuaded that its destination was elsewhere, ideally as far away as possible in the eastern Mediterranean.

The potential for leaking disinformation to the Germans through their Spanish sympathizers had been emphasized a few months earlier. A plane had crashed and a body had been washed ashore in Spain, as a result of which some fortunately un-compromising papers had fallen into the possession of the Germans. It was therefore decided to plant on the Spanish coast a corpse with fake plans for an Allied invasion of Greece in his pouch.

The initial, and perhaps surprisingly the greatest, difficulty lay in the obtaining of a suitable body in complete secrecy. Montagu approached his friend, Sir William Bentley Purchase, the highly discreet Coroner of St Pancras, explaining his rather macabre needs. The body had to be that of a reasonably young man, the causes of whose death had to be consistent with an airplane crash should a post mortem be held.

By the end of January, 1943, Purchase had found a suitable body which he retained on ice. It was of a man of the correct age, height and weight, who had been ill for some time before his death. The father of the deceased was approached, and with certain under-standable misgivings granted his permission on the understanding that his son would ultimately receive a Christian burial.

The remains now lie buried in Spain. Despite rigorous attempts by certain researchers to establish the true identity of the deceased it remains to this day, quite properly, a closely guarded secret.

It was decided to give the notional officer, who was given the name of Major Martin, the status of an officer in the Royal Marines to keep administration in the hands of the Royal Navy. Dressing him proved something of a logistical nightmare. He was provided with a battle dress, as no service dress could be made to fit exactly. Thick underwear was donated from the wardrobe of the late Warden of New College, Oxford. Difficulty arose in fitting the boots onto the frozen corpse. Eventually it was decided to thaw the feet over an electric fire. As soon as the boots were on the cadaver was refrozen.

Major Martin was provided with a personality built up by a series of letters and other personal documents. These included a bank statement showing an overdraft of £7 19s 2d, the stubs of two tickets to the theatre, a newspaper clipping announcing Major Martin's engagement, a jeweller's receipt for an engage-ment ring, a letter from his fiancée and a photograph of her. The letter was signed 'with love from Pam'. The girl was real enough, although she knew nothing whatsoever of the dead man. She was in fact a trusted employee in the War Office who, without being told why, had been asked to write a fictitious letter to her future husband.

Martin became an officer on the staff of the Chief of Combined Operations. He was given a personal letter from Admiral Mountbatten to Admiral Cunningham, the Naval Commander-in-Chief Mediterranean, to explain why he was travelling as he was and carrying the main deception letter. He was also given an informal letter to General Alexander hinting that there were two operations being planned for the Mediterranean. The letter set out the thoughts of the Chiefs of Staff Committee intimating that Greece was their priority target for an invasion, although they did not discount Sicily as a secondary target.

To make certain that the papers were found even if the people who recovered the body did not go through Martin's pockets, he also carried a letter from Mountbatten to General Eisenhower, enclosing the proof of a Joint Operations pamphlet to which Eisenhower was due to pen the preface. This was sufficiently bulky to necessitate its being carried in a black government briefcase into which the other letters were also slipped.

After a detailed study of the tides and currents in the Gulf of Cadiz it was decided to release the body, with the briefcase chained to its wrist, close to Huelva, a town in which the German consul was known to be particularly efficient.

In the utmost secrecy the body was placed in a specially made container packed with dry ice to delay decomposition. It was then driven to the Clyde, conventionally marked for onward transit, and placed on board HM Submarine *Seraph*. The boat sailed on 19 April.

On 30 April Major Martin was launched from the submarine together with a capsized rubber dingy. When the body floated ashore the pro-German Spanish authorities permitted a German agent to have access to it, but made no official report of the discovery for several days. During that time the German agent opened, photographed and resealed the documents in the brief-case, which was subsequently handed to the British Embassy. 'Major Martin' was given a military funeral. At the same time anxious messages were sent from London to North Africa enquiring as to his whereabouts and the top secret documents in his possession. The signals gave details of the aircraft in which he had been travelling.

Both German High Command and the Abwehr were completely deceived by the deception. They accepted fully Major Martin's bona fides, thanks in no small part to the theatre ticket stubs, and became convinced of the authenticity of the letters which he carried. Hitler himself expected an Allied invasion of the Peloponnese. He was convinced that Churchill, instigator of the much-maligned Dardanelles Campaign in the First World War, would wish to vindicate his decision by returning to the same area. Reinforcements were sent to Greece and the construction of defensive emplacements in the western Mediterranean halted.

So convinced were the Germans that they had discovered the Allies' true intentions that when the Secretary of the US Navy, Frank Fox, inadvertently let slip their actual plans his words were discounted as a bluff by Minister of Propaganda Goebbels.

By its very nature clandestine warfare has to be top secret. Throughout the war potential agents, those working with Ultra, or those involved in the world of strategic deception, were regularly monitored to ensure that the acute mental strain to which they were constantly subjected was not having too drastic an effect.

Those who were perhaps beginning to drink too much or talk too freely were posted to different work. Acute security risks were posted somewhere distant and insignificant, typically to a series of workshops in the remote Highland village of Inverlair (said to be the inspiration for the television series *The Prisoner*).

CHAPTER FIVE
Maskirovka; A Powerful Soviet Concept

'War puts nations to the test. Just as mummies crumble to dust the moment they are exposed to air, so war pronounces its sentence of death on those social institutions which have become ossified.' (Karl Marx, 1855).

Maskirovka, the art of deception, formed the very bedrock of Soviet military practice and is still an important tenet in Russian strategic thinking. It has no equivalent in the West; indeed the word *Maskirovka* itself defies translation. It encompasses the arts of concealment (*skrytie*), the use of dummies and decoys (*imitatsiia*), disinformation (*dezinformatsiia*), and even the execution of complex demonstration manoeuvres (*demonstrativny manevry*). Indeed, anything capable of confusing, and therefore weakening, the enemy may be incorporated.

Maskirovka, according to the *Soviet Military Encyclopaedia*, complements surprise by covertly 'securing military operations and the routine activity of troops and by confusing the enemy with regard to the presence and position of the forces, military complexes, their position, level of preparation and activity as well as the plans for the command structure.'

Although both the Tzars and Bolsheviks recognized the potential of *Maskirovka*, neither exploited it fully. The Leninist secret service organization, the Cheka, adopted the term *dezinformatsiia* in the 1920s, but was subsequently frustrated by Stalin who actively distrusted the concept.

In the late 1920s the Ukrainian Military District was allowed to organize a special partisan task force charged with the demolition of critical facilities along the border with Poland and Romania in the case of invasion. The task force was responsible for the development of demolition technology, the establishing of explosives caches and the training of special teams to carry out covert demolition tasks. Primary targets for such teams were to be the key points and rolling stock of the Soviet railway system, their objective being to deny use of the system to an invading enemy.

More than sixty demolition teams were formed with an average strength of twenty-three persons each (including some females). Every demolition expert was also a parachutist, a radio operator and a master of camouflage (then defined as *maskirovka*). In the winter of 1932 a number of teams jumped into the Leningrad Military District on an exercise to demonstrate their skills on operations in the enemy rear, their mission being to capture a headquarters and destroy transportation facilities. The mission was an unqualified success and the teams were able to place ten mines on a 10km stretch of track before their presence was detected (by a mine which blew up under the wheels of a commuter train before it could be removed).

Although primarily an engineer effort, the programme was closely related to the GRU's creation of a special partisan cadre trained for 'stay behind' operations in the enemy rear in the event of invasion. Gradually, however, as the threat of foreign invasion subsided, the partisan groups were absorbed into the Red Army and the programme destroyed. Most of the personnel associated with it were killed during Stalin's purges in the late 1930s, possibly because he feared that the programme was a destabilizing threat to his own régime.

The Great Patriotic War

Maskirovka was employed to limited effect by the military during the Great Patriotic War (the Second World War). It was exploited during the counter-offensive to relieve Moscow in 1942, and later in the encirclement of the Sixth Army attacking Stalingrad. Its large-scale use was otherwise limited to the Manchurian Campaign described below.

The NKVD, however, almost immediately formed a Special Tasks unit of 20,000 men and women, including 2,000 foreigners and 140 former intelligence and security officers arrested in the

pre-war purges and now released under licence (many were subsequently re-arrested once their usefulness was over). In October
1941, the unit was enlarged and reorganized into Independent
Department Two of the NKVD reporting directly to Beria, and in
February, 1942, became the Independent Directorate Four for
Special Tasks and Guerrilla Warfare. As such it assumed responsibility for the vast majority of major intelligence operations
against Germany, including the running of clandestine groups in
the occupied territories, the creation of deception plans at home
and the planting of disinformation rumours.

During the course of the war the unit infiltrated 212 guerrilla
detachments comprising 7,316 men behind the enemy lines. It
trained over 1,000 military and 3,500 civilian technicians and
saboteurs and was responsible for the deaths of eighty-seven high-
ranking German officials and the liquidation of 2,045 Soviet
collaborators in the service of the Germans. Twenty-three of its
officers (including a few former prisoners) were awarded the
highest honour, Hero of the Soviet Union, and more than 8,000
of its members received lesser decorations.

One of the most successful deception exercises of the war was
Operation Monastery, undertaken by the NKVD in conjunction
with the GRU in July, 1941. Monastery was intended as a
counter intelligence operation aimed at penetrating the Abwehr
(German intelligence) network within the Soviet Union, but
quickly expanded. A few members of the former Czarist intelligentsia who had somehow survived the Stalinist purges of the
1920s and 1930s were recruited by the NKVD and formed into a
psuedo pro-German organization in the hopes that they would be
targetted by the Abwehr.

Control of the group passed to Aleksandr Demyanov, a veteran
NKVD agent with an otherwise impeccable White Russian background. His grandfather had been the founder of the Kuban
Cossacks, his father an officer in the Imperial Army, killed in action
fighting the Germans in 1915. His uncle had been chief of counter-
intelligence for the White Army in the Northern Caucasus, had
been captured by the Chekists and had died of typhus en route to
interrogation in Moscow. Demyanov's mother, a well-known
socialite, had received but rejected several invitations to emigrate
to France, but had returned instead to Leningrad. There

Demyanov's background had denied him a formal education and, indeed, had led to his arrest in 1929 on false charges of possessing illegal weapons and anti-Soviet propaganda.

Unusually, Demyanov had not been sentenced to administrative exile in Siberia, but had instead been recruited by the NKVD. Tired of violence and political intrigue, he had agreed to work towards the neutralization of White immigrant groups returning to the Soviet Union. He had later moved to Moscow where he had obtained a job with the Central Cinema Studio, Moscow's Hollywood. His intelligence and easy going nature had made him many friends among the actors, directors and writers, and had brought him to the attention of the Abwehr.

On the eve of the war, when Demyanov was first approached by the Abwehr, he already had ten years counter-intelligence operational experience with the NKVD. Having gained the trust of Germany, Demyanov let it be known that he led a pro-German underground organization which would feed the Abwehr information in exchange for a promise of positions in the German provisional government once the Soviet Union had been conquered.

The deception operation was originally planned as a means of exposing Russian collaboration with the Nazis, but quickly expanded into a far more deadly confrontation between NKVD and Abwehr. In December, 1941, Demyanov crossed the front line on skis, pretending to be a deserter from the Red Army. To make the crossing, he skied over a recently laid minefield, unaware of the danger. The Abwehr group to whom he surrendered did not trust him and, as a deserter, treated him with contempt.

They were, however, most interested in how he had crossed the minefield and could not believe that he could have done so without knowing the pattern of the mines in advance. They took no interest in his covert activities and, indeed, on one occasion staged a mock execution to compel him to admit his collusion with Soviet intelligence. That failing, they transferred him to Abwehr headquarters in Smolensk. There, to his surprise, the Germans took no interest in his political motives but instead recruited him as a full-time agent of the Abwehr with the task of setting up a spy ring based on his connections in Moscow.

The Abwehr became certain of Demyanov's bona fides when

they checked their own files and discovered that not only was he of impeccable pedigree but that he had been targetted by one of their agents. Demyanov was not allowed to mix with the Russian emigrés then serving the Nazis. Their organizations had been heavily infiltrated by the NKVD and Berlin was adamant that their new find would remain untainted.

In February, 1942, after a period of intensive Abwehr training, Demyanov and two assistants were parachuted into the outskirts of Moscow. The landing went badly, the three men lost contact with each other in a snowstorm and had to reach Moscow independently. Demyanov quickly contacted his NKVD masters and with their assistance set up a Nazi rezidenzia in the city. His two assistants were arrested.

In the months that followed, the Abwehr sent in excess of fifty agents to Moscow. All were quickly and quietly arrested. Faced with the stark option of death, a number agreed to become double agents and assisted the NKVD in the creation of a fiction in which Demyanov was receiving considerable intelligence from a number of undisclosed ex-czarist officers.

Railway accidents were fabricated and reported to the Abwehr as successful sabotage missions. Occasionally Nazi sabotage groups were left at liberty for a few days, but covertly followed to establish their contacts. In one instance Demyanov's wife doped a team by dropping knockout pills into their vodka. While they slept a team of demolition experts entered her flat to disable the saboteurs' explosives. Effectively disarmed, the team was allowed considerable leeway before being arrested.

A few German couriers, mostly of Baltic origin, were allowed to return to the Abwehr to whom they reported that the network was functioning successfully. Operation Monastery proved highly successful, causing the German High Command to make a number of fatal errors. Because Demyanov ensured that all information sent to the Abwehr contained at least an element of truth they began to accept the whole unreservedly.

In one instance, on the eve of the Battle of Stalingrad, Monastery predicted that the Red Army would unleash a massive offensive in the North Caucasus and in the areas to the north of Stalingrad. Such an attack did take place, but it was only a diversion planned by Stalin in absolute secrecy to divert German efforts away from Stalingrad itself. Even Zhukov, in command of the diversionary attack, was not told that the Germans had been fore-warned, and in the process of pursuing the feint to its vigorous and bloody conclusion paid a heavy price in the loss of thousands of men.

Later, during the Battle of Kursk in April and May 1943, Monastery reported that the Soviets held strong reserves in the east and south of the theatre but that these lacked manoeuvrability. This resulted in the Germans moving much of their reserve to meet an anticipated, though non-existent, attack to the north, leaving themselves vulnerable to the actual Soviet thrust when it came from the south.

With the aid of Enigma the British were able to intercept many of Monastery's messages to Berlin and reported these in sanitized form to the Soviets. In February, 1943, London warned Stalin that the Abwehr had a source in Moscow. Only years later did the British discover that this was in fact Monastery.

Although the largest of the Soviet deception plans, Monastery was far from unique. In all, Moscow operated in excess of forty minor radio deceptions, few if any of which fell under Nazi sus-picion. In theory the Abwehr was an excellent intelligence organization. In practice it lacked versatility. It would not easily accept the possibility of error, nor the likelihood of infiltration. Soviet disinformation fed to the German High Command via the Abwehr seems to have been accepted almost at face value, and certainly did much to influence the course of several crucial battles.

The Manchurian Experience

The attack against the Japanese in Manchuria in August, 1945, was the last great campaign of the war, and was the only example of the successful use of strategic surprise by the Soviets. In eleven days of savage fighting they secured approximately 1.5 million square kilo-metres, an area the size of France.

The Soviets had fought the Japanese Kwantung Army in numerous border incidents in the years preceding the invasion, most notably at Lake Khasan in 1938, but tensions had eased somewhat with the signing of the Soviet-Japanese Neutrality Pact in April, 1941. The Soviets had, however, continued to maintain a force of 1.3 million men, including between forty and sixty rifle divisions, on the Manchurian border.

Stalin had promised at the February, 1945, Yalta Conference to assist the Allies in the war against Japan within three months of the surrender of Germany, but in fact had intended to attack into Manchuria in late summer-early autumn 1945 to clear the Japanese from the area before the onset of winter. In the event his hand was forced on 6 August when the United States dropped an atomic bomb on Hiroshima. On 9 August the Soviets crossed the Manchurian frontier taking the Japanese completely by surprise.

Preparations for the campaign were actually begun in late 1944, although formal planning did not begin until February, 1945. From December, 1944 to the end of March, 1945, the Soviets moved 410 million rounds of small-arms ammunition and 3.2 million artillery shells to the Far East. Between April, 1945 and 25 July, 1945 the Soviets shipped two military fronts, two field armies, one tank army and supporting war material from Europe, via the Trans-Siberian railroad to the Manchurian border. Over 136,000 rail cars and up to thirty trains a day were employed in the move, which led to the redeployment of the equivalent of thirty divisions, yet the entire manoeuvre was kept a closely guarded secret, not just from the Japanese but from the Soviet's Anglo-American allies.

Key personnel travelled in disguise to preserve the myth of normality, while many units moved only at night, staying camouflaged during the day. Soviet troops closest to the border built massive defensive emplacements to reinforce the Japanese feeling of security. By August the newly created Far East command had just under 1.6 million personnel under arms, supported by 27,000 guns and mortars, 1,200 multiple rocket launchers, 5,600 tanks and self-propelled guns, 3,700 aircraft and 86,000 vehicles along a 5,000km frontage.

The Kwantung Army was taken completely by surprise. Although it occupied good defensive positions it had not expected to fight and was in any case a mere shell of its former self. Its better troops had long been transferred to other theatres, all but six of its divisions were new and some of its veteran units were down to 15% efficiency. There can be no doubt that it could not have withstood the might of the Soviet onslaught under any circumstances. Equally, however, had the Soviets not been so effective in masking their intentions the Japanese would have been better prepared and might well have delayed, if not completely frustrated, their advance. The Soviets learned many lessons from Manchuria, not the least the absolute necessity for deception in tactical planning. When Stalin died in 1953 the art of *Maskirovka*, which had made the Manchurian Campaign so successful, was formally adopted by the Red Army.

Cold War Advances

By the late 1960s surprise had become an important ingredient in military operations. The *Soviet Military Encyclopaedia* described surprise as 'one of the most important principles of military art (which) consists of the selection of times, techniques and methods of combat operations, which permit delivery of a strike when the enemy is least prepared to repulse it and thereby paralysing his will for organized resistance.'

Painfully aware of the impact of *Barbarossa* on the Red Army in 1941, the Soviets determined that they would never again be caught unprepared. At the same time surprise and deception began to rank with superiority in arms and manpower as central themes for future victory against the West. From the outset the Soviets accepted that complete surprise was impossible, but nonetheless began to believe that they could neutralize most NATO early warning and surveillance systems by adopting a policy of absolute secrecy and by using *Maskirovka* at all levels.

Knowing that they were powerless to prevent the intrusion of United States spy planes and satellites into their air space, the Soviets took steps to disguise the true intentions of military factories and installations in their flight path.Phoney factories and arms dumps were built, and after May 1960 (when Francis Gary Powers' U-2 aircraft was shot down by an SA-2 missile near Sverdlovsk) dummy surface-to-air missile sites were constructed to deter further sorties over delicate areas. A massive arms park was constructed in East Germany, close to the railway used by the United States, France and Britain to resupply their troops in West Berlin. While every effort was made to disguise the quantity and type of real weaponry stored there, dummy tanks and guns were regularly deployed close to the compound perimeter to confuse the intelligence analysts travelling on the daily trains.

Disinformation, a core component of *Maskirovka*, became the responsibility of Department D of the Committee of State Security, or KGB. For years the KGB and its predecessors had been doctoring photographs to reinforce the myth that the Bolshevik seizure of power had been a mass movement headed solely by Lenin. Trotsky had 'disappeared' from many official photographs, including the famous photograph of Lenin addressing the troops in a packed square in Moscow in 1920. In the 1960s they even began to doctor parades. The May Day and October Revolutionary Parades through Moscow's Red Square began to 'exhibit' new weapon systems, tantalizingly tarpaulined to keep them a secret from prying Western observers. Only when the observers began to realize that the tyre pressures and suspensions on these often massive lorries were inconsistent with their carrying anything more than a light wooden mock-up did they come to realize that the whole thing had been an elaborate hoax.

Later, even after the introduction of Gorbachev's glasnost, topical subjects were cleverly distorted. Newspaper articles appeared describing the decadence of the West. In March, 1987, the influential state newspaper Izvestia carried a cartoon implying that AIDS had in fact been manufactured in the West. This was followed a month later by an article in the internationally read Moscow News implying that experiments were being undertaken at Fort Detrick, Maryland to spread the disease. The naked aim of this policy seems to have been to create pressure for the removal of US foreign bases, thus strengthening the influence of the Soviets abroad. Ultimately this somewhat crude propaganda attempt was overtaken by events and failed. Nonetheless the fact that it was even attempted gives an indication of the degree to which the Soviets were willing to project their policy of disinformation, even when fighting for their own political survival.

The Need for Strategic Surprise

At the height of the Cold War the Soviets were keenly aware that they could not hope to match the West economically, and fully appreciated that any conflict with NATO would have to be brought to a conclusion quickly and clinically before its sixteen participating members had the opportunity to mobilize and deploy their armies. West Germany would become the principal target, and would have to be overrun in a single pre-emptive offensive. The distance from the then Inner German Border (IGB) to the Ruhr was a mere 350kms across the North German Plain, a relatively short distance for the Soviet Union's highly mobile Third Shock Army if allowed to exploit its preponderance of armour, mechanized artillery and motor rifle regiments.

The Soviets fully appreciated that, if they were to stand any realistic chance of taking West Germany by surprise they would have to keep deployed in peacetime sufficient armed forces to reach at least the nearest strategic objectives before NATO had the opportunity to mobilize and bring into action its reserve echelons. The Soviets would not have time to call upon their own reserves, nor would they be able to mobilize them before hostilities for the fear of alerting the West to their intentions. In the words of Marshal of the Soviet Union V. D. Sokolovskii, 'He who, right from the start, can get his troops deepest into enemy territory will be best able to exploit the results of his nuclear strikes (or indeed to foreclose his nuclear option) and to prevent the enemy from mobilizing.'

Experience had taught the Soviets that troops moving fast sustained less casualties, and expended less fuel and ammunition, than forces moving slowly. By moving rapidly their strategists argued that they would be able to impose their style of war on NATO. Instead of having to conduct a difficult breakthrough operation, they would clash with NATO formations in a series of 'meeting engagements' – a form of battle for which they had trained and most of NATO had not.

They regarded surprise as a force multiplier which would enable them to achieve at least limited strategic objectives with much smaller forces than would be necessary against a prepared enemy. By moving fast they would be able to exploit the gaps and weaknesses enforced by NATO's maldeployment, and by obviating the need for breakthrough operations would remove the necessity for vulnerable concentrations of reserves and for strong second echelons. They would therefore simply not present NATO with sufficient battlefield nuclear targets to warrant the politicians agreeing to nuclear release, with its obvious ramifications.

In the world of deception the Soviets displayed a level of

flexibility and organization which NATO both failed to comprehend and was incapable of emulating. Officers were compelled by regulations to employ some form of *Maskirovka* to aid their exercise assaults and were severely censured if they failed to do so. Dummy equipment was introduced which not only looked like the equipment being simulated but possessed similar physical properties. Where possible it reflected light, heat and electromagnetic energy in the manner of the original to confuse photographic analysts with the array of infra-red and false-colour imagery available to them.

Control of deception plans was exercised at the highest possible level to reduce the possibility of lower-level deception schemes compromising each other and the main plan by revealing anomalies. All plans were clearly defined and subordinated ruthlessly to the aims of the overall operation. They were directed at specific targets, often the enemy commander, and were based on his known prejudices and likely reactions. NATO intelligence gathering and dissemination was analysed to insure that as many of its sources and agencies as possible would be able to corroborate the deception plan without realizing its implications.

The Soviets accepted that modern intelligence gathering made it difficult to conceal preparations for a large-scale offensive. Nonetheless they regarded concealment of the scale, and especially the direction and timing, of the main attack, as quite achievable. Soviet principles of *Maskirovka* were never tested on the North German plains. They, were, however exploited fully during the invasion of Czechoslovakia, and later in Afghanistan.

The rôle of Special Forces in Maskirovka

It was always accepted by NATO that any Warsaw Pact offensive would involve the widescale use of the Soviet Special Forces, or *Spetsnaz*, who would attack key targets behind the lines and who would almost certainly attempt the assassination of key military and political figures. Yet very little was known about *Spetznaz*. In fact *Voiska spetsialnogo naznacheniya,*to give it its full name, had no peer in the West. In the eyes of the Soviet Union it was a force of special designation rather than a NATO-style special purpose force, and was ideally suited to the art of *Maskirovka*.

As ever the Soviet paranoia for secrecy was all pervading. Until 1989 references in the Soviet press to the VSN were rare and usually couched in historical terms. Units were described in a special reconnaissance (spetsialnaya razvedka) or diversionary reconnaissance (diversiya razvedka) context, and never as special forces. The very existence of a multi-talented elite within the Soviet Army was discounted as Western propaganda.

In 1989 the Kremlin partly lifted the veil of secrecy and allowed a series of articles to appear in the Soviet military and civilian press referring in detail to the existence and performance of units of special designation. However, much of the information leaked was of low grade intelligence value. It was already known to NATO analysts and was almost certainly only released in an attempt to defuse the West's growing interest in Soviet special forces. Moreover, many of the units discussed, although doubtless elite, had little, if any, connection at all with Spetsnaz, nor were they directly involved in the growing art of Maskirovka.

The Prague Spring

Maskirovka was used to devastating effect during the suppression of the so-called 'Prague Spring', a Czechoslovak liberal-reform movement which began on 5 January, 1968. On that day the Central Committee of the Czechoslovak Communist Party met to formally end the fourteen-year reign of First Secretary Antonin Novotny. His replacement, Alexander Dubcek, at once began to implement a series of reforming policies which the Kremlin found unacceptable. For six months the Soviets tried to undermine the reform movement through political sabre-rattling, threats and covert action. When this failed they resorted to violence.

A series of large-scale Warsaw Pact exercises were initiated in and around Czechoslovakia and were accompanied by numerous visits by military and diplomatic delegations. Following the Warsaw Pact 'SUVAMA' exercise, 16,000 Soviet troops remained in Czechoslovakia awaiting their long delayed withdrawal. In a particularly clever ruse, shortly before the invasion the Soviets ordered the transfer of substantial Czech fuel and ammunition stocks to East Germany as part of an unspecified logistical exercise.

So as to mask their intentions from an unsuspecting world,

immediately prior to the invasion of Czechoslovakia the Soviets confined to barracks the majority of their conventional troops stationed throughout the northern sector of the Warsaw Pact. The Czechs were not unduly worried therefore when an unscheduled civilian Aeroflot aircraft landed at Prague's Ruzyne Airport late at night, taxied and eventually parked at the end of the runway. An hour later a second Aeroflot aircraft was granted permission to land. This time the aircraft disgorged its passengers, all of them fit young men, who, having cleared customs without incident, set out for the city centre. Two hours later the 'passengers', by now fully armed from caches stored in the Soviet Embassy, returned to take over the main airport buildings.

Almost at once one, possibly two, further aircraft, directed by the 'rogue' at the end of the runway, landed and immediately disembarked teams of uniformed Spetsnaz. A series of transports followed, each containing a nucleus of Spetsnaz supported by conventional airborne troops from the 103rd Guards Airborne Division. Within two hours of the first uniformed Spetsnaz troops landing, the airport and its immediate environment were firmly in Soviet hands and troops were advancing unmolested on the capital. By daybreak the Presidential Palace, the radio and television studios, the transmitters, all of the main railway stations and the bridges over the River Vltava were in Soviet hands.

Even now the Soviets maintained a level of total security. To the total surprise of Western military watchers (who openly admitted that they could not have done so themselves) the Soviets brought in reinforcements from throughout the Warsaw Pact in total radio silence. Quietly and with minimal fuss the advance units crossed the Czech border preceded by military police regulators. The latter deployed to the major crossroads, towns and larger villages en route to await the oncoming convoys. When these arrived they were flagged forward and onward to their destination without the benefit of a single radio transmission. The Nato EW (Electronic Warfare) units, which might have expected to gain a great deal of intelligence from the mass manoeuvres, were left confused and frustrated.

After the invasion the KGB embarked upon a propaganda campaign so virulent that it supposedly began to influence the actions of its political masters in the Politburo. Weapons caches supposedly hidden by Western sympathizers were 'discovered' near the West German border, fake documents were produced to prove the existence of CIA-supported counter-revolutionary activity, liberals were terrorized and untrue and exaggerated reports sent back to Moscow.

Maskirovka in Afghanistan

The rôle played by *Maskirovka* in the Soviet invasion of Afghanistan was no less critical. The aim of the invasion was to establish a new puppet government in Kabul which would ask for Soviet assistance, thus legitimizing the initial intervention. For this it was necessary for the exisiting government, itself pro-communist, to be destroyed completely. The actual invasion took place over the Christmas period when immediate Western condemnation would be difficult to orchestrate.

Nothing was left to chance as every aspect of *Maskirovka* was fully exploited. In April, 1979, a battalion of Soviet paratroops were deployed to Bagram Airport, notionally to release Afghan troops for operations against anti-government rebels in the hills. In late August General Ivan Pavlovskiy, who had commanded the invasion of Czechoslovakia, arrived with a sixty-man General Staff delegation to conduct a detailed on-scene reconnaissance that lasted into October. On 17 December, after an abortive attempt to assassinate him at his palace in Kabul, President Amin was persuaded by his Soviet advisers to move his court to the more 'secure' palace at Darulaman, some miles from the city.

Prior to the invasion, Soviet advisers actually managed to neutralize two Afghan divisions by persuading their commanders that their anti-tank weapons and ammunition needed to be checked and accounted for, and the bulk of their armour with-drawn for servicing.

Between 8 and 10 December, 1979, some fourteen days prior to the invasion, *Spetsnaz* forces accompanied by an airborne regiment deployed to Bagram, a key town to the north of Kabul, in order to secure the Salang Highway with its vital tunnel. Between 10 and 24 December a battalion from the airborne regiment, with *Spetsnaz* support, moved to Kabul International Airport less than 3kms from the city centre. Between 24 and 27 December troops from the 105th Guards Airborne Division, again supported by *Spetsnaz*, landed at and secured Kabul Airport and the Afghan Air Force bases at Bagram, Shindand and Kandahar.

During the course of the following night the full offensive began. Paratroopers arrested the Afghan government, much of it while attending a lavish Soviet social function in the city. At the same time *Spetsnaz* teams demolished the central military communications centre, captured the still-functioning Ministry of the Interior, the Kabul radio station and several other key points. Simultaneously two Spetsnaz companies, with KGB assistance and supported by an airborne regiment, attacked President Amin's palace at Darulaman. Amin, his family, security force and entourage were killed for the loss of twenty-five Soviet dead, including KGB Colonel Balashika, reportedly killed by 'friendly' cross-fire.

The Home Front

The importance of historical memory could never be over-estimated in the former Soviet Union. The glorious achievements of the Great Patriotic War were told and retold in ever more glowing and expansive terms until fact and fiction were allowed to merge into a single, plausible entity. Many Russians recognized that much of what they were told was an exaggeration, but nonetheless were comforted by its constant, often daily, repetition.

During the late 1960s Soviet propaganda began to evolve from a crude stereotype, until by the mid-1980s it was able to rival the West in presentation and sophistication. Under the auspices of the KGB, Moscow Radio was revamped. It began to transmit reasonably entertaining programmes interspersed with authentic news items. Patent lies were replaced by subtle intimations, although the inability of the average Soviet official to speak frankly, or to discuss his country's defence matters in depth, remained a hurdle.

Equally the inherent Soviet belief that they had a right to present their viewpoint in a way that the West should not question remained a stumbling block. The Soviets simply could not understand that their country could ever be wrong, or that their posture could ever be seen as threatening. For security reasons maps were rare in the Soviet Union, and where they did exist were often inaccurate. They showed the Soviet land mass not on the edge of the world but at its centre, surrounded in all directions by potential enemies.

Few Soviets had ever heard of the Molotov-Ribbentrop Pact of August, 1939, and had no real idea why their country was so unprepared at the time of the German invasion in 1941. All they knew was that they had suffered terribly as a consequence and were determined that their government would never be 'allowed' to make such a mistake again.

Soviet xenophobia made opinion-moulding at home easier, but opinion-moulding abroad more difficult due to the government's inability to address itself to legitimate Western doubts as to its policies. When the West began counter-Soviet propaganda by broadcasting impartial news the response was hysterical. Fearful that the more discerning and therefore influential listeners would learn to differentiate between Western news and domestic propaganda the transmissions were jammed.

Radio Transmissions to the East

Unfortunately for Moscow there developed in the West a large and diverse number of radio stations ready and willing to transmit to the Warsaw Pact contries in their own languages and dialects. Chief among these were the Anglo-Saxon networks, Voice of America (VOA) and the BBC External Services. Funded by government authorities but operating free from control (the VOA was funded from Congress' Board of International Broadcasting, the BBC External Services by the Foreign Office) both were able to report and comment on events from their own perspective.

Deutsche Welle and *Deutschlandfunk*, both operated by the West German Radio Council, Radio France Internationale and Radio Vatican fulfilled similar rôles, as did the East European surrogates, Radio Liberty and Radio Free Europe. Such was the authority of these stations that in October, 1986, a survey indicated that 36 per cent of Soviet citizens polled had first heard of the Chernobyl disaster on Western radio, while a further 13 per cent subsequently tuned in to hear of developments.

The Soviets firmly believed that Western broadcasts

orchestrated social unrest and during the final years of the old Communist régime frequently blamed them for inciting violence. Unable to prevent their transmission they did everything in their power to frustrate their reception.

The Soviets began to jam the radio stations of their ideological opponents as early as 1948, when Moscow first blocked the Russian language services of the Voice of America and the BBC. This treatment was extended to cover Radio Liberty and Radio Free Europe virtually at their inception and continued until the disintegration of the Warsaw Pact. Poland ceased jamming Radio Free Europe in 1956, the Soviet Union stopped jamming the Voice of America and the BBC in 1963 and Hungary followed their example shortly thereafter.

Jamming is an expensive activity requiring two transmitters and an additional coordinating installation for every signal targetted. By the time Poland gave up jamming in 1956 it was costing the country a sum equivalent to the entire budget of the Voice of America. At the height of the Cold War the Soviets were estimated to have been operating between 2,000 and 3,000 jamming stations employing some 15,000 personnel.

Despite the enormity of its jamming effort, Kremlin policy for many years was simply to ignore its existence. Although jamming was in direct contravention of a number of clearly-stated international agreements the Soviet Union argued that it had the absolute right to control the dissemination of information within its own borders.

In 1979 the Soviets sought to amend an earlier declaration concerning the use of the mass media in the strengthening of peace and international understanding. When it failed, they reverted to the long-forgotten League of Nations Convention of 1936, which they belatedly ratified in 1982. Drafted in a less complex era as a shield against Nazi propaganda, the convention allowed for arbitration in the event of a dispute over the acceptable content of foreign transmissions. Led by the United Kingdom in July 1985, the signatories almost immediately repudiated the Convention allowing for a reversion to the status quo, but by then events had taken a new turn in the Soviet Union.

Mikhail Gorbachev and the Western Media

Mikhail Gorbachev was elected General Secretary of the Communist Party of the Soviet Union in March, 1985, and almost at once introduced a series of radical policies under an umbrella of openness, or glasnost. The aim of glasnost was to make the Soviet Union more efficient, not to satisfy the wishes of the Western liberals. That September Czechoslovakia revived proposals for a United Nations 'New Information Order' condoning both jamming and government control of the media. Although the proposal was supported by several Third World régimes anxious to maintain a monopoly of information it was again blocked by the West. Gorbachev now sensed that further attempts to legitimize jamming were pointless and embarked on a radically new policy.

Instead of denying the existence of jamming he went on to the offensive, arguing that it was a necessary counter to Western 'large-scale psychological warfare' waged in contravention of international law. At the same time he hinted that stations which did not project a wholly unsympathetic line might be allowed to transmit freely. During the Reykjavik summit in October, 1985, Gorbachev became the first Soviet leader to declare unequivocally that jamming was his country's policy. At the same time he intimated that, were the West in general and the United States in particular to allow the transmission of Soviet propaganda internally, jamming of the less 'extreme' stations might cease. The United States was put in a dilemma. Under the terms of its constitution it could not allow foreign countries openly to transmit from within its shores. Instead it encouraged a broader and more sympathetic approach to the reporting of Soviet affairs on its established internal networks. Having won this not insignificant battle the Soviets subsequently allowed the Voice of America, and a little later the BBC, to transmit unhindered within its borders.

By 1980 the Soviets had come to realize that the tiny Western communist parties were poor conduits for propaganda. During the course of that year the veteran ideologist Boris Ponomaryev announced a change in emphasis. Moscow began to court the sympathies of the churches, of Social Democrats, in fact of anyone who would concede that they had a case to argue and would listen.

The results were highly encouraging and have been incorporated into current Russian policy.

Occasionally, by trying to spread dissent in the West the Soviets also kindled public opinion in their own camp. This proved extremely difficult to handle, particularly in Germany where East and West tended to receive the same television transmissions. Through television the peace movement in West Germany had enormous influence in East Germany, and ultimately in Hungary where great pressure ensued against the deployment of Soviet short range missiles.

The Russians dealt firmly and quickly with the peace movement in their own country, denouncing it as 'anti-Soviet' and locking up people who started a society for the promotion of trust between the Soviet Union and the United States. Problems arose when the official Soviet peace movement, led by the Cold War warrior Yuri Zhukov, visited the West only to be confronted with evidence of the suppression of the unofficial peace movements in the Soviet Union.

Maskirovka and Diplomacy

Military attachés are attached to the majority of major embassies. They are accredited diplomats and as such are immune from prosecution. The bulk of their duties are as open as they are innocent, revolving as they do around the worlds of liaison, arms sales and procurement. Occasionally, however, a few will stray into the world of low-level espionage. They will carry 'shopping-lists' of kit and equipment of particular interest to their intelligence departments and often prove surprisingly adept at taking close-up clandestine photographs in prohibited areas.

Although much of the information gleaned from their relatively primitive methods is comparatively low grade, in large enough quantities it may prove of value to technical intelligence analysts. Vehicle and (where possible) engine numbers are photographed as are suspensions and tyre pressures to establish the actual, as opposed to stated, weight of individual equipment pieces.

In the past Soviet military attachés worked in close co-operation with KGB-sponsored commercial attachés. These men and women were invariably accredited diplomats, although little of the work undertaken was in their stated field. According to Victor Suvorov, a medium-level Soviet defector of the 1970s, at the height of the Cold War up to 40 per cent of the entire staff of an average Soviet embassy were directly employed by the KGB, whilst a further 20 per cent were answerable to the GRU. Although the Soviet Union has now collapsed, Russia continues to operate a reduced security agency and certainly retains agents in the West.

Historically Moscow fully accepted that the Soviet Union was as much a target as a beneficiary of attaché espionage. The Kremlin knew that it could not prevent low-scale consular espionage activity without inviting retribution and therefore took every step to ensure that intelligence which passed was either tainted or of no practical use.

Every effort was made to disguise factory outputs, while areas of particular manufacturing interest were closed to foreigners. Diplomats were not allowed to travel beyond the limits of the major cities without permission, and when they did they were carefully monitored.

Gulf War Experiences

The Gulf War incorporated one of the most successful deception plans of modern military history, epitomizing as it did all the ingredients of Maskirovka. In total secrecy the Coalition forces moved several key armoured divisions westward through the Saudi desert, leaving them in a position to attack Saddam Hussein from a wholly unexpected quarter. The logistics required to support the Coalition move were as intricate as they were successful.

While the United Nations prevaricated and Saddam Hussein blustered the Coalition moved two United States airborne and several armoured divisions, the British 1st Armoured Division and the French Daguet Division to new training areas and ultimately to secret forming-up points close to the Kuwaiti border. In this they were aided by their ability to control absolutely press releases from the front.

The United States military was subsequently castigated, perhaps unfairly, for its handling of the media. Certainly the military failed to understand the journalists' rigid time scales, and all too often a psychological barrier of mutual distrust grew between the media and their military briefers. The majority of the press were tied to the briefing rooms in case they missed one of the several daily briefings. Only a few well-chosen (and compliant) reporters were allowed at the front, and their reports, and more particularly photographs, were rigidly censored.

The Coalition public information staff were determined that accidental leaks would not occur. On 28 May, 1982, during the Falklands Campaign, the BBC had inadvertently disclosed the British forward positions at Goose Green and Darwin, leading to the deployment into the area of massive Argentine reinforcements. When mistakes were made in the Gulf they tended to emanate from official sources. By way of example, the Captain of HMS *Cardiff* complained at one stage that reports of the still secret movement of a mines counter-measure flotilla north into the Gulf were prematurely released by the Ministry of Defence during a briefing, while considerable embarassment was caused in the Pentagon when the location of a number of elite Iraqi Republican Guard regiments was leaked to the press.

Ironically Iraq's handling of the press was more open. The various Western newsmen located in Baghdad were assigned 'minders' to whom they had to submit all reports before transmission. They could ask to go anywhere other than into Kuwait, and where practical were granted freedom of movement. They were prohibited from reporting operational facts for 24 hours after the event, but thereafter were free to do so.

Inevitably many came to trust, and in some cases even became protective of, their 'minders', accepting their explanations at face value. Thus, when two precision bombs delivered by a pair of F-117 Stealth fighter-bombers slammed into a nuclear-reinforced bunker in the middle-class district of Amiriya, killing approximately 300 sheltering residents, mainly women and children, Western pressmen invited to inspect the carnage were unequivocal in their condemnation.

The building was, as Coalition commanders were quick to emphasize, known by them to be a military command and control centre. Inspecting journalists however were shown no evidence of military use, nor, it would seem, did they pry too deeply. The extent of the civilian casualties, and the manner of their deaths, sent a shock wave around the world. In a vain attempt to placate the growing wave of hostility the Pentagon expressed the view that Saddam may have deliberately put the civilians in the target building as human shields. However, the images of death were too great as everywhere emotion replaced logic in the hunt for a scapegoat.

Anti-American demonstrations took place in Arab capitals as the first funerals took place in Baghdad. There was condemnation in the Soviet Union, where the newspaper *Izvestia* claimed that Moscow was 'siding with murderers'. Saudi and Egyptian diplomats voiced great concern, while Washington, to reduce the possibility of a recurrence, was forced to introduce a shift in policy. In future, it was announced, the presence of civilians would be enough to disqualify an otherwise legitimate target.

When, only a day later, fifty Iraqi civilians were killed in the market town of Fallujah by an RAF bomb, aimed at a bridge, which tragically missed its target the Coalition was forced to admit that the much-lauded art of precision bombing was not as accurate as originally claimed. It has been widely suggested that this admission, following so quickly upon the enforced change in Coalition bombing policy, did much to bring forward the ground war.

The Iraqis were not alone in attempting to manipulate the press. The Coalition did nothing to dissuade the media that, when it came, the land battle would include a substantial assault from the sea. The presence of a United States Marine Corps Expeditionary Force in the Gulf was frequently alluded to, while naval actions against the small Iraqi fleet received maximum coverage.

The battle for Khafji, described by General Norman Schwarzkopf as 'a mosquito on the elephant's back', was badly misreported by much of the press. The coverage, although negative in parts, was left largely unchallenged and ultimately did much to reinforce Saddam Hussein's belief that the major threat to his ground forces remained concentrated along the coastal plain. Khafji itself was a small, strategically unimportant town nestling close to the Saudi-Kuwait border. It was not even permanently garrisoned and could not conceiveably have controlled the axis for a major assault by either side.

Nonetheless, within minutes of reports being received by the press in Riyadh of an assault on the town many analysts were reporting the beginning of the land war. Bolstered by garbled and patently untrue statements on Radio Baghdad, and conscious of the need to meet television and news deadlines, totally inaccurate stories were filed without thought as to the effect that these would have on domestic public opinion and morale.

When it was found that the attack was nothing but a feint, those analysts who did not drop the story continued to depict it as a full-scale battle, even reporting it as an enemy victory.

In reality an inexperienced Iraqi mechanized regiment, equipped with old and unreliable Chinese armoured vehicles, advanced with a battalion forward into Khafji. At the time the town formed no part of the front line and was not even occupied by Coalition forces. The friendly troops in the area were in fact Saudi and Qatari National Guardsman and customs officials under the Gulf Cooperative Council (GCC) command. Their orders were to patrol the town and its environments, reporting on the enemy's movements without engaging him in battle.

When the leading Iraqi battalion entered Khafji the Saudis and Qataris obeyed their orders to the letter, retiring in good order. Only after Saddam's troops began to occupy Khafji in strength, and the press began to report an Iraqi victory, did the Coalition deem it necessary to assign US Marine Corps artillery and air assets to the battle. In over two days of hard fighting the Iraqis sustained thirty dead with forty-two tanks destroyed and 500 prisoners taken. Yet, in the eyes of certain 'experts', Khafji remained at the very least an Iraqi psychological victory.

CHAPTER SIX
Psychological Operations

'The method of imposing the will of one nation upon another may in time be replaced by purely psychological warfare wherein weapons are not even used on the battlefield, but instead the corruption of the human mind, the dimming of the intellect and the disintegration of the moral and spiritual fibre of one nation by the will of another are accomplished.' (V. I. Lenin *Selected Works*, 1921).

The psychological dimension of conflict is as important as the physical. It is those who operate the weapon systems, not the systems themselves, who control the eventual outcome of battle. This applies not only to combatants, but also to those on the domestic front, to the civilian population in the area of operations and to the international community as a whole.

In conventional military operations commanders must not only motivate their own troops, but constantly seek to undermine the morale of the enemy. Failure to do so may, at the very least, deny a Commanding Officer the potential to exploit the psychological factors in his favour. At worst, it may lead to major setbacks or defeat through his failure to recognize the growing disquiet in his own base.

The psychological dimension in internal security (IS) and counter-insurgency (COIN) operations is even more important. Insurgents tend to plan their actions with a view to the psychological effect on the often subservient and politically disinterested many, rather than the physical effect on the active few. Experience has taught them that conventional soldiers, especially conscripts, brought into an internal-security situation will quickly come to regard it as somebody else's war and will rarely fight well without motivation. Indeed they may refuse to fight at all if their very *raison d'être* is questioned by their families and loved-ones at home.

The Tet Offensive

The use of psychological operations by both sides in Vietnam will be discussed more generally later. However, the Tet Offensive of 1969 proved so successful that it remains a textbook caveat for what may happen when a Government neglects the sensibilities of its civilian population, and is thus worthy of particular mention as arguably the most successful use of mass Psyops in modern history.

By the winter of 1967/68 it had become clear to the Communist authorities in North Vietnam that the war for the South was not going according to plan. A huge increase in American military commitment over the previous two years had caused the North Vietnamese to lose the initiative. Their supply lines, crucial to their own morale, were being cut, denying them a regular flow of food and ammunition and they were sustaining increasingly heavy casualties in the field. More fundamentally, they were losing the trust and respect of the once largely sympathetic Southern rural population. Without an immediate victory there appeared to be little hope for the future.

The North conceded that she would not be able to defeat the United States in open battle. She therefore sought to carry the war to domestic America. Reasoning that America's weakness lay not in her military firepower but in her civilian resolve, Hanoi determined to turn public opinion against the war. If United States prestige could be dented it was anticipated that popular support for the war would crumble, leaving Washington with no alternative but to withdraw.

An offensive was launched on the morning of 31 January during the Tet festival. Traditionally Tet, the Vietnamese New Year, had been marked by an informal cease-fire. The bulk of the South Vietnamese Army was therefore on leave and security was lax making the smuggling of weapons into the target areas comparatively simple. Plans were put into effect for the execution of a series of simultaneous mass attacks against designated cities and

Government centres throughout the South. Regular troops of the North Vietnamese Army (NVA) were fed down the Ho Chi Minh trail and local Vietcong units enhanced. Feint assaults against remote outposts drew American reserves away from intended targets without alerting the Pentagon to the impending attack.

The offensive when it was launched came as a complete surprise to South Vietnam and her allies. In the space of less than twenty-four hours a total of 84,000 Communist troops assaulted the capital city of Saigon together with thirty-six of the South's provincial capitals, five of its six autonomous cities and sixty-four of its 242 district capitals. For the first time in history the realities of combat were brought nightly to the living rooms of the American public courtesy of live television. Yound G.I.s died in the sight of their loved ones as inevitably the whole morality of intervention came under increasing scrutiny.

The US Marines in particular fought magnificently in an urban environment completely alien to their training to recapture the ancient capital of Hue and in the expulsion of Vietcong suicide squads from the grounds of the American Embassy in Saigon, but their victory was pyrrhic. The minutiae of combat had been allowed to explode before an incredulous and horrified audience in America. The single-minded bravery and determination of the Communist enemy, a factor already recognized by the military, became apparent to the armchair strategists back home. Victory over an alien ideology, the sole purpose for prosecuting the war, ceased to be regarded with certainty. Militarily North Vietnam had lost the battle, but psychologically she had won the war.

The Art Of Propoganda

An effective PsyOps campaign must be based on thorough research and intelligence; it must be consistent with Government, military and political policy; it must stem from a deep understanding of the target audience and must get the right message to the right audience at the right time. Propaganda, a crucial factor of PsyOps, should be based on information which, to the enemy, is credible. It should be presented in a form which will both attract and excite, while exploiting the targets' physiological and psychological needs which it should then seek to satisfy. It should be neither excessively rigid nor dogmatic, nor unnecessarilly hostile or contentious.

Propaganda must of necessity be selective. Only in exceptional circumstances, however, should it be untrue. Inconsistencies will quickly be identified by enemy PsyOps teams and exploited. When William Joyce broadcast from wartime Nazi Germany his lies, exaggerations and half-truths were so patent that the Ministry of Propaganda in London had little difficulty in discrediting him. Only after his execution in 1946 did the tens of thousands of British listeners who had frequently tuned into the rantings of 'Lord Haw Haw' for light relief learn that much of what he had claimed, particularly in the early stages of the war, had been in large part true.

Although propaganda should generally be true it need not identify its source and may indeed purport to emanate from a source other than the true one. It may include rumour, but only if the target is suffering a shortage of factual information and if the subject of the rumour is of immediate interest or importance to the audience. Thus the wartime theme 'oversexed, overpaid, over here' proved remarkably successful when insinuated by German propagandists to home-sick British troops worried about the behaviour of the newly-arrived G.I.s at home.

Rumour should not be allowed to become folklore, nor should it be allowed to damage the morale of the instigator's own military or populace. In 1982, during its ill-fated defence of the Falklands, the Argentine Government attempted to bolster its men with completely unfounded stories of Gurkha atrocities. Its efforts proved disastrously counter-productive and led to the precipitous surrender to the British of several conscript units terrified at the prospect of meeting the Gurkhas in open battle.

Counter-Propaganda

Counter-propaganda is designed to counteract or capitalize on hostile psychological operations and may be offensive or defensive. It may concentrate on easily refutable mistakes made by the enemy, such as Lord Haw Haw's frequent sinkings of the aircraft carrier *Ark Royal* during the Second World War, or may seek to minimize the impact of an unpalatable truth, such as the fall of Tobruk. Several techniques are available, although each has its weaknesses, making the art of counter-propaganda far from simple.

An enemy's statement may be rebutted, although in so doing it will usually be necessary to repeat his message in its fuller context, giving added publicity and credence to aspects of it which might be true. The impact of an anticipated propaganda coup may be limited by a frank and early admission of error or by the introduction of a new theme of greater potential interest or impact to the target audience. However, the growth in the last decade of investigative journalism has led to an underlying cynicism in the European and American psyche which will not easily be fobbed off by part-truths and platitudes.

Steps may be taken to blot out completely the influence of the outside world, but few countries are self-sufficient and such methods often have drastic consequences for the national economy. For nearly four decades until his death in 1985 Enver Hoxha succeeded in isolating Stalinist Albania from all but Chinese influence. In so doing he left it politically, economically and militarily moribund, a state from which it has yet to recover.

Rigid censorship may be enforced by a totalitarian régime. For many years radios sold in North Korea were fitted with tuner-switches rather than dials to prevent the domestic population from listening to foreign stations. However, modern satellite communications have made this unrealistic in more sophisticated societies, where a lie will quickly become apparent and may well debase the future value of its instigator as a reliable source for the truth.

The Dissemination Of Propaganda

Numerous visual, audio and audio-visual electromechanical systems exist for the transmission of propaganda to the chosen target. Of various cost and complexity they may be used to supplement or replace direct communication and are invaluable in places where the audience is inaccessible, unreceptive or simply too large to be approached by simple non-mechanical means.

Visual dissemination, the oldest and least sophisticated means, remains the most popular. It embraces not only posters and leaflets but silent films, cartoons, exhibitions and static displays. Despite its relatively low degree of effectiveness its simplicity and low cost ensure its continued usefulness, particularly at the tactical level and in third-world conflicts.

Leaflets and Posters, to be truly effective, must be subjective and capitalize upon the target's immediate situation and needs. However, in large-scale operations it may not be feasible to release sufficient design staff to produce the volume of specialist material required. Under such circumstances standard material may be used, although its effectiveness is likely to be severely diminished. Standard material is easier to produce in bulk but lacks topicality.

The way in which the material is presented is critical as a misspelt word or a confused symbol may have a devastating counter-effect. Equally a layout which seems somehow alien to an audience may be dismissed as an example of foreign interference and therefore prove counter-productive. An enemy may take punitive action on those caught reading propaganda material. Leaflets should therefore be both interesting and capable of overcoming the proposed recipient's natural fears. It is not uncommon to disguise one side of a leaflet as a bank note. Although the truth becomes apparent once the leaflet has been picked up, few people can resist picking up what purports to be money on the off chance that it is genuine. As well as being credible, leaflets should uncover and feed the target's latent or patent psychological needs and, where possible, should offer him a reasonably attainable short-term course of action by which he may fulfil such needs. Safe-conduct passes, dropped at the end of a campaign, often have a devastating effect.

Leaflets may be disseminated in a variety of ways including balloon, artillery shell, aircraft bomb or fused bundle. The choice of means will often be dictated by availability, but might otherwise be influenced by the size and location of the target, its vulnerability and prevailing winds. Britain has no dedicated delivery system and has traditionally relied upon free-dropping from aircraft, a policy which cost RAF Bomber Command dear in the early stages of the Second World War.

Until comparatively recently Germany retained two balloon battalions dedicated to the preparation and release of propaganda material over the Eastern block. Platforms were suspended beneath the balloons and were timed to open and effect a controlled release when over the target area. As timing was crucial, and wholly dependent on the vagaries of barometric pressure coupled with the force of the prevailing winds, the system was somewhat unreliable. Perhaps fortunately it was never tested in combat.

Leafleting was used to great effect against Germany during the final stages of the First World War. In 1918 the Minister of Information, Lord Beaverbrook, appointed his fellow newspaper magnate, Lord Northcliffe, as Director of Propaganda in Enemy Countries. Established authors of the calibre of H.G.Wells and Rudyard Kipling were instructed to write propaganda material aimed at growing German fears and susceptibilities.

Leaflets, which were sympathetic in tone and struck closely to the truth, highlighted Allied territorial gains while emphasizing German casualty figures. Building on these indisputable facts, they encouraged the German people to take control of events themselves so that an Armistice could be arranged to end the suffering brought upon them by their Government. The inevitability of an Allied victory was made clear, coupled with the veiled threat that the longer the Armistice was delayed the more onerous its terms would be.

The leaflets were delivered by shell, balloon and aeroplane over the vicinity of the German trenches, and by long-range aircraft deep into Germany itself. Specialist leaflets dropped round German ports included details of 150 U-boats that had failed to return from the North Sea and Atlantic.

Ironically it was Operation Michael, the German spring offensive of 1918, which did most to emphasize the accuracy of the Allied message. When the exhausted and often ill-equipped German veterans stormed the Allied front lines they found them amply supplied with food and ammunition, and the Anglo-French prisoners taken well clothed and comparatively fresh. It quickly became apparent to all but the most blinkered that the territorial gains recently made at a tremendous cost in lives were short-term and that defeat was inevitable. As the Germans were forced from their newly captured positions withdrawal turned into rout. During October and November morale and discipline plummeted, while the number of desertions soared until finally the Navy mutinied. Dock and factory workers sided with the mutineers and troops at home refused to intervene. By the time of the final Armistice on 11 November, 1918, the entire fabric of German domestic society was in danger of disintegration, a victim as much of Allied propaganda as of the fear of her advancing armies.

An interesting form of ancillary visual propaganda was introduced by Northcliffe. Knowing that many influential Germans relied upon neutral newspapers for the truth he arranged for a series of letters, supportive of the German cause and therefore not liable to censorship, to be sent to their editors. Each was posted through the embassy in a neutral capital to disguise its origin, and contained a subtle comparison of the hardships being endured in Germany with the life of luxury being enjoyed in Britain and France. At a time when German civilians were suffering devastating privations in order to keep the front-line armies fed the letters began to have an accute effect on the morale of the German intelligentsia, which quickly permeated down to the masses.

At the same time German troops in the front line were confronted by trench newspapers openly critical of the war. Unknown to them these were Allied creations carefully written and matched to the original. During the final weeks of the war half a million phoney newspapers per week were printed and dropped behind the German lines.

Audio Reproduction

Audio reproduction, the use of radio, loudspeakers and various sound recording devices, is more complex and costly than the majority of its visual competitors, but has the advantage in terms of audience appeal and impact. The audio-visual approach, the use of television and the cinema, is by far the most sophisticated and costly, but can be highly influential on a medium and long term basis. Even relatively sophisticated societies such as Iran have recently banned the use of satellite dishes lest Western television, much of which is perceived as propaganda, somehow undermines the religious fundamentalism of the general population.

Loudspeakers are used by the civilian community for many purposes throughout the world. They are therefore easily obtainable and are regarded as a natural means of information transmission. Due to their short range their usefulness is limited to tactical and consolidation operations. However, within this very real constraint, they have a number of immediate advantages. They may be used selectively to target a specific audience with a particular message, are mobile and simple to use. While transmissions are limited by the physical factors of climate and terrain and are vulnerable to enemy action, particularly when the equipment is aircraft-mounted, loudspeakers nonetheless continue to offer an excellent localized platform for the dissemination of propaganda.

Whether loudspeaker messages are live or pre-recorded the transmissions should be kept short, particularly when an aircraft is being used, and only in exceptional circumstances should they exceed twenty seconds in duration. The message should be kept clear and simple, with key words and phrases repeated several times to maximize their effect.

Messages should be transmitted in the language and dialect of the target audience. A wrong accent may grate, emphasizing the alienness of the transmitter's culture, which if anything will add to the target's determination to continue the fight. Locals should therefore be used wherever possible. Defectors make ideal propagandists, although steps must be taken to ensure that they are genuine in their conversion and that their messages neither breach security nor offer subliminal support to the enemy.

Under certain circumstances loudspeakers may be used to transmit disorientating noise in the direction of the enemy. If the enemy is confident this will have little effect. If, however, he is apprehensive, perhaps in anticipation of a coming assault, it will deny him sleep, play on his already frayed nerves and reduce his willingness and ability to fight. Such transmissions were used both by the Japanese and Americans in the Pacific War of 1942-45 and by the Japanese in their jungle campaign against the British Fourteenth Army. They were later used to maximum effect by the Communist North during the Korean War.

More recently they were employed by the US Army to force General Noriega from the protection of the Papal Legation after Operation Just Cause, the United States intervention in Panama. Loudspeakers were placed round the legation and music blasted incessantly at the unfortunate occupants. Many analysts openly scoffed at what they regarded as the amateurishness of the American tactics. However, they worked and Noriega surrendered after a few days, much, it must be imagined, to the relief of his unwilling hosts.

By virtue of their simplicity printed matter and loudspeaker broadcasts comprise the bulk of purely military psychological operations. However, on an international or long-term scale radio transmissions may well be introduced.

Radio broadcasting is particularly suited to the world of propaganda. Its range, timeliness and versatility enable it to reach a mass audience denied any other media. Material can be prepared quickly and, depending on the frequencies available and the receivers in the possession of the audience, transmitted over great distances. Crucially it can take advantage of new information or rapid and unexpected changes in the military and political status quo.

Used to maximum efect it may intersperse subtle propaganda with news from home, popular music and current affairs to produce a potent cocktail which the target audience will find difficult to ignore. If the announcers are well chosen and the local news both accurate and interesting, transmissions may have a devastating effect on enemy morale leading to bouts of near-uncontrollable homesickness.

During the Falklands War of 1982 Britain began transmissions to the Argentinian troops on the Falklands from a temporary radio station on Ascension Island. The station employed broadcasters of South American origin who were able to speak to the troops not only in their own language but dialect. Radio Malvinas, as the station was known, did not transmit overt propaganda and was therefore not regarded as an enemy by even the most fervent of the invasion force. Instead it transmitted to individual soldiers, advising him that his wife had given birth to a baby boy and that both were well, that tragically his father had died or that his cousin had married. The station gave football results and commentaries, even local weather reports, anything to make the troops feel unsettled and homesick. In an environment in which news from home was scarce and local information heavily censored the effects on Argentinian morale were said to have been devastating.

How the information was obtained remains a closely guarded secret. Broadly similar tactics were used by the North Vietnamese in their dealings with American prisoners of war, although in this instance much of the information passed was not true. United States sympathizers obtained as much information as they could on individual prisoners. This was then fed to the North Vietnamese and used by their Psy Ops teams to create a blend of truths, half-truths and innuendoes which many prisoners found difficult to sustain.

Despite their obvious advantages even radio transmissions have their limitations. They are relatively simple to jam and may be distorted by atmospheric conditions and other natural hazards. In certain societies the ownership of receivers may be limited to the upper income groups, usually the least susceptible to propaganda. Their message, being of necessity non-visual, is transitory and may quickly become forgotten or distorted unless repeated on a regular basis.

The Visual Arts

Television is the most influential of all communications media. It enjoys the immediacy of radio and can respond very quickly to new or changing situations. There is no requirement for a television viewer to be literate; indeed Western television has developed an ubiquitous style almost universally accepted. However, as a medium of propaganda it has obvious limitations; it is extremely expensive to operate, has a relatively short range and is easy to jam. Furthermore the cost of television receivers severely limits their availability in many parts of the world, as does the need for a source of electrical power.

The growth in satellite transmission has brought with it its own problems. Reports may now be sent, with or without permission, from almost any part of the world and received immediately in the living rooms of every subscribing family. At a time when networks seem increasingly unwilling to accept censorship, or even to enter into a code of conduct, the possibilities of a second Tet Offensive 'own goal' are very real.

The cinema remains an influential medium in many parts of the world, particularly where television is not widely available. It is, however, readily controllable, difficult to export to a hostile environment and expensive to produce. Live performances, such as theatre and dance, still attract mass audiences in many parts of the third world but suffer the same limitations as the cinema. As audiences are becoming more sophisticated they are showing less inclination to accept obviously 'politically correct' productions.

All aspects of psychological operations were brought together during the Second World War. Black propaganda, that which attempts to disguise its source, was used to great effect by the Germans during the early stages of the war, and later even more successfully by the Allies.

After the German breakthrough in May, 1940, German radio propaganda spread rumours about enemy agents, the collapse of the French Government, the treachery of the British, the duplicity of the Jews and much more. As the German breakthrough continued new transmitters began to send streams of meaningless coded messages to non-existent agents and saboteurs supposedly working behind the crumbling French front line. After the fall of France in June German black propaganda transmissions to Britain played so successfully on the population's latent xenophobia that the regular army and Home Guard wasted thousands of valuable hours in a fruitless search for non-existent Fifth Columnists and disguised German parachutists.

With the Battle of Britain won and the threat of invasion lifted Britain was able to go onto the offensive. Duff Cooper, as Minister for Information in the Churchill Government, recruited Sefton Delmer, the pre-war Berlin correspondent for the *Daily Express*. Delmer knew the German psyche well and was able to set up two black propaganda radio stations, one run by émigré German Marxists and aimed at left-wing workers in the Reich, the other run by a former Weimar Republic politician living in England. The latter, which evolved into the 'underground' radio station 'GS1', simulated a station transmitting from somewhere in Germany; its tone was pro-Nazi, patriotic and militarist, yet it allowed itself the luxury of criticizing the Government when it felt that the ordinary soldier or citizen had been let down.

Delmer recruited a Berliner, Paul Sanders, who had left Germany in 1938 at the height of Jewish persecutions and who was then serving as a corporal in the Pioneer Corps working on bomb disposal. Sanders was given the code name '*Der Chef*' and began transmissions in May, 1941. He made an immediate impact by deriding the abortive attempt by Rudolf Hess to persuade Britain to sue for peace with Hitler by flying across the North Sea and crash-landing his Messerschmitt in Scotland.

'GS1' painstakingly built up a VIP portfolio, supplementing it with a card-index system of ordinary people. It gained its information routinely by debriefing German refugees, reading German newspapers and monitoring broadcasts. More covertly it was supplied with information from German letters secretly opened in transit in neutral countries and from snippets gained from conversations overheard by German-speaking guards in prisoner-of-war camps. The result was a highly efficient radio station able to inflict considerable psychological damage to the German war effort.

On one occasion 'GS1' spread the damning rumour that blood taken from Polish and Russian prisoners had been given to German wounded without screening and had subsequently been found to have been infected with venereal disease. Such transfusions had never taken place, but the fact that 'GS1' was able to support its fabrication with the names of actual transfusion centres, and of the personnel working within them, did much to give it credence.

Der Chef died a dramatic and violent 'death' in October, 1943, by which time the authorities felt that he had passed the peak of his usefulness. His last broadcast ended with the sound of machine gun fire as the Gestapo discovered his underground location and stormed it. A new station, '*Soldatensender Calais*,' went on the air as the Allies were preparing to invade Northern Europe. It operated with great effect until the final German surrender, targeting first the German Army fighting in France, and later in Germany itself. When the Nazi authorities tried to jam the station many of its faithful listeners assumed that they were witnessing a bungled attempt by the British to jam a bona-fide German station.

As the Battle of the Atlantic slowly turned in the Allies' favour the British created a new station, the '*Deutsche Kurzwellensender Atlantic*' (German Short-Wave Station Atlantic). Aimed at the U-boat crews, who quickly christened it '*Atlantiksender*,' it gained their attention by playing the latest German dance music, either bought on the open market in Sweden, recorded in America or fabricated in a studio in London.

Request programmes, which where possible were introduced by 'turned' navy prisoners, contained dedications for genuine birthdays and anniversaries gleaned from censored mail passing between German navy prisoners of war and their families. Up to date information was received courtesy of Goebbels' news agency which had abandoned a radio teleprinter when fleeing London on the outbreak of war. Into this cocktail of popular music current news and requests were slipped subversive information, morale-sapping innuendo and highly accurate details of the situation on the home front.

Photo-reconnaissance bomb damage imagery was super-imposed on old German street maps to give up to the minute raid damage reports which were then transmitted in great detail. The effect on U-boat crews, cramped, in constant danger and thousands of miles from home in the mid-Atlantic, can well be imagined. Even when it became common knowledge that *Atlantiksender* was in fact a British propaganda station most U-boat crews, starved of reliable information from more conventional sources, continued to listen.

Allied attempts at visual propaganda proved less successful. Counterfeit publications, letters and leaflets were distributed by agents in an attempt to encourage German soldiers on leave to desert or surrender, but in virtually every case failed. It has been suggested that this had more to do with the élan of the German soldier than to a weakness in the visual content of the propaganda.

The German Army of the day had a hard corps of officers and men imbued with ideals of 'toughness', manly comradeliness and group solidarity (*'Gemeinschaft'*). Only when soldiers were sepa-rated from their comrades or suffered a loss of leadership through battle casualties did they begin to consider their own physical survival and countenance surrender or desertion.

It is estimated that between D-Day and the final surrender some 70 per cent of all German soldiers serving on the Western Front listened to an Allied radio broadcast or read, however briefly, a propaganda leaflet. Many leaflets were passed from soldier to soldier, but their contents rarely seem to have been discussed. However, as the war reached its inevitable conclusion many soldiers claim to have been influenced by the promise of good treatment as Anglo-American prisoners of war, and it may be that this theme went some way to inducing large numbers of troops to surrender in the West rather than fall into the hands of the Soviets.

Tactical propaganda, particularly the use of loudspeakers, proved more successful. In early 1945 the British Fourth Armoured Division psychological warfare unit captured over 500 prisoners in its four-day dash from the Kyle River to the Rhine by fitting loudspeakers to its tanks. Later similar tactics would be adopted, albeit less successfully, by United States Psychological Operations Groups (POGs) in Vietnam.

Home Persuasion

Domestic propaganda is a subject in its own right and as such will be dealt with in detail in Chapter Seven. Suffice it to say at this stage that during the Second World War both sides used audio and visual propaganda to the full. Initially Goebbels had no difficulty in maintaining German morale, for during the early stages of the war the Nazi propaganda machine had an abundance of successes on which to work. Huge maps were displayed in public squares on which civilians could follow the advance of the panzers deep into Eastern Europe.

Weekly newsreels followed the stormtroopers into the front line to bring the feats of German arms to the cinema screens. Goebbels took a great interest in the newsreel; indeed, to increase its impact he insisted on a five minute pause after it finished, to enable the audience to savour its full impact before the main film began. The films themselves were mainly sugary entertainments, although a number showed the stupendous virtues of the German people. A few were openly political, notably *Jew Suss*, a popular tale of Jewish wickedness and German virtue set in the eighteenth century.

Goebbels' ministry organized heart-lifting talks and rallies in all forty-two of the Nazi party districts. Speakers were schooled in style and projection, although none was allowed to ape the highly distinctive style of the Fuhrer himself.

Manipulating the news was not an admissible notion in Britain. Editors were free to print what they liked, but risked penalties for printing that which could help the enemy. 'D' notices, so called because they were issued under the Defence Regulations, gave guidance on what was unsafe to publish. On the outbreak of war the embryonic television service was closed down. Cinema newsreels, often weeks old, were initially uninformative and ludicrously jocular.

Matters improved when the BBC War Reporting Unit was expanded until there were twenty-seven radio correspondents plus recording and transmitter engineers covering the post-invasion campaign in north-west Europe. Reporters such as Richard Dimbleby, Wynford Vaughan-Thomas and Chester Wilmot gained the trust and affection of the nation as they risked their lives with the front line troops to bring a true taste of combat to the living rooms and cinemas of the families at home.

It was Dimbleby who, after the other stars of war reporting had left Germany, first dared to air the puzzling behaviour of the Soviets, who had been lauded by the media for the past four years. After his temporary arrest by suspicious Red Army soldiers in Berlin he broadcast to the West, questioning Stalin's motives and warning his listeners of the problems to come. Few transmissions have been more prophetic.

Psyops In Malaya

After the war Western psychological warfare experts found themselves facing two threats – the advent of the Warsaw Pact in Europe and the growing influence of Communism in the Far East. To counter the latter Britain in particular found herself prosecuting a series of 'brush fire' wars during which the PsyOps lessons of the Second World War were honed to perfection.

When the Japanese overran the Malay Peninsula at the end of 1941 the members of the Malay Communist Party (MCP), which with other political parties was proscribed by the Japanese, took to the jungle. There they joined with a number of non-communist organizations to form the Malay People's Anti-Japanese Army (MPAJA) and engaged in guerrilla warfare against the common enemy. With little military experience, few arms and no logistical plan, they were initially little more than an irritant to the enemy. However, when Britain created Force 136, a guerrilla group of expatriate policemen, rubber planters and tin miners, and began to infiltrate its best operators back into Malaya, matters rapidly began to improve. The MPAJA was armed and trained, and by the end of the war was operating as a highly efficient and co-ordinated guerrilla force.

With the coming of peace rewards of 250 Straits Dollars were offered by the British to any member of the MPAJA who would leave the jungle with his weapon. Many accepted the offer, although a hard corps of the original MCP refused. Chin Peng, Secretary General of the MCP and leader of the MPAJA, joined elements of Force 136 in a victory parade in London and was subsequently awarded the OBE, although he never received it. On returning home he prepared the MCP for an armed struggle with the aim of turning Malaya into a Communist republic.

By altering one letter Chin Peng changed the entire emphasis of his party. The MPAJA became the Malay People's Anti-British Army (MPABA) and embarked upon a campaign of terror in remote areas, manifested in the first instance by the cold-blooded murder of British and other European estate and mine managers. When the indigenous population largely refused to be coerced, torture and terror followed. As the purely anti-British nature of the struggle changed, the 'Army' again changed its name to the Malay Races Liberation Army (MRLA).

Between 1948 and 1962 the British Government turned the near certainty of a Communist takeover in Malaya into a victory for democracy. Painstaking steps were taken to turn the hearts and minds of the Chinese minority against the Communist Terrorists (CTs) whom they had once supported. Tough controls over the sale and movement of food were introduced in an attempt to eliminate supplies reaching the CTs with every crop recorded in minute detail. The SAS were reformed and introduced into the jungle to pursue and destroy the enemy in his own lair. Up to 25,000 British troops with 15,000 Gurkhas were employed in supporting search and destroy missions. In 1957, when Malaysia finally gained its independence, there were no more than 1,500 CTs still operating, of whom 309 were killed that year and 209 surrendered. In 1960 the insurrection was finally abandoned, the remaining terrorists fleeing to Thailand.

There can be no doubt that the ultimate victory was accelerated by the insertion into the theatre of highly skilled intelligence and psychological warfare teams. SAS troopers and FINCOS (Field Intelligence NCOs) moved deep into the jungle to live with the locals, offer them protection and establish in depth their fears and aspirations. Armed with this information, the PsyOps experts were able to conceive a plan based on a combination of visual and audio propaganda enhanced by the much improved art of prisoner turning.

At the outset the principle motivation for those organizing the PsyOps effort was revenge. They had seen their friends, families and colleagues tortured and murdered and their way of life threatened, and wished for nothing more than to see the perpetrators dead or captured. Early propaganda comprised little more than threats of what the CTs might expect on capture and consisted of lists of the names of terrorists killed or captured, supported by pictures wherever possible. Little thought was given to the counter-propaganda opportunites thus offered. The MRLA countered by depicting the dead as heroes of the revolution whose demise had to be avenged with the murder of yet more innocent civilians.

All this was to change, however, in September 1950 when Hugh Carleton Greene (later Sir Hugh Greene, Director General of the BBC) was appointed Director of Emergency Information Services, Malaya. He persuaded Lieutenant-General Sir Harold Briggs, the equally perceptive Director of Operations, to introduce a policy of surrender and rewards for former terrorists, whatever their crimes. Despite vigorous police and civil service opposition the policy slowly but steadily bore fruit, as increasing numbers of exhausted and dispirited terrorists surrendered.

Cartoons as a Weapon

Every form of mass communication (save for television, which was virtually unknown in much of the area) was used to spread the message, although the leaflet remained the principal and most successful means of communication. Over 100 million leaflets were dropped annually and in 1953 alone resulted in the voluntary surrender of 372 guerrillas. In one of the most famous leaflets, designed to exploit the growing rift between the Communist leaders and their men, cartoon characters were used to depict their differing lifestyles.

The officer had big eyes to watch the faults of his men, yet little ears to enable him to ignore their complaints. He had a large mouth with which to give orders and a big stomach to store nutrition from good food, yet only a small chest to avoid the bullets. His bottom was large from excess sitting down while others worked, and his fingers small for untying knots. He wore a clearly defined pistol, the mark of a leader among the communist bands.

The man, on the other hand, was blind so as not to notice the mistakes of his superiors, yet had big ears to listen to their false propaganda and orders. He had no mouth with which to criticize, had a big chest to stop the bullets aimed at his leaders and a small stomach to minimize his consumption of rice. The analogy was pictorially crude, yet in the prevailing situation of mistrust and recrimination it proved remarkably effective.

Propaganda in the Air

Vehicle-mounted loudspeakers were employed in the early stages of the campaign, but their limited reception range and need to keep to the tracks proved too much of a disadvantage and their use was largely discontinued in late 1953. Voice aircraft were introduced in 1952, and after a series of teething troubles proved highly successful. Initially messages were broadcast in Malay, Tamil and a variety of Chinese dialects. However, the lack of suitable dialect linguists caused this policy to be abandoned and eventually Mandarin, the lingua franca of the jungle, was used for all but the most specialist of transmissions.

As the PsyOps teams became more proficient it became possible to broadcast news of an event within two or three hours of its happening. Thus details of the killing of a key terrorist in an ambush could be relayed to his men before they had had time to recover from the impact. Such messages were always supported by a request to the survivors to give themselves up, with a promise of fair treatment if they did.

In one instance a list of the names of terrorists killed in a major ambush was broadcast. It was reported that the bodies of a number of the terrorists had been recovered by the security forces and had been buried according to religious custom. The bodies of other named terrorists, however, had not been recovered until later by which time their remains had been largely eaten by wild pigs. The effect of this transmission, which in all respects was wholly accurate, was devastating on the morale of the already shaken Muslim terrorists below.

As the campaign progressed well known surrendered personalities were employed in visits to remote areas where their popularity did much to persuade the politically disinterested to side with the government. Later, small groups of former terrorists were organized into troupes of actors who toured the remotest areas to perform playlets depicting the generosity of the authorities to former terrorists who surrendered. Despite the patent crudity of their theme these plays were well accepted by their target audience and proved most successful in facilitating the surrender policy.

Hearts And Minds

While maintaining a psychological war against the guerrilla it is crucial to conduct a 'Hearts and Minds' campaign with the ordinary people.

In Malaya White Areas, heavily patrolled and free of communist influence, were set up in 1954. Initially these were heavily controlled, with curfews, food restrictions and body searches. However, the restrictions were quickly lifted to allow the privileged occupants of such areas to enjoy a near normal existence. Before long the occupants of peaceful villages surrounding the white areas began to demand incorporation, until all but a few of the most hardened pro-communist areas were involved.

At the same time power passed from the military to a civilian High Commissioner, while steps were taken to broaden the base of Tunku Abdul Rahman's government-in-waiting to make it more acceptable to the Chinese and Indian minorities.

The policy of 'Hearts and Minds' was later extended by the British to her 'brush wars' in Borneo and the Oman and did much to facilitate her comparatively bloodless withdrawal from Empire. British involvement in Borneo began in 1962, when President Sukarno of Indonesia declared a state of Confrontation with the neighbouring states of Sabah and Sarawak in an attempt to coerce them into joining a Greater Indonesia.

Initially the Indonesians fought the war by proxy, employing local guerrillas to mount small-scale cross-border raids against isolated police and army posts. As the war intensified Sukarno introduced regular troops, including special purpose forces, trained in deeper infiltration. These received limited assistance from the Clandestine Communist Organization, mainly supported by the Chinese in the coastal towns and by a few Indonesian labourers in the timber trade along the southern border of Sabah.

To counter these incursions the British employed some 15,000 troops, mainly infantry. Borneo was a small-unit war in which patrols often spent weeks in the jungle seeking out and ambushing the enemy. In 1964 top secret British and Gurkha 'Claret' patrols began to infiltrate across the border in an attempt to drive the Indonesians back from their forward bases, without escalating the war or inviting intervention by the United Nations.

At the same time RAF helicopters worked closely with the British and later Australian and New Zealand SAS. Using their language and medical skills to win the hearts and minds of the Murat and Kelabit peoples and the numerous smaller groups living deep in the jungle SAS patrols amassed huge amounts of intelligence on enemy movements. The indigenous peoples were mainly pro-British, although some were quite introverted and resistant to outside influences. Others, like the Punans, were hard to find, migrating back and forth across the border.

Patrols were moved close to target villages, although at night they moved to jungle hides to maintain security. The comparatively simple medical and engineering services provided by the patrols vastly improved the villagers' lot without fundamentally altering their way of life, which many SAS troopers came to respect and admire. Health education programmes were introduced and preventable illnesses treated, while malnutrition was overcome, initially by gifts of food and later by the introduction of better farming methods.

As contact increased, gifts of radios, medical kits, beer and even luxury hampers sealed the friendship. Ideology was rarely, if ever, mentioned. It was simply accepted that the tribesmen, to whom national borders were irrelevant, had no interest in politics and would happily support those who best served their very subjective interests. In appreciating this, and reacting to it, the British in Borneo proved the worth of 'Hearts and Minds', a policy which they were to adopt again with equal success in the Oman but which few other Western countries ever seem fully to have grasped.

In 1970 Britain was drawn with some trepidation into what was to be her last major colonial war. Since 1962 Sa'id bin Taimur, the aged and despotic Sultan of Oman, had been engaged in a losing battle with Marxist inspired guerrillas in the southern province of Dhofar. Using the recently independent People's Democratic Republic of Yemen as a base, they had mounted an increasingly successful campaign against the small government presence in the region and were now threatening to destabilize the entire region. In 1970 the unpopular and totally out of touch Sultan was replaced in a bloodless coup by his son, the Sandhurst-trained Anglophile Sultan Qaboos bin Said.

Qaboos requested and was immediately granted British military assistance to crush the insurrection. SAS teams were introduced within days (there is some suggestion that elements may already have been in position) and at once began to implement Operation Storm, the regaining of the initiative in the South.

The area of operations was alien to the SAS troopers, most of whom were fresh from the jungle. It comprised a narrow coastal plain some 60km long and 10 km wide centred on the regional capital of Salalah. Inland the region was dominated by the mountainous Jebel Qarra, with its deep wadis and numerous caves running south and west to the Yemeni border. The Negd, a generally flat and treacherous area of desert between the mountains and Empty Quarter completed the uninviting panorama.

The Dhofari people were largely unknown to the SAS. The town tribes of the coastal plain were basically of Kathiri origin, industrious, comparatively sophisticated and unsympathetic to the Marxist cause. By contrast the Qarra Jebalis of the mountains were hot tempered, highly intelligent and fiercely independent. Their loyalty was to self, livestock, family and tribe in that order. As the SAS discovered to their advantage, the Jebalis made loyal friends if exploited sensibly, but bitter enemies if crossed. The Bedu of the Negd were nomadic herdsmen drawn from the Mahra and Bait Kathir tribes. They had their own languages and were equally independent.

Lieutenant-Colonel Johnny Watts, commanding 22 SAS, fully appreciated that his greatest battle would be for the hearts and minds of the indigenous population. A PsyOps team was formed to counter the Adoo, or Marxist rebel, propaganda. Initially most Dhofaris offered at least tacit support to the rebels, until the British were able to exploit the Marxists' hatred of family and religion, the two main cornerstones of local society. Once it was safe to do so doctors and SAS paramedics visited the local villages, inoculating the tribesman and their families against preventable but previously fatal diseases. At the same time veterinary teams treated the camel and goat herds in the Negd, providing the nomadic Bedu with new-found economic security.

Watts then gave the Dhofaris the opportunity to take up arms against the Adoo. Newly formed groups of fighters were trained, armed and paid, but never actually commanded by, the SAS. Known as 'firqat' they were allowed to elect their own leaders, after which they were given almost total autonomy. By 1975 the SAS administered some 1,600 men deployed in twenty-one separate 'firqat' units. With skilful handling they became a key element in operations to recover lost territory and win the hearts and minds of the Dhofari people.

Defection

Causing the enemy to defect is a crucial part of the PsyOps battle. Although defections do not follow a set pattern, a number of studies have been undertaken in the last thirty years which would suggest a series of common denominators. Andrew Molnar, in his study of the Viet Cong, argued that communist defectors more often came from rural areas than from cities despite its having been easier to defect from an urban environment. He put this down to the fact that life was not so hard for guerrillas in a city, whereas active units often experienced considerable privations in the hills and jungle.

Certain types of cadre member were more prone to defection: covert intelligence operators often had to assume a pro-government façade, and sometimes actually came to believe in it; liaison agents had the opportunity to defect at any time and were particularly susceptible to amnesties. On the other hand cadre leaders, who gained considerable satisfaction from their positions of power, were unlikely to defect. Equally PsyOps specialists, although not always committed from the outset, invariably came to believe in what they wrote and quickly became unshakeable.

One of the largest studies of defection, of 1369 Viet Cong, showed that the harshness of irregular warfare, food and medical shortages in particular, were the chief reasons for defection. Three-fifths defected for these reasons, others because they became disillusioned with the failures and shortcomings of the organization. A few cited government promises as their ground for 'turning' – most often the promise of land, less often the promise of no recriminations and occasionally the offer to buy their weapons.

Most defectors, claimed Molnar, gave no thought to defection during their first year. The most vulnerable period came some six months thereafter when the individuals began to worry about their futures. Very often the men developed personal difficulties, perhaps with another member of the unit, which, if allowed to fester, developed into a political disagreement with the movement as a whole. Sex, or the lack of it, often led to strain. Although approximately ten percent of Viet Cong were women, sex was not usually allowed in the jungle or other remote areas. When it was, the leaders took their pick, adding to the subordinates' feelings of alienation.

Defections usually occurred after several minor personal crises. Once defection had been decided upon, the guerrilla invariably began to detach himself from his unit. According to Molnar most of the defectors decided to defect first, and only then became susceptible to government propaganda. Although subsequent studies have questioned this finding, and indeed much of Molnar's report, it is an important point to take into account when planning a PsyOps campaign, particularly against an unsophisticated opponent.

Vietnam Experiences

The United States reaction to the threat of revolutionary warfare was (and indeed remains) fundamentally different to that of the British. Tragically the Pentagon would not accept the worth of the North Vietnamese as a foe. Relying almost exclusively on superior firepower for victory, they regarded stealth, subtlety and subterfuge as the prerogative of the enemy. While US troops travelled mainly by road and helicopter, were dependent on well established supply routes and moved by day, the North Vietnamese Army (NVA) were ubiquitous. They used the low ground by night, were far more logistically self sufficient and became the masters of the nocturnal attack.

Left to their own devices the North Vietnamese and their Viet Cong allies were easily able to win the battle for the hearts and minds of the rural population. Coercion was not always required. Between March and May, 1964, the Viet Cong distributed a staggering 418 different leaflets to their countrymen and women. Of these 45 per cent dealt with military and paramilitary topics. A further 36 per cent were of general public interest while 8 per cent either targetted named government officials or were aimed at the American audience. A mere 1.3 per cent carried a religious theme, although 7 per cent were designed for specific groups such as students, women and small traders.

Besides these a number of additional ad hoc leaflets were produced for instance warning the local civilian population of a secret United States plot to militarize women. Letters from captured Viet Cong prisoners were produced in leaflet form to show how badly they had been treated. In one sterling example of PsyOps a leaflet was distributed within 24 hours of the Kennedy assassination advising that the new President, Lyndon Johnson, had been slightly wounded in a separate and unrelated incident.

When peaceful intervention failed the Viet Cong were rarely slow to resort to violence. Government agents and hostile village headmen were publicly beheaded or ritually disembowelled. Official projects aimed at improving life in the villages and bridging the gulf between the Government and the peasants came in for special attention. When the authorities attempted to introduce a programme to eradicate malaria the Viet Cong responded with violence. Hundreds of children continued to die from this wholly preventable disease due to communist coercion, yet in its eyes the North scored a psychological victory.

Many U.S. soldiers on the ground viewed psychological operations in general, and deception in particular, with suspicion. It was an enemy tactic, offered no immediate solution to the problem and was thus somehow un-American. When leaflets were employed by the United States forces they lacked subtlety, ignoring the Indo-Chinese psyche and concentrating too firmly on an immediate result. The five major vulnerabilities exploited were hardship, fear, loss of faith in victory, disillusionment with the enemy cause and family concerns. These might have worked had the United States not been dealing with a battle-hardened enemy who had defeated not only the Japanese but the French. Furthermore the behaviour of many G.Is. towards the indigenous population did nothing to suggest that a communist government, with its promises of reform, could be any worse than the existing status quo.

The B-52 Follow-Up Program epitomizes the United States train of thought. Some four hours after a bombing raid leaflets were dropped into the area informing the victims that they had just experienced (in case they had failed to notice) a B-52 sortie. The leaflets reminded those on the ground that the B-52s would return to strike again and therefore urged them to defect. The leaflets were designed to engender friction between the soldiers and their officers, but in this they were largely ineffective.

As the Allies had discovered in the final stages of the Second World War, an enemy which has just been pounded from the air learns to hate rather than submit. The B-52 was a blanket bomber and as often as not caused considerable collateral damage to the innocent civilian population, even when well targetted against an established enemy. Whatever the military worth of the B-52 sorties, psychologically they were of little value.

Occasionally the United States resorted to wholly peaceful PsyOps techniques. The 7th Psyop Group developed a method of disseminating propaganda messages embedded in successive layers of soap 'thus enabling the originator to convey several messages to the user over a considerable period of time'. Grocery bags with a propaganda message were also distributed. As bags were in short supply many were kept for household purposes and were thus able to spread their message through the crowded market places. Flexagons and puppets provided much the same function for the children, who were generally starved of toys and who therefore tended to make those which they had last. Propaganda messages were stamped on them or they were made in the image of a well-known personality.

In May, 1966, the Battelle Memorial Institute experimented with a series of 'stink' bombs designed to impair the Viet Cong whilst not affecting the battle potential of the American forces. Odours were sought which the Vietnamese would find offensive and which might even induce nausea or fright. Had the programme succeeded, smell bombs would have been developed designed to flush the guerrillas from the jungle. Conventional explosive bombs would have been impregnated with offensive smells, so that the mere presence of the odour would, in time, have come to signal fear and thus disrupt ordinary life by its continual and dangerous associations.

Usually United States attempts at PsyOps in Vietnam were far more direct. Operation Tintinnabulation, which was undertaken by elements of 10th Psyop Battalion and the 5th Special Squadron USAF and which employed two C-47 aircraft, was typical. One aircraft, nicknamed 'Spooky', was equipped with miniguns, the other, 'Gabby', with loudspeakers. During the initial phase of each sortie, which took place during the hours of darkness, a 'Gabby' deploying a frequency pulsating noisemaker and protected by a 'Spooky' overflew the enemy's position, harassing and confusing him. As dawn broke the noise was replaced by more conventional tapes of senior politicians exhorting the Viet Cong to surrender. Despite the patent crudeness of the operation it occasionally succeeded in its aim. During a particularly successful series of twenty-four missions, each of approximately two hours' duration, the number of defectors in the target area more than doubled from an average of 120 a month to 380.

In November, 1969, the 1st Infantry Division began to employ a combination of armed propaganda teams by day and loud noise by night to deny the Viet Cong time to rest. Each propaganda team comprised a highly trained platoon of three sections, one a propaganda squad and the other two security squads. The latter were extremely heavily armed, while the former contained at least one 'turned' rebel, ideally a local. The heavily armed units cordoned off a village, locating and neutralizing the possible ambush sites before the much more lightly armed propaganda squad entered, moving from door to door to distribute literature and seek snippets of local intelligence.

At night the targetted village or villages were overflown by helicopters broadcasting loudspeaker music. For two hours between midnight and dawn psywar tapes were played, their themes being either nostagic to make the Viet Cong homesick, or eerie, intended to represent the souls of dead communists who had yet to find peace. This tactic, known as 'Wandering Souls', played particularly on the Viet Cong fear of being buried in an unmarked grave, and as such was not dissimilar to the highly successful British tactics then being employed in Borneo. It is reported that, although they realized that the sounds were coming from a helicopter, in their sleep-deprived state many of the less experienced Viet Cong quickly became agitated and disorientated.

Northern Ireland

The fight for control of Ireland is now more than 800 years old. Its latest phase, centred in the six counties of Northern Ireland, began as a comparatively bloodless confrontation between the rival mainly Protestant Loyalist and predominantly Nationalist communities, but quickly developed into something far more sinister. The British Army was first involved in August, 1969, after the Royal Ulster Constabulary (RUC), supported by the highly sectarian B Specials, had proved incapable of controlling local rioting.

Responsibility for the maintenance of public order passed to the army whose numbers gradually swelled until, by 1972, they had peaked at around 22,000.

However the shooting in Londonderry of thirteen demonstrators by the 1st Battalion The Parachute Regiment in January of that year led to an inquiry into the army's behaviour and long-term rôle. It quickly became clear to both politicians and senior officers alike that the time had come to reduce the army's profile on the streets.

By 1977 the army's presence had been reduced to fourteen battalions of about 650 men each, together with a small number of support elements. The majority of units were by then serving on a four-month unescorted tour of duty and were deployed in defined areas known as Tactical Areas of Responsibility (TAORs). A few battalions however, served for two years and were generally held in reserve to come to the assistance of any unit within its own area of responsibility which found itself particularly heavily committed.

Despite attempts to integrate army and police activities there remained an antipathy between certain RUC and army officers on the ground. Few in the army wholly trusted the mainly Protestant police to act impartially when dealing with Loyalist extremism. Conversely elements of the RUC (with perhaps more justification) began to regard the army as outsiders, who after short tours returned to the comparative safety of the mainland without ever really coming to terms with the true parameters of the Irish problem.

Between 1977 and 1979 rivalry between the police and the army became acute, so much so that it began to threaten the all-important process of intelligence gathering. At the time the majority of RUC intelligence was gathered by E Department, the Special Branch. However, the Department had lost responsibility for interrogations to C Branch, the CID. Simultaneously the army relied upon volunteer FINCOs (field intelligence NCOs) and relatively untrained officers from the roulement battalions to run its own agents. The army and police rarely talked to one other, the sub-units within each relying on the time-honoured principle of 'Need to know' to guard their information jealously. In addition both MI5 and MI6 ran agent networks in Northern Ireland, occasionally employing the same contacts but rarely sharing intelligence.

In 1970 Brigadier Frank Kitson, then in command of 39 Brigade in Belfast, was given permission to form the Mobile Reconnaissance Force (MRF). Drawing on his experience of counter-insurgency campaigns in Kenya, Malaya, Oman and Cyprus he gathered together a group of 'turned' IRA members, nicknamed the 'Freds', whom he sent to live in a British Army married quarters attached to Palace Barracks in Holywood, County Down. Initially the military element of the undercover unit comprised a mere handful of soldiers under the command of a Captain and answerable directly to Kitson. Its early operations were basic. Soldiers in plain clothes and unmarked cars would sit in places where they expected the IRA to plant bombs. Others would cruise Republican areas accompanied by 'Freds', who would point out characters or places of interest.

Within months, however, the unit's activities became more unusual, and in many instances more complex. In one instance it set up its own massage parlour; in another female soldiers posed as door-to-door cosmetics saleswomen. One particularly daring, and ultimately tragic, operation involved the setting up of the Four Square Laundry. Laundry vans were used to carry out surveillance in Republican areas, while dirty washing actually deposited for laundering was submitted for forensic testing before return. The operation was compromised when a 'Fred' was 're-turned' by the IRA. A laundry van containing two MRF soldiers, one of them a woman, was ambushed in West Belfast. The male soldier was killed but the woman escaped. The 'Fred' was subsequently executed by the IRA.

It gradually became clear that the MRF suffered a number of weaknesses. Its almost total reliance on intelligence provided by the far from reliable 'Freds' left it vulnerable, as did its inability to call upon the assistance of dedicated quick-reaction troops in an emergency. In 1973 the unit was disbanded and its place taken by a new surveillance group, later to become known as 14 Company.

Early attempts were made to disguise the name of the new unit to afford it greater cover. Originally volunteers posted to it were said to be joining one of the Northern Ireland Training Advisory Teams (NITATs). However, when it became felt that this was beginning to compromise the true rôle of the NITATs all implied connections were severed.

Subsequent attempts to disguise the unit as part of the Intelligence and Security Group based at Ashford, Kent, were abandoned when the very real division between the covert rôle of the unit and the more overt rôle of 12 Intelligence and Security Company, actually serving in Northern Ireland, began to blur.

Although the rôle of 14 Company remains secret, Mark Urban, in his excellent analysis of the unit in his book *Big Boys' Rules*, has succeeded in identifying certain of the major incidents attributable to it. Most missions carried out by 14 Company involved either the setting up of covert observation posts (as opposed to conventional vehicle check points) or the observation of targets from unmarked 'Q' cars.

However, the use of covert OPs and 'Q' cars in an area such as Northern Ireland in which strangers were treated with paranoia was fraught with danger. In 1974 Captain Anthony Pollen of the Coldstream Guards, attached to 14 Company, was cornered and shot while trying to take photographs on the edge of the Bogside, a Catholic estate in Londonderry. Three years later three soldiers manning a covert observation post in South Armagh were compromised. They were targetted from across the Irish border by an Active Service Unit (ASU) armed with an M60 machine gun, stolen from the US National Guard, and shot dead.

On 12 December, 1977, a lance-corporal attached to the unit became the victim of a potential hijack when two members of the Irish National Liberation Army (INLA) attempted to steal his car. In the process one of the terrorists, Colin McNutt, was shot dead. A day later, in an unrelated incident, Corporal Paul Harman was stopped by an unknown number of assailants in West Belfast. It seems likely that he tried to talk his way out of it rather than use force. He was shot dead, his car was set on fire, and a considerable amount of delicate communications intelligence was captured by the Provisional IRA.

Since 1977 varying numbers of SAS have been employed in covert rôles in Northern Ireland. Their very presence has had a marked effect on the terrorist propaganda machines. Numerous conventional incidents have been attributed to the SAS and sitings reported, so much so that were even half of these to have been true it would have required the constant presence of the entire Regiment in the Province.

Lessons For The Future

Perception Management has been defined by John M. Collins, the author of the perceptive *Green Berets, SEALs and Spetsnaz*, as: 'Overt, covert, or clandestine employment of deception, controlled disclosures, military demonstrations, psyop, psychotropic biological and chemical agents, and other special operations to influence and exploit the emotions, thoughts, and motives of targetted governments, groups, and individuals in ways that help users achieve objectives.' It is the way ahead.

In the world of counter-terrorism the major powers have come to accept that prevention is often better than cure. Whereas it is appreciated that armed intervention must always remain an option, in certain circumstances its use may prove positively counter-productive. It is impossible to keep cameras from the battlefield and the televising of heavily armed foreign troops forcing their will on a group of ill-equipped, confused and frightened local militia will often send wholly inappropriate signals to the voters back home.

Political and economic pressures may have little effect on subnational or terrorist groups. However, when applied to the more structured states supplying such groups with arms, equipment and sanctuary they may prove devastating. Economic sanctions bite slowly and do not afford good radio or television. They are therefore rarely questioned domestically, particularly if they can be tied to a specific atrocity (such as Lockerbie), but within years, or sometimes even months, can lead to the destabilization of the target régime.

International co-operation is essential if an economic embargo is to work successfully, but, as the United States in particular has frequently learned to her cost, too often friends are inhibited by fear of losing commercial opportunities or by fear of provoking a bully. Therefore allies often have to be coerced covertly as a precursor to coercing the target nation overtly, a costly and potentially politically dangerous game. Unilateral United States sanctions against Libya, Nicaragua and (in the early days) Iran proved less than satisfactory. However, United Nations sanctions against Serbia quickly caused its government to temper its aspirations towards expansion into neighbouring Bosnia.

During her ill-fated Afghan campaign the then Soviet Union operated a relatively successful carrot and stick policy in its dealings with Pakistan. While Pakistan offered the Muslim Mujahideen shelter and allowed them to purchase arms it remained ambivalent in its attitude to the United States. Despite the strongest of CIA pressure, Soviet economic inducements combined with cross-border bombings, subversion and other pressures served to limit Pakistani involvement in the affairs of her neighbour.

CHAPTER SEVEN:
Lies on the Home Front

'It may seem melodramatic to say that the United States and Russia represent good and evil. But if we think of it that way, it helps to clarify our perspective on the world struggle.'
Richard Nixon.

As a rule, human beings do not kill other human beings. Before man enters into war or genocide, he must first dehumanize those whom he means to destroy. Before the Japanese performed medical experiments on human guinea pigs in the Second World War, they named them *maruta*– logs of wood – to destroy any latent tendencies that they may have had to identify with their victims.

Propaganda, and with it deception, have long been used to paralyse thought, to prevent discrimination and to condition individuals to act en masse. 'The' enemy becomes a singular entity capable of the greatest evil, yet seemingly incapable of the higher emotions of fear and remorse. When war begins, clarity and charity are exiled for the duration as the whole economy dedicates itself to the victory of good over evil.

When Western countries go to war against Asians, they often portray them as faceless hordes, incapable of individual thought or personal suffering. The old image of Genghis Khan and the Mongol hordes still haunts the European and is unashamedly pressed into service when needed.

British and American tacticians ignored Japanese victories against the Chinese in the late 1930s and convinced themselves, wholly erroneously, that the Japanese soldier was incapable of firing his rifle accurately and would prove no match for an army of European extraction. A few years later United Nations forces in Korea found themselves swamped by an 'ochre horde', a yellow tide of faceless masses, cruel and nerveless subhumans, the incomprehensible and inscrutable Chinese. Less than a generation later the United Sates learned to its cost the dangers of degrading the enemy as 'gooks,' 'dinks' or 'slopes' in Vietnam.

With God on My Side

God and country may be quite separate in theory, but in time of war scarcely a government fails to invoke its deities. God sanctifies a social order, a way of life and national values to create a 'just' war in which hardships and danger have to be endured as a price for victory of good over evil. Often the enemy becomes the devil, particularly in religious wars when the terrible self-righteousness of the 'holy' cause is all too often used as an excuse for carnage of the most terrible kind.

The Western Judeo-Christian tradition of holy war has its roots in the invasion of Canaan, when Yahweh reputedly commanded the Israelites to slay or enslave the native population and destroy its gods. The sin of the enemy was not only that it occupied the land which had been given to the chosen people, but that it worshipped 'false' gods. The old divinities – Astarte, the Queen of Heaven, and Beelzebub, the god of fertility – were seen as idols and demons whose existence could not be tolerated.

Holy war was continued by the Puritans and their successors, who believed that they had a 'destiny' to inhabit America from coast to coast, and who therefore considered the native Americans, whose prior presence was socially and economically inconvenient, as 'the bond slaves of Satan' to be subjugated or destroyed.

Within Islam the *Jihad* continues the tradition of holy war. Historically it was the duty of all good Moslem princes to undertake an annual campaign to extend the faith, and to fight it until all men bore witness that there was no God but Allah. Thus when the Crusades pitted Moslem against Christian a macabre situation arose in which both sides assumed without reservation that the other was the enemy of the one true God.

Every nation with a Christian heritage has accused its enemies of being Christ-killers. In the First World War the Kaiser was pictured as the devil. In the Second World War, the Germans claimed '*Gott mit uns*'. Occasionally religion has proved a political embarrassment, in which instance it has been conveniently ignored by those wishing to pursue the cause of war. Thus clerics who in 1854 railed against Britain and France for going to the defence of infidel Turkey against Christian Russia were hounded as traitors to the cause of British imperialism. A century later those few brave German clergymen who risked all to denounce the evils of Naziism from the pulpit found themselves hounded into concentration camps for daring to question the ethicacy of the Third Reich.

It has become traditional to regard an enemy as a barbarian and a destroyer of culture. He will be portrayed as rude, crude and uncivilized. Usually the barbarian image is used by advanced cultures against simpler, less technically advanced peoples. To the Greeks, anyone who did not speak their language and share their customs was considered a barbarian, and even the gentle Aristotle did not object to the slaughter of non-combatants and the selling of the children of conquered people into slavery.

To the Romans, anyone living beyond the civilizing pale of the empire, especially the fierce Germanic tribes, were barbarians. For centuries Europe grew rich on the enslavement of 'inferior' black Africans, and in the nineteenth century fought a series of wars against the Chinese to keep alive the trade in opium.

The barbarian theme was widely used in Second World War propaganda by all participants. Nazi anti-semitic tracts contrasted the healthy Arians with the inferior dark races with contaminated blood – Jews, Gypsies, Slavs and Orientals. In turn the Allies frequently depicted the Germans as a Nazi horde of dark monsters on a mindless rampage.

President Truman created a rhetoric for the Cold War which, in the words of Robert Ivie, an expert in the propaganda of the period, 'coloured a picture of the enemy as brutal, bestial, domineering, inexorable, impersonal, blatant, blunt, immoral, powerful and destructive.' Ronald Reagan continued with the theme; indeed it was only with the fall of the Soviet Union that the majority of the United States press began to regard it as other than unpatriotic to pay compliments to anything with an Eastern European theme.

But What of the Truth?

It is difficult to preserve the theory of the just war when the body bags begin to come home in large numbers. Today war is televised in all its stark horror. However, during the First World War there was no television, radio technology was primitive and it was comparatively easy to dilute, if not completely hide, the growing casualty figures. In the bloodbaths of 1916 and 1917 the comrades who had queued for hours in 1914 to enlist into the Pals battalions were massacred. Small towns and villages lost the flower of their youth in a single morning. Yet to reduce the shock at home the casualty figures were often suppressed by the authorities and released in stages to lessen the shock.

Censorship was rigidly enforced. Soldiers could neither keep diaries nor sketch the carnage about them, while letters home were subject to prior clearance. Soldiers could describe the environment about them, provided they did not do so in too geographically explicit terms, but could not easily criticize their conditions or leadership. Despite the rigours of censorship soldiers could not be silenced when on leave, yet surprisingly few seem to have wanted to frighten their loved ones by relating the true horrors of the trenches.

Where possible journalists and politicians were kept clear of the front lines, unless of course their views coincided with those of the general staff in which case their presence was welcomed.

Thus it was with the evolution of the tank. The tank was first used by the British in 1916, during the Battle of the Somme. Its effect on the military front was minor, but on the home front it was enormous. By then the readership of national and local newspapers had increased dramatically to the extent that they were regularly pinned to notice boards to ensure maximum exposure. Newspapers craved for facts on the tank but official reports were scarce and photographs were censored. When journals began to carry fanciful stories of tank successes enhanced by futuristic cartoons depicting the new wonder-weapon the Government actively encouraged the fiction.

In January, 1917, the first moving pictures of the tank were made available to the general public. Crowds queued at the 107 London cinemas showing a film containing pictures of the tank, cheering, yelling and applauding whenever the beast appeared on screen. To those at home the tank became the weapon which would break the stalemate on the Western Front and bring ultimate victory. The somewhat naive attitude of the civilian masses was resented by many soldiers in the Tank Corps who were all too aware of the harsh realities of early armoured warfare. Nonetheless Brigadier Elles, who later became Colonel Commandant of the Royal Tank Regiment, deliberately sought maximum publicity to further the cause of the tank and in 1917 arranged for King George V to witness a highly contrived demonstration of the new weapon's potential.

In the presence of the King a tank was made to cross an ammunition bunker. When the King enquired after the health of the crew three of the members were introduced to him. Neither he nor the other onlookers were told that the other five members of the crew had been knocked unconscious. It was patently clear that early tanks were simply not capable of taking such punishment. However, the truth was not allowed to get in the way of propaganda and the entire exercise was publicized as a great success.

During the Battle of Cambrai 400 tanks advanced along a six mile front. Church bells rang out for the first time in three years when it was announced that the armoured monsters had helped force a breakthrough five miles into the enemy rear. The military realities were less impressive, with a large number of tanks lost to artillery fire in the early stages of the engagement. More than fifty tanks were captured by the Germans, although this fact was never disclosed to the press, and when the Germans counter-attacked after a few days they recaptured virtually all the ground lost.

The shortcomings of the tank were massaged to such an extent that the public at large kept faith with the new wonder-weapon. Tanks appeared in the towns and cities of Britain to enhance the sale of war bonds. Ironically the Germans also used footage of captured British tanks for the same purpose, describing the weapon as evil, barbarous and an affront to civilization.

In truth the tank was more significant as a tool of propaganda than as a weapon of war. It was Germany, and not Britain, which in the two decades which followed the war closed the gap between tank propaganda and military reality.

Lions Shot By Donkies

The attitude of the military to battle-related illness was little short of barbaric and remained hidden from the public at large for decades after the end of the war.

Illnesses such as post-traumatic shock disorder were not recognized by the authorities and even shell-shock was as often as not incorrectly diagnosed. Psychiatry was in its infancy and there was thus a tendency to view mental disorder as a reflection of moral weakness. In army circles this reinforced the view that shell shock was bad for morale and was thus to be discouraged rather than pitied.

Many victims of shell shock were court-martialled and executed in a series of courts martial details of which the authorities did all in their power to suppress. According to the official records of the British Army 346 officers and men were summarily executed by firing squad during the First World War. Both during and after the war the military did its best to keep these executions secret. Sparse details were given in the 1922 *Statistics of the Military Effort of the British Empire During the Great War, Para 23-Discipline*, but requests for specific information on individual cases were blocked. Anthony Babington, a circuit judge of some experience, was granted limited access to the files when researching for his book *For the Sake of Example*, but otherwise researchers had to wait until January, 1994, for access to the files, most of which were then begrudgingly released under the 75-year rule.

They made astonishing reading. Some 3,800 men were condemned to death during the period of hostilities and 11 per cent of them were shot. On average 160 courts martial a day sat, 87 per cent of them resulting in convictions. Most of the accused had no one to defend them, and until 1918 the courts were without legal advice of any kind. Executions were invariably carried out in front of the victim's battalion by a firing squad drawn from the accused's own unit.

The bandleader Victor Silvester was 17 when he volunteered for the Army (he had lied about his age). He was caught by a senior officer reading a document marked 'For the eyes of officers only'. It contained a list of soldiers condemned to be shot and Silvester's punishment was to be ordered to serve in the firing squad. Some of the other members, he recalled in an aide-memoire published after his death, were drunk, as their first victim was to be a member of their own battalion, the Argyll and Sutherland Highlanders. So inept was the firing squad at its macabre duty that it missed and an officer was forced to shoot the accused with his pistol. Silvester suffered a breakdown as a result. He was sent home when details of his age were released. Had he been a few months older he might have been returned, a sick man, to the line where no account of his mental state would have been taken. The consequences may only be imagined.

With wholesale disregard for the basic mores of jurisprudence, and totally unknown to the general public at home, young officers fresh to the front found themselves with more power than High Court judges. Most played safe, imposing the extreme sentences demanded by their commanding officers in the hope that higher authority would commute them. But often they did not. Cases of cowardice were invariably punished by death, whatever the medical circumstances. Not that the Army doctors often intervened in mitigation. Shell-shock, accepted by every other European army, was brushed aside by the medical officers, even when on one occasion the accused had been a lunatic before being called up.

Typical was the case of Harry Farr, a regular soldier of the West Yorkshire Regiment who joined the army in 1910 aged 16. His unit transferred to France on 5 November, 1914, and was almost immediately in action. The following March two members of the battalion were shot for desertion. Two months later Farr was himself evacuated from the front suffering from shell shock. Five months later he returned to active service on the Ypres front, but by now conditions in the trenches were worse. During the course of 1916 Farr was treated twice for mental exhaustion. When he failed to see a doctor on a subsequent occasion and disobeyed a series of orders to return to the front, he was court-martialled for cowardice and shot. The court martial, the transcript of which is contained on seven hand-written sheets of foolscap paper, lasted no more than thirty minutes. Four witnesses were called for the prosecution. Farr gave evidence on his own behalf and attempted to call his Medical Officer. The officer had, however, been wounded and was not available. Farr was certified medically fit for trial, but no other medical evidence as to his previous history or state of mind at the time was offered.

The young man was sentenced to death and executed in October, 1916. Shortly thereafter his widow, Gertrude, received a terse telegram from the War Office stating simply:

> 'We regret to inform you that your husband has died. He was sentenced to death for cowardice and shot at dawn on 16th October.'

She heard nothing further until a subsequent communication advised her that, as her husband had been executed, the military pension on which she and her daughter were relying would be stopped.

Men who had been gassed and were found choking behind the lines were shot; a 44-year-old Welshman, married with three children, whose defence was that he had been unable to keep up with his fellows, was shot as a deserter. In one of the most macabre cases of all a deserter whose mother had died and whose father, a prisoner of war, was going blind, became worried about the fate of his little brother and sister who had been left in the care of a neighbour. He deserted, was apprehended en route to the coast, was condemned to death and shot.

The Corporals of Souain

France, faced with wholesale mutiny in 1917, shot far fewer than the British. However, in 1915, they too became party to one of the most shameful and public abuses of law in military history. On 8 March 22nd Company the 336th Infantry Regiment was ordered to assault the heights of Souain, an enemy strong point in the Champagne region. When it refused (the rest of the battalion had earlier been slaughtered making an equally pointless attack) the brigade commander, General Reveilhac, ordered his artillery to fire on the company's position. He had no authority to do so and the Artillery Colonel refused.

The General dared not put the order in writing, but instead instructed that from each section of the Company a corporal and four privates be ordered into no-man's-land in broad daylight to cut the German wire. Naturally the Germans opened fire, forcing the men to shelter until nightfall. Taking this failure personally, the General ordered the Company to be relieved and the names of the two youngest men in each section, together with six corporals, to be taken. There was not a single shred of evidence to support the contention, yet the 36 men were charged with 'collective refusal to obey an order,' and confined to the cellars of the local town hall to await a court martial.

The court martial convened on 16 March and, despite pressure put on it by General Reveilhac, dismissed the charges with the exception of those against four of the corporals, whom it sentenced to death with a petition for mercy. The firing squad was told off for 2.00pm. Fearful that the petition might reach sympathetic ears the General brought the executions forward to 1.00pm.

The widow of one of the victims, Corporal Maupas, tried for fifteen years to clear her husband's name but the authorities closed ranks against her. With the assistance of the League for Human Rights she finally won her case on 27 May, 1933. The court martial was recognized as a legal sham and a travesty of justice and the four men were pardoned. Even so the authorities failed to acknowledge the extent of their guilt and damages were confined to 1 Franc. In 1935 Humphrey Cobb used the shameful incident as the basis for his best-selling novel *Paths of Glory*. Stanley Kubrick adapted the book into a film, which was subsequently banned in France for twenty years.

Coldly and clinically the trials of the First World War were lawful. Nonetheless from the point of view of military discipline they were unnecessary. Australia had no death penalty, despite which its troops were among the best on the Western Front. During the Second World War there were only four executions for military offences in the British Army, yet the discipline and spirit of the ordinary soldier remained inviolate through the bloodiest of battles.

To date all attempts to gain a pardon for those soldiers executed for purely military offences has failed. It is to be hoped that one day, perhaps in the not too distant future, wiser, more humane counsel will prevail. Until it does government after successive government will continue to maintain one of the greatest deceptions of all time; that the judicial murder of nearly

350 men was other than a gross travesty and a violation of natural justice.

The Making of a Collective Madness

Adolf Hitler was appointed Chancellor of Germany on 30 January, 1933, and within months transformed a hitherto democratic country into a dictatorship. He persuaded the ailing President Hindenburg to hold fresh elections on 5 March and in the intervening weeks conducted a political campaign of unerring savagery. Opposition newspapers were suppressed, opposition meetings disrupted by uniformed thugs and their speakers beaten up.

In Nazi-controlled Prussia Minister for the Interior Hermann Goering ruthlessly purged the police, replacing large numbers of senior officers with Nazis, supported by 30,000 SS and SA men drafted into the auxiliary police force. When the Reichstag was burned down on 27 February Hitler published a decree 'for the protection of the people' suspending all guarantees of civil liberties. When it became clear that the fire had been caused by a young Dutch communist, Marinus van der Lubbe, left-wing leaders were summarily arrested and the Communist party outlawed.

The combination of terror on the streets and the growing power of Nazi propaganda brought Hitler victory at the polls and brought to an end the final vestiges of German democracy. When the newly elected deputies arrived to take up their places at the disused Kroll Opera House (the Reichstag's meeting place after the fire) they were greeted by rows of armed SS guards and SA Brownshirts. When Hitler introduced an Enabling Act designed to give him dictatorial powers to rule without reference to the Reichstag few deputies dared to argue.

In the months that followed all sources of potential opposition to Nazi authority were destroyed. In May trade unions were banned and the workers forced to join the Nazi Labour Front. In June the Social Democrats were banned and in July the Roman Catholic Church made a shameful Concordat with the Nazis, by which the Vatican accepted that no Catholic party would operate in Germany and agreed to consult the government when appointing bishops.

Thousands of left-wingers and Jews were arrested and all other political parties dissolved. On 14 July, 1933, Hitler proclaimed that the National Socialist Party was Germany's only political party, and in December that it and the German state were one. When President Hindenburg died in August, 1934, Hitler announced that the offices of president and chancellor would be merged and that in future the armed forces would swear a personal oath of loyalty to him.

Hitler could never have come to power without the tacit support of the people. That he obtained this must remain a testimony to the brilliance of the Nazi propaganda machine, which in its skill, cunning, lies and sheer frenzy was unprecedented in world history. The depression, which at its peak saw 30 per cent of the German workforce unemployed, proved an ideal breeding ground for the spread of Naziism. Feeding on a combination of fear and frustration Nazi propaganda blamed the country's woes on the political left, on the 'traitors' who had surrendered Germany's heritage at Versailles, on the weak politicians of the Weimar Republic and above all on the Jews.

In 1931 the Nazis forged a link with the ultra-conservative Nationalist Party with its strong industrial and commercial credentials, and in so doing placated many business magnates who might otherwise have baulked at their strong-arm tactics. Two years later, its usefulness over, the Nationalist Party was banned.

Huge public spending schemes were introduced to reduce unemployment. Over 3,000kms of canals were dug and a new network of autobahns constructed, giving Germany a transportation system the envy of her European neighbours. At the same time the country was put on a war production footing, adding impetus to the Nazi-inspired economic 'miracle' which by then was beginning to affect the daily lives of much of the population. It was clear to the far-sighted that Germany, once rearmed, would have little option but to go to war. Yet few foreigners heeded the danger, indeed many became deferential, preferring to appease Hitler rather than provoke him.

To ensure that there could be no doubt as to the source of the country's new-found prosperity cheap radios were mass-produced and sold at a subsidy to allow Goebbels' propaganda machine easy access to the homes and work places of the population as a whole. Those who had gained temporarily from Naziism quickly began to accept at face value its lies and deceits, particularly when spread by a medium as 'official' as German radio.

The Nazi Party was careful to spread its tentacles deep into the countryside, where it found a willing audience among the peasants many of whom had been sadly neglected by the Weimar Republic. Harvest festivals were politicized to emphasize the rôle of National Socialism in bringing about the renaissance of Germany's prosperity, while Hitler Youth teams toured the villages extolling the virtues of health and fitness through Party-inspired mass training programmes.

The mood of nationalist exultation which enveloped Germany during the early months of Nazi rule found greatest favour with the professional classes. Most middle-class Germans found much to admire and relatively little to condemn during 1933. The assault on the left was widely popular. The 'Emergency Decrees' following the Reichstag fire, which made devastating inroads into civil liberties, were by and large warmly welcomed as the more affluent succumbed to the deluge of withering anti-Bolshevik propaganda. Even the majority of those middle-class Germans not organized into the Party were generally sympathetic towards at least some of its stated aims and supposed intentions, whatever their misgivings about the more violent aspects of National Socialism.

From 1934 onwards the professional classes were exposed to direct Nazi influence from the more or less compulsory membership of craft guilds, chambers of commerce and professional associations, all of them by now run by proven National Socialists. When discontent was voiced it manifested itself in complaints against increased taxation, low productivity, high interest rates and the patent corruption of many local party officials. Much of this died a natural death when the SA Brownshirt leadership was purged in June, 1934, and the policy of rearmament began to lead to a highly superficial improvement in the standard of living. What could not be improved was blamed upon external influences and the alleged corruption of the Jewish business community which was still surprisingly strong in large parts of Germany.

Those in the Church who dared to question the ethicacy of National Socialism were shown little mercy. However, the Nazi Party was careful to court the Church during its rise to power and it was only later that many clerics learned to their cost the full extent of the ideological rift between National Socialism and Christianity.

Defeat and revolution in 1918 left the Protestant Church in Germany in disarray and brought into the open a series of fundamental theological and ideological rifts which the Nazis were able to exploit. Liberal theology was discredited in favour of a new wave of revivalist fundamentalism, which led on the one hand to a renewed assertion of the truths of Lutheran orthodoxy and on the other to a growth in nationalism. Though many Protestant ministers remained sceptical about the advancing Nazi movement in the late 1920s and early 1930s, there was no denying its appeal for others, particularly those who supported a spiritual as well as a political revival based on Christianity and the politics of national resurgence.

To a number of Protestant ministers the Nazi appeal to self-sacrifice, idealism and the overcoming of selfish materialism and cultural decadence was so attractive that they publicly proclaimed the destruction of the Weimar Republic as a day of liberation. Many were to rue the day. In 1934 a group of Nazi extremists within the Protestant Church began to denounce the Old Testament 'with its Jewish morality of rewards, and stories of cattle-dealers and concubines'. It began to argue that the whole concept of 'Christ Crucified' was flawed, and that in future the Church should depict him as the epitome of Nordic supremacy over a lesser world. When those pastors who a few months earlier had lauded the arrival of Nazi supremacy began to object they became the subject of gestapo persecution.

On 6 October, 1934, Bishop Wurm of Wurttemberg was placed under 'protective custody' in Stuttgart and five days later Bishop Meiser was placed under house arrest in Munich. A series of mass demonstrations so alarmed the Nazi régime that both men were released on 1 November, 1934, but by then the damage had been done. Many Protestants came to realize that they had been widely deceived by the Nazi phenomenon. Even so most remained true to its nationalist goals and social aspirations and few did anything actively to oppose it.

The Catholic Church initially banned all association with the Nazi Party, but in 1933 came to accept the inevitable and sought a compromise. Even so the government pursued a relentless, albeit piecemeal series of attacks on Catholic traditions and customs, on its institutions and above all on its educational structure. However, in the Catholic clergy Goebbels met his propaganda match. Highly contrived 'immorality trials' of members of religious orders in 1936-37 were countered effectively by priests pointing out to their congregations not only the patent fabrication of most of the allegations but also the demonstrably much wider prevalence of gross immorality and corruption within the Nazi Party itself.

The pro-government press was openly denounced by the clergy which successfully recommended the boycotting of several newspapers. Banned church flags continued to be flown in place of the swastika and services increasingly became excuses for demonstrations of religious solidarity and defiance. Numerous priests were arrested and punished in one form or another, but this only served to exacerbate the situation.

The violence and sacrilege perpetrated on the Church by roving bands of Hitler Youth, SA and SS caused widespread criticism and resentment, even among moderate members of the Party. The crucifix became a symbol both to the Church which demanded its retention and to the Party which agitated for its removal from all public places. When attempts to remove crucifixes from school rooms in Oldenberg in northern Germany led to stiff resistance the Party relented and even replaced some crucifixes which it had earlier ordered removed from the schools. However, the Nazis continued their policy of secularization by restricting Church possessions and abolishing a number of important feast days.

In 1936 the government forced the introduction of non-secular community schools. Convent schools were dissolved and nuns in teaching orders dismissed without compensation. Initially this created a furore, particularly in the more devout south. However, as Germany moved closer to war massive Party and State propaganda, mixed with not a little intimidation, took its toll and the complaints abated, enabling the State to control education in its entirety.

The Jewish Problem

The Nazi theories of Aryan superiority were based on one of the most dangerous and fundamentally flawed misconceptions in modern sociological history. The word Aryan, from the Sanskrit for 'noble', was first penned to describe a prehistoric people who settled in Iran and Northern India. During the early 19th century there arose a notion, propagated by the Comte de Gobineau, of a modern 'Aryan race', those who spoke Indo-European languages and were considered responsible for all the progress made by mankind. They were superior to 'Semites', 'yellows' and 'blacks' whom they might subjugate at will.

Gobineau was a successful writer, diplomat and ethnologist, but in his theories on race allowed the objectivity of his usually painstaking research to become tainted by his fundamental belief in racial superiority. In his *Essay on the Inequality of Human Races*, published between 1853 and 1855, he argued that the fate of civilizations is determined by racial composition, that Aryan societies flourish as long as they remain free of black and yellow strains, and that the more a civilization's racial character is diluted through inter-marriage the more it is likely to lose its vitality and creativity and fall into the abyss of degeneration and corruption.

Gobineau's theories were generally discredited by the later 19th century. Nonetheless they had a marked effect on the thinking of Germans such as Richard Wagner and Friedrich Nietzsche, and later on Adolf Hitler. The notion that the Nordic, or Germanic, peoples were racially supreme became the basis of the Nazi government policy of exterminating Jews, Gypsies and other 'non-Aryans'.

The worst excesses of Hitler's anti-Semitic policies were kept from the German people. Although newspapers carried occasional articles alluding to the 'final solution', relatively few Germans knew of the existence of the extermination camps. Nonetheless, from 1933 the Nazi anti-Semitic propaganda machine was so powerful that virtually the entire country allowed itself to be drawn into a consensual paranoia. The anxieties and guilt of the previous two decades, indeed all the negative traits which the German people did not wish to recognize in themselves, were transferred to a loyal and hardworking minority.

Few German Jews were physically very different from their Christian neighbours, many had been highly decorated during the First World War and most were fully assimilated into German society. Nonetheless, through a combination of threats, lies and innuendo the propagandists slowly but steadily succeeded in building up in the mind of the ordinary German dangerous seeds of anti-Semitism which had lain only semi-dormant for many generations.

Jews were banned from state education, from the professions and from government service, and in 1933 from marrying outside of their religion. They were attacked as 'Christ Killers' by pro-Nazi clergy and defamed as mutants and sub-humans in the schools. Books, such as a children's missive depicting the Jews as poisonous mushrooms threatening a field of good Aryan crops, were encouraged and many became best sellers.

Racist theories discredited a century earlier were returned to prominence; the crania of Jews, gypsies and other undesirables were even measured to 'prove' that they were inherently less intelligent than their Aryan neighbours. Those who dared to point out that these patently flawed theories were not born out by empirical fact were fiercely reminded, often physically, that the Jews had gained their pre-eminence in commerce and the professions through centuries of lies and deceit. As Germany moved towards a war footing most of her citizens withdrew within themselves and only the bravest dared to argue. Many of those who did disappeared into the secret and terrifying world of the concentration camps.

Ironically the Nazi's first consolidated attempt at anti-Semitism failed. A nationwide boycott of Jewish shops and businesses called in April, 1933, met with no more than limited success and in many areas was largely ignored. Equally, rural attempts to coerce the local peasants into selling their produce exclusively to Aryan traders failed, not because the pragmatic and ultra-conservative farmers wished to antagonize the government but because the Jewish buyers had an established record for fairness and a habit of paying immediately in hard cash.

There followed an uneasy truce for about a year during which anti-Jewish activity was largely confined to localized outrages while the Party attempted to undo the harm that the boycott had caused on the international front. By late 1934, however, leading Nazi newspapers were again carrying tirades of wholly unsubstantiated anti-Semitism, setting the tone for the renewed and heightened violence which afflicted the whole of Germany in 1935.

The renewal of anti-Jewish agitation was in large measure a reflection of the discontent of the Nazi Party at grass-roots level to the progress of the State in solving the Jewish Question. Even so the general public, by now subject to daily, virtually unquestioned media propaganda, did little, or in most cases nothing, to stay the excesses. Signs depicting '*Juden Sind Hier Unerwuenscht*' (Jews not welcome here) began to appear on the outskirts of towns and villages as once docile populations began to turn on their Jewish neighbours, forcing them into the temporary safety of the larger towns and cities.

Nazi-inspired anti-Semitic violence grew steadily until November, 1938, when it reached a new peak of barbarity in *Kristallnacht*. When a 17-year-old Polish Jew shot Ernst von Rath, a German Embassy official in Paris, he gave Propaganda Minister Goebbels a pretext for putting into effect a well-rehearsed plan of anti-Semitic destruction. That night SA and SS squads throughout Germany began 'spontaneous' acts of violence against Jews and Jewish property.

During the next day over 7,000 Jewish businesses were destroyed, nearly 200 synagogues burned and 76 razed to the ground. Nearly 100 Jews were killed and 36 severely wounded. More than 30,000 were arrested and sent to concentration camps. Two days after *Kristallnacht* (literally 'Crystal Night' from the smashed windows) a fine of 1,000 million Reichsmarks (US $250 million) was imposed on the Jews for damage done during the violence; it was levied by collecting 20 per cent of the property of every Jew in Germany.

In April, 1939, a law was passed preventing Jews and non-Jews from living in the same tenement blocks, causing the formation of ghettoes in the large cities and further isolating the rump of the Jewish population which had not by then fled abroad from the bulk of the German people. By the outbreak of war most Germans had forgotten that they had ever had Jewish neighbours.

Remarkable as it may sound Nazi propaganda was so efficient that the Jewish Question became of no more than minimal interest to the vast majority of Germans during the early stages of the Second World War. Under the growing pressures of war most citizens became too worried about relatives at the Front, fears about bombing raids and the intensified strain of daily existence under an increasingly totalitarian régime to feel any concern for a generally unloved minority from whom they had been skilfully isolated.

To the majority 'the Jew' became a completely depersonalized image, incapable of human thoughts and needs and beyond the protection of the law. Few even noticed when, in September, 1941, the ghettoes began to empty and their recent occupants began their lonely journeys east to supposed 'resettlement'.

Radio Deceptions

The Nazi propaganda machine was the first to exploit the full potential of the airwaves. The first international political event in which the radio played an important, even crucial rôle was the campaign leading up to the plebiscite in the Saar. In 1935 the Saarlanders were asked to decide whether they wished the administration of their land to remain with the League of Nations or be annexed by France or re-united with Germany.

The Saar was unusual in Europe in having no radio transmitting station of its own. As a consequence its citizens had taken to listening to programmes produced by their neighbours. As most spoke German the majority naturally looked eastwards for their entertainment. With entertainment came news and current affairs broadcasts, and with these highly sophisticated propaganda. While French radio made few if any concessions to the social and national aspirations of the Saarlanders, Goebbels fed his listeners a heady diet of patriotism and sophistry designed to convince them that their fate lay with the Nazi cause.

Unlike subsequent plebiscites held by the Soviets in the Baltic, in which voting was made compulsory, the issuing of ration cards being made contingent on the casting of a vote for the sole candidate, the Saar plebiscite was scrupulously fair. The election was held under the closest international scrutiny, was secret and offered three clear choices. There were Germans in the Saar who for political or religious reasons campaigned vigorously for a retention of the status quo; yet the vast majority, elated by the words of Goebbels, elected to join a National Socialist Germany whose totalitarian nature was becoming daily more obvious.

In the certain knowledge that victory would be theirs, the

German authorities gave the international press every opportunity to record and report the proceedings. The American broadcaster Cesar Saerchinger, working in conjunction with the BBC and operating from the flat of an American member of the plebiscite committee, Miss Sarah Wambaugh, transmitted live, concluding with the sound of festivities in the street.

Eight years later, their countries now at war, American broadcasters attempted to return to the theme of the Saar plebiscite, but this time painted it as a travesty of justice. The total conflict between the two accounts demonstrates ably how truth can be strained under the stress of total war. What was unquestionably true was that radio had played a fundamental part in the German victory. It would soon do so again, but this time under cicumstances in which the propagandists would find themselves less constrained by the truth.

The next major propaganda exercise set by Goebbels was the 1936 Olympics. At the time the Olympics retained an unblemished amateur ethos and was regarded by the vast majority as nothing more than a great sporting event. However, Goebbels saw them as a political opportunity and, through the medium of the radio, used them to spread the message of Nazi superiority. The short-wave transmitting station at Zeesen, near Berlin, was expanded prior to the Garmisch-Partenkirchen winter Olympics to ensure the most up-to-date facilities for any foreign correspondents wishing to use them.

The result was a great success for Nazi Germany. Day after day broadcasts went out to the world with an increasing note of euphoria. Closer to home radio provided not only the instrument for news-distribution but also for the marshalling of crowds. Loudspeakers placed strategically, particularly in Garmisch, relayed in detail news of the day's events, particularly when these involved German triumphs.

The undoubted success which Germany made of the winter Olympics gave her a new presence in the world. In the wake of the public euphoria Hitler took an amazing risk. He decided to occupy the Rhineland with a token force, even though he knew that his Army was not yet strong enough to counter the French should they resist. Hitler agreed with his generals to withdraw his troops should there be the slightest show of resistance. However, he need not have worried. The Wehrmacht goose-stepped into the Rhineland unmolested, supported by cheering crowds, their euphoria transmitted to the world by German radio broadcasters.

The success of the Rhineland occupation was crowned by yet another political coup involving the skilful use of radio crowd-martialling. A ballot was arranged for March, 1936, prior to which the fullest use was made of the radio, culminating in a formal instruction to all Germans to listen to Hitler's speech to be broadcast from the Krupp armament works in Essen. Beforehand announcements appeared in the press ordering all factory owners, department stores, offices, shops, restaurants and blocks of flats to put up loudspeakers an hour before the broadcast to ensure that the Führer's speech reached the maximum audience.

The electors voted 98.79 percent in favour of Hitler; but here, unlike in the Saar plebiscite less than a year earlier, the ballot was patently rigged. The ballot papers had only one space for a vote, voting was effectively compulsory, and was supervised by the Nazi Party itself.

Radio played a crucial rôle in the chain of events leading to the Anschluss, the annexation of Austria into Greater Germany. Anschluss was not a new concept. It had been proposed at the time of Versailles, but had been rejected by the victorious powers despite the overwhelming wishes of the Austrian and German people. Opinion in Austria had polarized after Hitler's coming to power. Parties of the left had begun to talk of independence while those on the right had begun actively to press for annexation. Austrian Nazis in large numbers had been imprisoned and deported after July, 1934, when a failed coup had resulted in the assassination of the Prime Minister, Dr Engelbert Dolfuss.

Radio had been crucial to the Austrian Nazis' plans. They had anticipated seizing the radio station in Vienna and broadcasting a programme which would have been a signal to their comrades all over Austria to rise. However, their planning had been flawed. The radio station studios were in Vienna, but the transmitters were outside the city, enabling those loyal to the government to switch off the transmitters when they realized what was happening.

The coup attempt was accompanied by sympathetic broadcasts from Germany which ceased as soon as it became clear that the attempt had failed. Prime Minister Schuschnigg took over from

Dolfuss and immediately attempted to restore order. However Goebbels took this as a key to increase German propaganda transmissions to Austria, in which he not only extolled the virtues of Nazidom but began to issue increasingly open threats to those who would resist the inevitability of its advance.

In so doing he brought about a premature crisis in Vienna, unexpected either by the Austrian Government or himself. In early 1938 Schuschnigg was made aware of the plans for a second clandestine Nazi plot. He travelled at once to Germany to protest, but, instead of being met with sympathy, became the victim of one of Hitler's legendary tirades. He returned home a broken man, with a new cabinet forced upon him and the National Socialist, Seyss-Inquart, installed in the key post of Minister of the Interior and Public Safety.

On 23 February Seyss-Inquart made his first broadcast to the Austrian people, using what was soon to become his customary address, 'My German fellow-countrymen.' He ordered the removal of the prohibition on Nazi insignia, including the swastika, and in so doing deliberately engineered a confrontation with Schuschnigg. A few days later the Prime Minister made a fateful decision to hold a plebiscite on the matter of an Anschluss. Infuriated, Hitler at once demanded that the referendum be cancelled, a blatant intrusion into a friendly neighbour's internal affairs which Schuschnigg rejected.

There followed a radio war more politically savage than any seen to date. Schuschnigg allied himself with the left and for the first time since 1934 allowed them access to the media. Two broadcasts were announced for the evening of 11 March, one by Minister Rott, a leading member of the Christian Social Trade Union movement and member of the government, the other by the young workers' leader, Sailer.

Prior to this announcement, virtually non-stop broadcasts from Germany had spread a ceaseless tirade of alarmist, pro-Nazi disinformation, claiming that the plebiscite was no more than an excuse for a communist takeover. It was stated that Czechoslovakia was supplying arms, including artillery, to left-wing mobs in Vienna, while Schuschnigg was openly accused of forming a popular front with the Communists. When news broke of the Socialist leaders' proposed broadcast many Austrians who until then had been sceptical of the worst excesses of Nazi propaganda began to believe it in its totality.

Berlin heard within minutes of the proposed broadcasts and immediately attacked the proposal. Hitler, who had already decided upon a coup, brought the date forward and issued an ultimatum. The socialist broadcasts never took place. Instead, after a slight delay when music was played, Schuschnigg came to the microphone to announce his resignation. A pre-recorded speech by Seyss-Inquart followed, interspersed with the Horst Wessel song, played over the Austrian air waves for the first time.

The next day Hitler entered his home town of Linz and from there made an historic broadcast announcing the Anschluss. The contrast between Schuschnigg's tired if impassioned plea for a free Austria and Hitler's equally impassioned and spontaneous appeal to his 'fellow Germans' could not have been greater. Austrians everywhere were intoxicated by the moment. Swept up in the immense enthusiasm, they welcomed the German troops with a fervour which took seasoned foreign commentators by surprise.

The duel for the soul of Austria, between democracy and totalitarianism, had been played out on the radio waves before an international audience of millions. Reason, analysis and debate had been swept aside by saturation propaganda. The day of wholesale media manipulation had come one dangerous and tragic step closer.

The Necessary Lies of War

No country, however dedicated it may be to democracy, can afford to tell the whole truth in time of war. Whether it is forced to revert to open lies or merely be economical with the truth depends on a series of circumstances. It is usually impossible to hide a defeat, although suppression of the full extent of the catastrophe may often avert a wholesale decline in morale. Occasionally, skilful manipulation of the facts coupled with the brilliant oratory of a trusted and revered figure, such as Churchill after Dunkirk, may actually serve to turn a military defeat into a moral victory.

Throughout the Second World War the British press was subject to censorship. The BBC, however, was self-regulatory, yet there seems to have been little attempt by it to abuse its privileged status.

When the Government made it clear that it wished a story suppressed the BBC invariably complied, particularly in the early years of the war when the prospect of victory seemed far from certain.

The Government's grounds for suppressing individual stories seems to have been at the best ad hoc. On 17 June, 1940, the 20,000 ton Cunard liner *Lancastria*, converted into a troopship, was sunk by German aircraft off St Nazaire, resulting in a record loss of life. The number of dead will never be known, but estimates have ranged from between 4,000 and 7,000. When the news reached Churchill that afternoon he forbade its publication, on the basis that 'the newspapers have got quite enough disaster for today at least'. He subsequently claimed in his own *History of the Second World War* that he had 'intended to release the news a few days later, but events crowded upon us so thick and so quickly that I forgot to lift the ban, and it was some years before the knowledge of this horror became public.'

In fact, on 26 July, 1940, the *Daily Mirror* reported the tragedy on its front page and gave a figure of 2,823 men lost. Why the ban was in fact not lifted, or why the *Daily Mirror* was not prosecuted for publishing the story in contravention of it, has never been fully explained.

Radio propaganda entered a new phase in April, 1940, with the rapid development by Germany of a new type of English language radio station. Goebbels operated three black-propaganda stations, each claiming to be transmitting from within Britain. These were the New British Broadcasting Station, or NBBS; the Workers' Challenge, purporting to be run by a determined band of Socialist revolutionaries from industrial Britain; and, in contrast, a passivist station, The Christian Peace Movement.

The British authorities reacted vigorously and on occasions actually broke their own guidelines by jamming the NBBS and Workers' Challenge broadcasts. The existence of the stations was kept a closely guarded secret and all references to them in the press or BBC was strictly forbidden.

The Government's attitude to the white-propaganda broadcasts of Lord Haw-Haw was wholly different. British news broadcasting during the early stages of the war was plagued by self-imposed censorship. It was only natural therefore for the general public to seek the 'truth' elsewhere by scanning the air waves for other English language broadcasts. They quickly found that German broadcasts were providing vivid and up-to-date reports of great accuracy produced by specialist teams at the front. The Authorities realized that any attempt to jam these stations would be divisive, and instead set about the introduction of one of the most skilful counter-propaganda campaigns of all times.

When a *Daily Express* reporter, Jonah Barrington, gave the principal German white-propaganda announcer the nick-name 'Lord Haw-Haw of Zeesen' the name stuck, although references to Zeesen, the German overseas transmitting station, were soon dropped. Barrington gave Lord Haw-Haw a wife, 'Winnie of Warsaw', and created other characters, 'Auntie Gush and Uncle Smarmy'. Thus depersonalized, the announcers became far easier targets for the establishment to ridicule.

Contrary to public opinion the original Lord Haw-Haw was not William Joyce, who did not travel to Berlin until well after the transmissions subsequently attributed to him had begun. The voices were in fact provided by a variety of broadcasters, including, embarrasingly for the BBC, Mrs P P Eckersley, the wife of one of its pioneer engineers. He did, however, write many of the scripts. Later in the war he made the mistake of deciding to trade on the British propaganda triumph of Lord Haw-Haw by starting a programme in which he spoke as the 'real' Lord Haw Haw. After the war this deceit was to take Joyce to the gallows as a traitor.

Joyce's scripts were so convincing that they created problems for the appropriately-named 'Anti-Lie Bureau' of the Ministry of Information. The Bureau was formed originally to counteract German black-propaganda with the truth. Ironically, in the early stages of the war it found itself countering the white-propaganda of 'Lord Haw-Haw' with government-inspired lies.

Joyce did not rely upon spies for the bulk of his information, but upon the British newspapers which he obtained within twenty-four hours of their publication. Newspapers, however well censored, contain a wealth of damning information if fully exploited and presented credibly. Shortly after Dunkirk a number of German agents were parachuted into Britain in contemplation of an invasion. Rumours of their arrival spread rapidly and were compounded by the German-English radio. The 'Anti-Lie Bureau' countered these by spreading stories likely to ridicule the reports, some even involving troops disguised as nuns with heavy boots being seen descending by parachute. In this instance the Ministry of Information was only partly successful; there are ample reports of nuns having suffered the indignity of a search until their bona fides could be established.

The whole matter of rumour and the activities of the 'Anti-Lie Bureau' might have remained an embarrassing irrelevancy had the Authorities not attempted to adopt the tactics of Nazi Germany by prosecuting rumour-mongers. Establishing evidence against an individual for spreading a 'Haw-Haw rumour' was never easy, particularly when the 'rumour' was known to be true and was only being denied for reasons of security or morale. Typically, an individual spreading a rumour and attributing it to 'Lord Haw-Haw' was arrested and the BBC approached to establish whether or not their monitoring stations had registered the rumour. If they had not the prosecution took place and the BBC gave evidence. Many prosecutions were fundamentally flawed. Most rumours were of too general a nature to be attributed to a single transmission and, in any case, the BBC did not monitor all broadcasts from Germany. A number of individuals who were convicted and sentenced subsequently had their convictions quashed.

The BBC also relied upon more conventional means to counter the Haw-Haw broadcasts. The Ministry of Information commissioned Norman Birkett to write the script for a weekly broadcast from an anonymous commentator to counter some of the more scurrilous 'truths' broadcast during the previous seven days. Birkett was quickly replaced by J. B. Priestley, whose somewhat irreverent attitude towards the establishment permeated to his scripts and found favour with the general public.

Occasionally Priestley's left-wing opinions produced scripts so political that the MOI attempted to intervene. However, such was the author's popularity that he was invariably given *carte blanche*. Alas Priestley did not always translate his political convictions into his private affairs. As his popularity grew he began to demand fees far in excess of those which the BBC was prepared to pay. Eventually, exasperated, the BBC declined to renew his contract.

The Blanket Bombing Campaign

Contrary to public opinion the decision to bomb Germany into oblivion was taken before Sir Arthur Harris assumed command of the offensive. In the early stages of the war British planners deceived themselves into believing that the comparatively few bombs that their aircraft were able to drop were hitting their targets. It was also assumed that British bombs were as effective as their German equivalents. Neither fact was true. By early 1941 post-strike imagery reports produced by the RAF's Photographic Reconnaissance Units were making it clear that the vast majority of RAF bombs were not falling within 5km of their targets. Equally, the 100lb General-Purpose bombs being dropped by the RAF were no more than half as effective as the German light-cased (ie blast) bombs of the same weight. Both facts were kept a closely guarded secret from the general public.

On 14 February, 1942, six days before Sir Arthur Harris assumed control, Bomber Command issued a new directive transferring the aiming points of individual raids from specific targets to general, usually residential, areas. The undermining of the morale of the German people by the wholesale destruction of their homes and infrastructure at any cost became paramount. During an attack on the town of Wuppertal on 29/30 May, 1943, the bomber crews had their conventional ordnance survey maps withdrawn and were issued with 1941-style red and grey target maps showing the major industrial centres. Unlike in 1941, however they were now told to ignore the targets marked on the map and instead to concentrate on the residential areas at the eastern end of the city.

To exploit the known failing of the 'rabbits', the Bomber Command crews who perpetually dropped their bombs as early as possible then scuttled away from the target area, the raid was routed over an area of high population density. It was recognized that if the marker flares were dropped at one end of the target area and the bomber stream were routed in along the length of the target, then any bombs dropped early by the 'rabbits' would still do useful damage somewhere in the target city. Again, the British public was told nothing of this change in tactics.

Wuppertal's industrial production as a result of the raid was set back by 52 days, compared with 32 days after the Luftwaffe's saturation raid on Coventry. The loss of life was far greater – 2,450 people killed in Wuppertal as against 380 in Coventry. This was the first raid to cause civilian casualties on such a scale and as such attracted special attention from the German Propaganda Ministry. Even in London there were some horrified murmurs when photographs of the damage to Wuppertal were published.

The Ministry of Information went on to the offensive. *The Times* Leader of 31 May 'recognized and regretted that no matter how accurate Allied bombing of military objectives may be – and the degree of accuracy is very high in the RAF – civilian losses are inevitable.' The newspaper, which was still regarded by many as wholly accurate in its reporting, went on to remind the general public that, in 1940, the Luftwaffe had turned its aircraft loose against undefended Rotterdam and had killed 'many thousands of civilians – men, women and children.' The true figure had been 980 dead, but not for the first time the truth was not allowed to interfere with the potency of black propaganda.

The Authorities made it clear that all bomber crews had specific targets and were particularly ordered to ensure that they did not damage hospitals. The crews themselves, who by late 1943 were undertaking regular blanket-bombing raids, were forbidden to discuss their orders in public. Only after the war, when the awful effects of the saturation bombing became apparent, were the raids seriously questioned.

Japan sustained far greater loss of life from the raids on Tokyo and its other major cities in the latter half of 1945. However, so incensed was the West by the treatment of its prisoners of war at the hands of the Japanese that few post-war objections seem to have been raised.

Censorship and Today's Press

'The essence of successful warfare is secrecy; the essence of successful journalism is publicity.' These words were uttered during the Suez crisis in 1956 and were later repeated during the Falklands War. They remain equally true today.

The issue of media access to combat information is as complex as it is vexatious. Many countries exercise ongoing censorship, or so control their national newspapers that censorship is unnecessary. Others traditionally rely upon the inherent patriotism of their media proprietors to ensure that nothing detrimental to the government or to its war effort is printed.

In the United Kingdom, while elements of the press insist on publishing lurid scandals involving politicians and members of the Royal Family, none would dream of deliberately compromising national security, nor of putting the lives of servicemen at risk. During the Falklands War of 1982 the Government controlled the means of communication and was thus able to exert considerable influence on the timing and method of press and casualty releases.

The public came to trust the slow, measured tones of the Ministry of Defence's press information officer, Ian MacDonald, as he issued the daily bulletins. MacDonald later stated that he had believed everything which he had released to have been true and that he would not have deliberately lied to the general public. He was not asked to. Throughout the campaign the British Government relied on a policy of scrupulous honesty, giving as complete a picture of the situation as circumstances permitted.

Occasionally this superficially unimpeachable policy has backfired. When the LSL *Sir Galahad* was bombed at Fitzroy, realizing that the tragedy could not be kept secret for long, the Ministry of Defence released the fact almost immediately. It admitted that at the time of the incident the ship had been heavily laden with troops, but declined to give details of their regiment. Friends and relatives of those serving in the theatre were kept on tenterhooks until it was at last announced that the majority of losses had been sustained by the 1st Battalion, The Welsh Guards. Even then a further delay ensued while the Army gathered together sufficient trained personnel to break the news to those who had suffered a bereavement.

In this instance, however well meaning, the policy of open and immediate reporting did more harm than good. The Ministry of Defence undertook to ensure that such a mistake was never made again, but at the same time had to concede that this would only be possible if rigid sensorship were to be introduced to the battlefield. Sensorship is deeply unpopular in the Western world. However, where it does not exist, innocent leaks will occasionally lead to tragedy.

During the Falklands campaign, immediately before the historic assault of the 2nd Battalion The Parachute Regiment on the Argentine positions at Goose Green, a representative of the BBC inadvertently disclosed the unit's position and intentions. The Commanding Officer, Lieutenant Colonel 'H' Jones, who was subsequently awarded a postumous Victoria Cross, was beside himself with rage and threatened to sue the BBC. It has never been suggested that the actions of the BBC were either malicious or particularly negligent, and fortunately they did not, in the end, add to the carnage of the battle. Such events are, however, indicative of what may happen when something as seemingly innocuous as a situation report (SITREP) is transmitted without considering the omnipresent demands of long-term security.

Gulf Lessons

No war, not even Vietnam, has been so directly affected by the mass communications media as the Gulf War. Israel, Jordan, Saudi Arabia and Iraq all imposed severe controls without provoking significant outcries from their journalists. Iraq, Jordan and Israel in particular attempted to manipulate the media. Jordan reported consistently that Iraqi forces were winning, and only after the Coalition proved victorious finally admitted the devastating degree of the Iraqi defeat.

Israeli censorship was most evident in the reporting of Scud missile attacks. The sites of impacted Scuds were quickly cordoned off and the press only granted acccss once the government had decided its response. Press reports thereafter stressed the public demand for retaliation and depicted the government's difficulty in coping with the general demand for a military response. This complemented precisely Israel's demand for defensive missiles and led not only to the provision of several high-profile United States Patriot anti-missile batteries but to a marked increase in the Coalition's special forces' Scud-busting activities.

The state-owned Iraqi media, through a series of blatantly false news reports, led the Iraqi public to believe that they were winning and never publicly informed them that they had lost the war. Although foreign reporting was encouraged it was totally mani-pulated, with reporters' movements controlled to ensure that they saw only what the government wished. The Authorities used the language barrier and the lack of fuel to ensure that guest journalists saw only what was intended. This affected even the experienced CNN's reporting and reached a climax when the highly respected Peter Arnett reported on the precision bombing of the Amiraya bunker.

The Coalition had struck Amiraya because it knew it to be a military installation, not knowing that its upper levels were being used as a shelter for the families of local government officials. Clearly distressed by the loss of life, the CNN crew emphasized the civilian dead rather than the building's military importance. In so doing they gave Baghdad a major propaganda victory and forced a reconsideration of the Coalition bombing policy; thereafter the politicians, and not the military, controlled the bombing.

In a subsequent interview with David Frost, General Schwarzkopf described the reporting of the incident as 'aiding and abetting the enemy'. Perhaps with a degree of justification, he claimed that it implied that he was 'deliberately lying to the American people that (he was) targetting civilians.' In this instance the General, a man of considerable honour and integrity, had not lied. However, to suggest that lies and deceptions do not form an integral part of the pursuit of war would, at the very least, be foolishly naive.

BIBLIOGRAPHY

ANDREW Christopher/GORDIEVSKY Oleg: *KGB The Inside Story of its Foreign Operations* (Hodder & Stoughton)

ANDREW Christopher/GORDIEVSKY Oleg: *Instructions from the Centre: Top Secret Files of the KGB* (Hodder & Stoughton)

BABINGTON Anthony: *For the Sake of Example: Capital Courts Martial 1914 – 1918* (Leo Cooper)

BELLAMY Christopher: *Expert Witness: A Defence Correspondent's Gulf War 1990 – 1991* (Brassey's)

BICKERS Richard: *Friendly Fire* (Leo Cooper)

BINYON Michael: *European Security: Public Opinion and Influence* (RUSI/Brassey's)

BULLOCK John/MORRIS Harvey: *Saddam's War* (Faber & Faber)

BURGESS Maj. Wm. H. III: *Inside Spetsnaz – Soviet Special Operations* (Presidio)

BURUMA Ian: *My Enemy's Enemy is My Friend* (The Independent)

CHANDLER David: *The Art of Warfare in the Age of Marlborough* (Batsford)

CHANDLER David: *Marlborough as Military Commander* (Batsford)

CLARK Alan: *The Donkeys* (Pimlico)

COLLINS John M.: *Green Berets, SEALS, and Spetsnaz: US & Soviet Special Military Operations* (Pergamon-Brassey's)

COOPER Alan: *The Men Who Breached the Dams* (Airlife)

DEACON Richard: *A History of the British Secret Service* (Panther)

DEACON Richard: *Spyclopaedia* (Futura)

DERRY Archie: *Emergency in Malaya, The Psychological Dimensions* (National Defence College)

DEWAR Colonel Michael: *The Art of Deception in Warfare* (David and Charles)

DICK Charles: *Soviet Views on Strategic and Operational Surprise and Deception* (RMA Sandhurst)

FOOT M.R.D.: *SOE: The Special Operations Executive 1940–1946* (Mandarin)

FOSTER Edward: *Mikhail Gorbachev and the Western Media: How Open is Openness?* (RUSI/Brassey's)

GIBSON Charles: *Death of a Phantom Raider* (Hale)

HAMPSHIRE Cecil A.: *The Secret Navies* (William Kimber)

HARCLERODE Peter: *Para: Fifty Years of the Parachute Regiment* (Arms & Armour)

HASTINGS Max: *Bomber Command* (Michael Joseph)

HORNER D.M.: *SAS Phantom of the Jungle* (Allen & Unwin)

HYDE H. Montgomery: *Solitary in the Ranks* (Constable)

IRVING David: *The Destruction of Dresden* (Macmillan)

KEEGAN John: *Who Was Who In World War II* (W H Smith)

KEEN Sam: *Faces of the Enemy* (Harper Collins)

KERSHAW Ian: *Popular Opinion and Political Dissent in The Third Reich* (Clarendon Press)

LAWRENCE T. E.: *Revolt in the Desert* (Jonathan Cape)

LENIN V.I.: *Selected Works*, 1921

LLOYD Mark: *The Guinness Book of Espionage* (Guinness Publishing)

LLOYD Mark: *The Guinness Book of Helicopter Facts and Feats* (Guinness Publishing)

LLOYD Mark: *Tactics of Modern Warfare* (Brian Trodd Publishing)

MACDONALD Lyn: *They Called it Passchendaele* (Macmillan)

McLACHLAN Donald: *Room 39* (Weidenfeld & Nicholson)

McLACHLAN Ian: *Night of the Intruders* (Patrick Stephens)

MONTAGU Ewen: *The Man Who Never Was* (Evans Bros)

NUTTING Anthony: *Gordon* (Constable)

PAINE Lauran: *The Abwehr: German Military Intelligence in the Second World War* (Hale)

PIMLOTT John/BADSEY Stephen: *The Gulf War Assessed* (Arms & Armour)

PIMLOTT John: *The World at Arms* (Reader's Digest)

POCOCK Tom: *War Correspondents* (The Sunday Times)

PRESTON Adrian: *In Relief of Gordon* (Hutchinson)

PUTKOWSKI Julian/Sykes Julian: *Shot at Dawn* (Leo Cooper)

REGAN Geoffrey: *The Guinness Book of Military Blunders* (Guinness Publishing)

SIMPSON Andy: *Hot Blood and Cold Steel: Life and Death in the Trenches of the First World War* (Tom Donovan Publishing Limited)

STEVENSON William: *A Man Called Intrepid* (Macmillan)

SUDOPLATOV Pavel: Special Tasks: *Memoirs of an Unwanted Witness* (Little Brown & Company)

SUN TZU: *The Art of Warfare* (Wordsworth Reference)

URBAN Mark: *Big Boys' Rules* (MacKays)

WATSON Bruce: *Military Lessons of the Gulf War* (Greenhill Books)

WATSON Peter: *War on the Mind* (Hutchinson)

WEST John L.: *The Loss of Lancastria* (Millgate Publishing Limited)

WEST W.J.: *Truth Betrayed* (Duckworth)

WHITE Terry: *Swords of Lightning* (Brassey's)

WILLIAMS Eric: *The Wooden Horse* (Collins)

WILSON Robert: *The Destruction of Troy* (Owlett Books)

YAZOV Army Gen Dimitri: *Soviet Military Doctrine* (Brassey's)

INDEX

France, 7

Franco, General Francisco-Bahamonde, 53, 106

Franco-Prussian War, 50, 94

Franklyn, Maj Gen Harold, 44

French, Fld Mshl Sir John, 42, 52

'Freds', 166, 167

Frere, Sir Bartle, 21

Frost, David, 199

Gage, General, 20

Gala, 104

Gaza, 15, 16, 17

Gelb, Operation, 87

General Assembly, 29

General Staff, 51, 173

Germany, 10

Gestapo, 87, 96, 100, 150

Giap, Vo Nguyen, 76, 77, 78

Gibraltar, 6, 62, 111

Giskes, Herman, 96, 99, 100

Glasnost, 123, 132

Gobineau, Comte de, 184

God, 171

Goebbels, Joseph, 60, 114, 151, 152, 180, 183, 186, 187, 188, 192

Goering, Reichs marshall Hermann, 55, 59, 60, 179

Gorbachev, Mikhail, 123, 132

Gort, Fld Mshl John, 55

Greece, 30, 46, 172

Greene, Sir Hugh, 155

GRU, 116, 117, 134

GS1, 149, 150

Guderian, Heinz, 19, 44, 53, 55

Guernica, 53

Gulf Co-operation Council, 137

Gulf War, 32, 134, 135, 198

Gurkhas, The, 141, 154, 158

Haas, Lt Hendrich van, 98

Hague, The, 86, 87, 97

Haig, Fld Mshl Sir Douglas, 11, 12, 14, 42, 43, 52

Haldane, Richard, 40, 50

Hall, Admiral 'Blinker', 10

Hamburg, 75

Hamilton, General, 15, 24

Han River, 29

Han Xin, 3

Hanoi, 76, 139

Harbinger, 37

Harman, Cpl Paul, 168

Harris, Air Marshal Sir Arthur, 74, 75, 195

Hart, Maj Gen, 26
Haw Haw, Lord (see Joyce, Wm)
Hearts and Minds, 79, 154, 157, 158, 162
Heathrow Airport, 32
Hemert, Gerard, 99
Hess, Rudolf, 149
Hindenburg, President Paul von, 179, 180
Hiroshima, 120
Hitler, Adolf, 53, 54, 55, 56, 57, 58, 69, 60, 81, 89, 90, 91, 94, 106, 114, 150, 152, 179, 180, 184, 186, 191
Hitler Youth, 181, 183
Hittites, The, 2
Ho Chi Minh, 140
Hobart, 10
Holland, 54, 63, 64, 96, 99, 100, 102
Hollis, Sir Roger, 102
Homberg, Piet, 98
Home Guard, 149
Home Security, Ministry of, 81
Hoover, J. Edgar, 101, 108, 110
Horrocks, Lt Gen Sir Brian, 65
Hoth, Gen Hermann, 58
Howard, Leslie, 108
Hoxha, Enver, 142
Hue, 140
Huelva, 113

Huguenots, The, 6
Human Rights, League of, 178
Hungarian Revolution, 34
Hungary, 30, 131, 133
Hunstanton, 10
Hussein, Saddam, 134, 136
Hussein, Sherif of Mecca, 48, 49
Hu Yi, General, 5

Inchon, 29
Indo-China, 75, 76
Inner German Border (IGB), 30, 124
Inshore Patrol Flotilla, 71
Intelligence Corps, 62, 101, 167
Intelligence Division, 25
Internal Security (I.S.), 138
Intrepid (see Stephenson, Wm)
Inverbank, 69
Inverlair, 114
IRA, 166, 167, 168
Iran, 49, 145
Iraqi Air Force, 32
Irish Brigade, 26
Ironside, Operation, 94
Ithica, 46
Israelites, The, 2, 171
Ivie, Ronald, 172
Izvestia, 136

Souain, The Corporals of, 177
South Africa, 25, 26
South Vietnamese Army, 78
Soviet Union, 56, 117, 130, 131, 132, 133, 134, 136, 169, 172
Spahis, 39
Special Branch, 107, 166
Special Forces, 125, 126
Speer, Albert, 75
Spetsnaz, 31, 125, 127, 128, 129
Speybank, 69
Spain, 6
Spy Planes, 122
Staff College, 42
Stalag Luft III, 47, 48
Stalin, Joseph, 56, 57, 58, 89, 106, 116, 117, 120, 121, 122, 153
Stalingrad, 116
State Department, 107, 108
Stephenson, William, 105, 107, 108, 109, 110
Stevens, Captain Henry, 86, 87
Stockton, 10
Storm, Operation, 159
Storrs, Ronald, 49
Strong, Maj Gen Sir Kenneth, 64
Stuart, General Jeb, 9

Stumme, General Georg, 57
Sukarno, President, 157, 158
Sun Ping, 3
Sun Tzu, 1, 3, 4
Sunshield, 85
Suvorov, Victor, 134
Sverdlovsk, 122
Switzerland, 56, 106, 111
Sydney, HMAS, 70
Sykes-Picot Plan, 48, 49
Sylt, 11
Syria, 49

Taconis, Thys, 97
Tallard, General, 7
Tank, The, 43, 44, 174
Tea Act, 19
Tehran, 84
Television, 148, 155, 169
Ter, Laak, 97
Terwindt, Beatrix, 99
Tet Offensive, 80, 139, 148
Thornton, Air Vice-Marshal, 91, 92
Thutmose III, 2
Tian Dan, 3
Times, The, 36, 197
Timoshenko, Marshal, 56
Tintinnabulation, Operation, 164
Tobruk, 141
Tonkin, 76
Tokyo, 56